THE SPY WHO WAS
LEFT BEHIND

RUSSIA, THE UNITED STATES, AND THE
TRUE STORY OF THE BETRAYAL
AND ASSASSINATION OF A CIA AGENT

.

MICHAEL PULLARA

SCRIBNER
New York   London   Toronto   Sydney   New Delhi

Scribner
An Imprint of Simon & Schuster, Inc.
1230 Avenue of the Americas
New York, NY 10020

First Scribner hardcover edition November 2018

SCRIBNER and design are registered trademarks of The Gale Group, Inc.,
used under license by Simon & Schuster, Inc., the publisher of this work.

For information about special discounts for bulk purchases,
please contact Simon & Schuster Special Sales at 1-866-506-1949
or business@simonandschuster.com.

The Simon & Schuster Speakers Bureau can bring authors
to your live event. For more information or to book an event,
contact the Simon & Schuster Speakers Bureau at
1-866-248-3049 or visit our website at www.simonspeakers.com.

Interior design by Kyle Kabel

Manufactured in the United States of America

1   3   5   7   9   10   8   6   4   2

Library of Congress Cataloging-in-Publication Data is available.

ISBN 978-1-5011-5213-9
ISBN 978-1-5011-5215-3 (ebook)

This book is dedicated to my father,
Captain Angelo Pullara, USAF.

He died so that someone else could live.

CONTENTS

A NOTE ON GEORGIAN NAMES

At first glance it might seem like almost everybody in Georgia is related because their names sound so similar—all those -dze's and -shvili's. However, these suffixes are merely the Georgian equivalent of the Western -son (as in Ericson, which originally meant "Eric's son").

The suffix -dze is Old Georgian for "son" and the suffix -shvili is Old Georgian for "child." Whether someone is a -dze or -shvili depends on which side of the country his or her family comes from: the -dze (like Eduard Shevardnadze) are from western Georgia and the -shvili (like Mikheil Saakashvili) are from eastern Georgia.

When a Georgian name is rendered into Latin script, it is written phonetically. You pronounce each letter and place the accent or stress on the suffix. For names ending with -dze, the "e" is stressed (e.g., sheh-vard-nad-ZEH); and for names ending with -shvili, the first "i" is stressed (e.g., sah-kash-VEE-lee).

KEY PLAYERS

THE PEOPLE IN THE NIVA

Eldar Gogoladze

Marina Kapanadze

Elena Darchiashvili

Freddie Woodruff

THE YOUNG MEN ARRESTED BY GOGOLADZE

Anzor Sharmaidze

Gela Bedoidze

Genadi Berbitchashvili

THE GEORGIAN GOVERNING COUNCIL

Jaba Ioseliani

Tengiz Sigua

Tengiz Kitovani

Eduard Shevardnadze

GEORGIAN INVESTIGATORS AND FORENSIC EXPERTS

Irakli Batiashvili

Avtandil Ioseliani

Zaza Altunashvili

Shota Kviraya

Otar Djaparidze

Levan Chachuria

GEORGIAN POLITICAL FIGURES

President Zviad Gamsakhurdia

President Mikheil Saakashvili

Zurab Zhvania

Temur Alasania

Giga Bokeria

Daniel Kunin

U.S. POLITICAL AND DIPLOMATIC FIGURES

President Bill Clinton

Ambassador Strobe Talbott

Ambassador Richard Miles

Ambassador John Tefft

Ambassador Kent Brown

President George W. Bush

Vice President Dick Cheney

Secretary of State James Baker

Vice Consul Lynn Whitlock

FBI SPECIAL AGENTS

George Shukin

Robert Hanssen

Dell Spry

Dave Beisner

CIA OFFICERS

Director William Casey

Edward Lee Howard

Bob Baer

Dayna Baer

Director James Woolsey

Aldrich Hazen Ames

Milt Bearden

G. L. Lamborn

THE WOODRUFF FAMILY

George Woodruff

Chery Woodruff

Georgia Woodruff Alexander

Dorothy Woodruff

Jill Woodruff-Pully

Meredith Woodruff

THE JUDGE AND LAWYERS AT THE TRIAL

Chief Judge Djemal Leonidze

Tamaz Inashvili

Prosecutor K. Chanturia

Avtandil Sakvarelidze

MEMBERS OF THE PROSECUTOR GENERAL'S OFFICE

Irakli Okruashvili

Zaza Sanshiashvili

Zurab Adeishvili

SELECTED JOURNALISTS

Thomas Goltz

Peter Klein

Jamie Doran

Adam Ciralsky

Sopiko Chkhaidze

Andrew Higgins

Eliso Chapidze

Natasha Gevorkian

Magda Memanishvili

Inga Alavidze

WITNESSES ON THE OLD MILITARY ROAD

Badri Chkutiasvili

Giorgi Tserekashvili

Lali Tserekashvili

Merab Gelashvili

Ramin Khubulia

Tamaz Tserekashvili

Eteri Vardiashvili

Vasiko

RUSSIAN INTELLIGENCE OFFICERS

Victor Cherkashin

Alexander Litvinenko

Stanislav Lekarev

"Igor"

SELECTED MEMBERS OF GROUP ALPHA

Igor Giorgadze

Vladimir Rachman

Kote Shavishvili

THE BILLIONAIRES

George Soros

Bidzina Ivanashvili

HELPERS, GUIDES, AND FRIENDS

Lali Kereselidze

Carolyn Clark Campbell

Nana Alexandria

Maria Semenova

Lance Fletcher

CHAPTER I

DEATH ON A LONELY ROAD

"Mr. President, I am an American lawyer and I represent surviving family members of a US diplomat who was murdered near Tbilisi in 1993."

It was November 2004 and Mikheil Saakashvili had just finished two hours of remarks in the Tbilisi State University auditorium. Twelve months earlier this thirty-six-year-old former justice minister had scrambled to the front of a popular revolt in the former Soviet Republic of Georgia. In a made-for-TV moment, he handed his predecessor a rose and demanded that the old man quit elected office. Riding a wave of patriotic euphoria, Misha (as he was popularly known) had been elected president of the tiny Eurasian nation and given a mandate to lurch toward the West.

The young chief executive felt comfortable with the invitation-only crowd and agreed to take a few questions from the audience. I had tagged along with two guests in hopes of having a few minutes with a minor government official. The opportunity to talk to the president himself was too good to pass up.

The murdered diplomat was Freddie Woodruff, a forty-five-year-old former preacher with a gift for languages. I remembered him mostly as the strawberry-blond older brother of one of my junior high classmates. He was a Bible major who played college football and (in my world) that made him a Samson-like hero. But those who knew him better recalled a more complicated character. As one of his friends told me, "Freddie was an extraordinarily outgoing individual—seductive on many different levels. He had an intuitive sense of what people wanted and he used it to manipulate them. But somehow, with Freddie, you just didn't mind."

I raised my hand and was chosen to address the president. The question before mine had provoked enthusiastic applause from the fifteen hundred in attendance: What wonders would Saakashvili do in the second year of his administration to match the glories he had accomplished in the first year? The response to me was less congenial. The crowd seemed to hold its collective breath and look to the president for cues on how to react. His displeasure was apparent: He was not happy to receive an unscripted question from a soft-spoken foreigner on live national television.

"We have obtained evidence proving that Anzor Sharmaidze— the young Georgian man who was convicted of killing the American diplomat—is completely innocent," I said.

An ominous murmur rolled over the crowd of handpicked supporters. I focused my mind on the job at hand: be polite, be respectful, be careful.

"My clients have sent me here to present this evidence and to ask the Georgian government to honor the promises made during the Rose Revolution. They have sent me here to ask you, Mr. President, will you let this innocent man go free?"

The crowd's murmur became a grumble; the president's scowl became a glare. One of Saakashvili's American-trained bodyguards stepped in front of me and put his hand on his gun. I felt the tingle of panic creeping up the back of my neck.

Saakashvili's answer was a blur of indignation. "Georgia is not some third-rate country that can be talked to in this way," he said. "We are a small country, but we have our rules and procedures. I'm not some dictator. I don't tell the courts what to do."

The president was spitting words at me, but the noise in my head made it hard to hear. His bodyguards had triangulated around me and were poised to spring at the first sign of aggression. I kept my hands in plain sight and tried hard to look benign.

"Imagine if my friend George Bush delivered a speech and some Georgian lawyer asked him to free a person whose case was being reviewed by an American court," Saakashvili barked. "This American lawyer should respect the Georgian system the same way we Georgians respect America's system."

The crowd cheered. The president had defended the honor of the plucky little country and addressed the insult of a stranger's appeal to fairness. Never mind that a grave injustice had been committed against one of their own citizens. No foreign lawyer could be allowed to point it out.

A terrible fear squeezed my chest. I was seven thousand miles from home and had just offended the most powerful man in the country. I had unintentionally provoked a lethal adversary and quite possibly killed the man I was trying to liberate.

I felt sick with doubt and fixated on a single thought: "How the hell did I get myself into this?" The answer to that question was twelve years earlier and a world away in Houston, Texas.

Like any respectable adventure, this one had started with a good breakfast and the *New York Times*. I had turned to page 4 of the paper with no inkling that I was starting a quest. The two-column headline proclaimed "CIA Agent Dies in Georgian Attack." An inset map identified the Georgia in question as the small Black Sea country wedged between the empires of Russia, Turkey, and Iran. The article made short shrift of the spy's cover story as a State Department regional affairs officer. A senior administration official identified the dead man as an employee of the Central Intelligence Agency. But it was the spy's name that caught my attention: Fred Woodruff of Stillwater, Oklahoma.

"Fred Woodruff?" I thought. "Freddie? I didn't know Freddie was a spy." When last I'd heard of him, he'd given up on preaching, divorced his first wife, and gone to work for the State Department.

The article said Woodruff had been shot dead on August 8, 1993, while riding in a car driven by one Eldar Gogoladze, the chief bodyguard for Eduard Shevardnadze. Known around the world as "the Silver Fox," Shevardnadze had been the Soviet foreign minister under Mikhail Gorbachev and, following the December 1991 breakup of the USSR, had become chairman of Georgia's governing State Council.

According to the *Times*, Freddie and Eldar were returning from a Sunday sightseeing trip to the mountainous northern border when Woodruff was mortally wounded by a single bullet to the head. The article quoted Gogoladze saying that the shooting occurred at night about twenty miles northwest of Tbilisi in a little village called Natakhtari.

High-ranking Clinton administration officials said Woodruff had been identified to the Georgian government as a CIA officer who was in country to train Shevardnadze's security force. It was a previously secret mission involving the CIA and US Special Forces, the first such effort inside the former Soviet Union. Woodruff had arrived in Georgia on June 3 and was scheduled to depart on August 20. It was his third visit to the country.

Georgian investigators from the Ministry of Internal Affairs, the national law enforcement agency, said that it was unclear whether the murder was a politically motivated assassination or a carjacking gone horribly wrong. "It may be an ordinary crime or political," said a ministry spokesman. "Ordinary because this is a dangerous region where car thefts are common; political because the car had Georgian state plates."

Notwithstanding this uncertainty, Shevardnadze had decried the killing as a crime justifying martial law. "There are mafioso structures and criminal elements which are very active," he said. "This speaks in favor of the emergency regime that I have mentioned before."

The US, however, remained officially cautious. "I know the Georgians would like to see this as a horrible accident," said an embassy spokesman, "but nothing can yet be ruled out. We're keeping an open mind as to whether it was an incredible accident or otherwise."

Accident or otherwise, the story of Freddie Woodruff was incredible to me. Someone from a family I knew, a family with whom I'd grown up, had joined the CIA and gotten himself murdered in a faraway and exotic land.

I scoured subsequent news reports for details about the shooting. Two women had accompanied Woodruff and Gogoladze on their sightseeing trip. The quartet made their journey in a Niva 1600, a Russian-made two-door hatchback. Just outside the village of Natakhtari a group of armed men allegedly tried to carjack the Niva and fired a single shot at the automobile as it raced away. Woodruff was sitting in the back seat on the right. The bullet struck him in the forehead and he died at the scene. Three young men—one of them in a military uniform—had been detained for questioning.

A number of newspapers reported that Gogoladze had been suspended as Shevardnadze's chief bodyguard. An equal number of newspapers denied the suspension and denounced the report. Apparently, Gogoladze's status was complicated and contentious.

James Woolsey, the hawkish and intellectual director of the CIA, flew to Tbilisi to retrieve Woodruff's body—a tribute described as both "highly unusual" and a tacit acknowledgment by the CIA that Woodruff was one of its own. The director and Shevardnadze talked for more than an hour on the international side of passport control. Afterward, Woodruff's flag-draped coffin was loaded onto the director's Boeing 707 for the long journey home.

Nine days after the murder, the Georgian Ministry of Internal Affairs announced that the crime had been solved. The American secret agent—a veteran of countless encounters with death—had been killed by a common criminal shooting blindly at a fleeing car. "It was an accidental killing," the spokesman stated. "Nobody knew who they were shooting at."

The name of the alleged murderer was one Anzor Sharmaidze, a twenty-one-year-old off-duty soldier. He was one of the three men detained for questioning on the night of the shooting. He had confessed and his two companions had implicated him. According to the government spokesman, all three men had been drunk at the time and Sharmaidze had shot at the car because it had failed to stop for him.

In 1993 Georgia was a lawless republic wracked by separatist rebellions and civil strife. Armed men walked the streets. The police were outmanned and outgunned. Nevertheless, the country's anemic central government had swiftly investigated Woodruff's murder and efficiently identified the perpetrator. As luck would have it, the facts of the crime turned out to be exactly what the government needed them to be: The murder of the American diplomat was not intentional, not political, and not their fault.

I considered the narrative arc of the official version: It described a triumph of professionalism over anarchy. "Very impressive," I thought. "Almost too good to be true."

The trial of Anzor Sharmaidze began on December 30, 1993. By then most newspapers had lost interest in the murder. I found a fleeting reference to it in the *Washington Times*. Sharmaidze testified that his own car had broken down near Tbilisi and that he had tried to stop the Niva in which Woodruff was riding. He said he fired one shot in anger when the car did not stop but that the killing of the American was unintentional. Five weeks later the Russian news service Interfax reported that Sharmaidze had been convicted and sentenced to fifteen years in prison.

About the same time, the US State Department announced the results of an FBI investigation into the murder: Freddie Woodruff had been killed by "a random act of violence." I thought that this was the end of the Woodruff saga. But things were about to get much more interesting.

On February 21, 1994, thirteen days after a Georgian judge rendered his verdict in the trial of Anzor Sharmaidze, the FBI arrested Aldrich Hazen Ames for espionage. They alleged that Ames, a senior CIA operations officer, had secretly been working for Moscow since 1985. During those years, Ames had been a branch chief in Soviet counterintelligence and, after the collapse of the Soviet Union, chief of an antinarcotics intelligence task force for the Black Sea basin. He was suspected of having betrayed to their deaths at least ten people who spied on the USSR for the CIA.

And he had been in Tbilisi a week before Freddie Woodruff was murdered.

Director Woolsey promised "a thorough damage assessment" of the extensive injury done by the traitor. This process, known in spy argot as "walking the cat backwards," involved a microscopic review of Ames's thirty-two years at the Agency: all the documents he'd looked at, all the people he'd talked to, all the secrets he'd known. It was an investigation that would take decades.

But in the days immediately after the arrest, the US government mobilized to reexamine a question of more personal interest to me: What role, if any, had Ames played in the death of Freddie Woodruff? Spokesmen for the CIA acknowledged that Ames's duties at the Agency's Counternarcotics Center involved tracking the flow of heroin and cocaine through Georgia, Turkey, Bulgaria, and Romania—a drug pipeline that both Senator Jesse Helms and the *Wall Street Journal* attributed to the KGB. Ames had traveled to Georgia in July 1993 in connection with this work. It now seemed plausible that Woodruff's murder two weeks later was connected either to Ames's desire to protect the Russians or the Russians' desire to protect Ames.

In October 1995 the former chief of Georgia's security service, Irakli Batiashvili, publicly asserted that Woodruff was killed at the behest of the SVR (the successor organization to the KGB First Directorate). Batiashvili had directed an independent investigation of the murder; however, the press linked his accusation to a government media campaign against Igor Giorgadze—a man accused of attempting to assassinate Eduard Shevardnadze. A former Soviet general and high-ranking KGB officer, Giorgadze had replaced Batiashvili as Georgia's security chief. After the failed assassination attempt, Giorgadze had fled to Russia, where he was living under Moscow's protection.

Nine months later the man who had replaced Giorgadze as security chief made a more explicit accusation. Shota Kviraya declared that his predecessor had arranged the murder of Woodruff on Moscow's orders and that Eldar Gogoladze (Shevardnadze's chief bodyguard and the driver of the car in which Woodruff died) was involved in the plot. A spokesman for the Russian SVR called the accusation "groundless, absurd and malicious." The service "is not involved in terrorism," he said. "It fights against terrorism, together with other countries, including the United States."

In addition to accusations of SVR involvement, the press reports provided a previously undisclosed fact about the Woodruff story: At his trial, Anzor Sharmaidze had testified that he was tortured into "confessing" to the murder. He claimed to be innocent of all charges.

The carefully constructed official version seemed to be coming apart and what was left in its place was a tantalizing mystery. As I considered the allure of this puzzle, it occurred to me that, with a modicum of effort, I might be able to offer the Woodruff family the comfort of reliable information. I already had deep reason to be suspicious about the sincerity of pronouncements by the US government. I had just completed a decade-long investigation into the circumstances of my father's death in the Vietnam War and had discovered that the air force had deceived my grieving family. Contrary to their earnest representations, my father did not die in a quaint hamlet in South Vietnam. Instead, he was killed in Laos fighting a war that no one would officially acknowledge.

So I decided to make a FOIA request about the death of Freddie Woodruff.

The Freedom of Information Act is a remarkable law. It compels agencies of the federal government to produce information in response to an individual request. Prior to being reluctantly signed by Lyndon Johnson, the FOIA was unanimously opposed by the executive branch agencies. They warned the president that the legislation granted extraordinary powers of intrusion and examination to people who were merely "idly curious."

And they were right, of course. I *was* merely curious and the federal government was going to have to tell me at least a part of what it knew about Woodruff's murder.

I initiated the process in November 1997 by mailing identical FOIA requests addressed to the Central Intelligence Agency; the Federal Bureau of Investigation; the National Security Agency; and the Department of State. I did so with no inkling of where my queries might lead. If I'd known, I might have been more careful.

The first document arrived from the FBI more than a year-and-a-half later: a three-page memo authored by a Special Agent George Shukin on August 11, 1993. The Bonn-based FBI legal attaché (legat) had arrived in Tbilisi on August 9, a little more than eighteen hours after the murder of Woodruff. Shukin, who spoke fluent Russian, had traveled to Georgia to make a preliminary assessment of whether Woodruff's death gave rise to a federal crime that could be prosecuted in the United States.

The Bureau had responsibility to investigate the shooting under a law that made it illegal to murder a US diplomat anywhere in the world. Thus, even though Woodruff was merely *posing* as a State Department employee, the FBI had jurisdiction to investigate the CIA officer's death.

The Georgians informed Special Agent Shukin that Woodruff had been killed by a randomly fired bullet that struck him just above his right eye. However, the FBI agent considered this explanation unlikely. His examination of the Niva revealed that the metal skin and glass of the car were *undamaged*. There was no evidence that a bullet had penetrated the vehicle from the outside.

In addition, a French wire service reported an alternative scenario that seemed to be more consistent with the forensic facts. Citing sources in Tbilisi, Agence France-Presse said that Woodruff had been killed by a shot fired from *inside* the car in which he was riding. AFP also reported that the driver of the car, Gogoladze, was in a "state of extreme drunkenness" when he arrived at the hospital and that he was "known for his excesses when drunk."

More troubling still was the condition of Woodruff's body. An American embassy employee who was present when Gogoladze first arrived at the Kamo Street Hospital at 10 p.m. on August 8 reported that Woodruff's body was already in an advanced state of rigor mortis, a stiffening that would not normally occur until several hours after death. Gogoladze explained the rigor and his apparent delay in reaching Tbilisi by claiming that after the shooting he had unsuccessfully searched for a hospital for three-and-a-half hours. The image of Gogoladze frantically hauling Woodruff's dead body from village to village searching for medical care seemed implausible to Special Agent Shukin. The shooting had allegedly occurred twenty miles from Tbilisi and, as chief of Shevardnadze's personal protection force, Gogoladze would have been expected to know every trauma facility in the area.

In light of these inconsistencies, Shukin said in his memo that he considered it possible that Woodruff had been killed somewhere other than the car and then put in the car. Shukin recommended that an FBI shooting team be dispatched to investigate each of the places visited by Woodruff on the day he died—but only if the Georgian government provided adequate security. It was clear to the special agent that Georgia was a very dangerous place. Shukin had already twice informed US ambassador Kent Brown that FBI investigators would not leave the United States until written assurances regarding their safety had been provided.

I read the memo a second time. It made me queasy. The memo was exculpatory evidence. In the hands of a skilled trial lawyer it could be used to liberate an innocent man from prison. And I was a skilled trial lawyer.

The absence of a bullet hole in the Niva meant that Sharmaidze could not have fired at the back of the car and struck someone inside. The presence of rigor mortis meant that Woodruff died long before Sharmaidze allegedly appeared at the scene of the crime. The official version of the murder was impossible.

It was a fantastically inconvenient discovery.

I spent weeks wrestling with my conscience. What duty did I owe Sharmaidze? I did not know him and he did not know me. I was not responsible for his imprisonment—but if I acted I might be able to set him free. And all the while I heard Edmund Burke, the eighteenth-century Irish statesman and philosopher, whispering in my ear, "All that is necessary for Evil to triumph is that good men do nothing."

It was 2001 and newspaper pundits were describing the rise of a uniquely modern phenomenon—the super-empowered angry man: agents of radical change who use wealth and technology to cause devastation on a scale that formerly only nation-states could do. I was no super-empowered angry man. But I was a moderately-empowered curious man.

"I wonder what I can do with a law license, a passport, and a credit card?" I thought.

I was about to find out.

CHAPTER 2

"DO THEY THINK WE'RE IDIOTS?"

Four years passed before the next tranche of documents arrived from the FBI. Three hundred fifty-six thoroughly censored pages, a kind of evidentiary Swiss cheese in which all the tastiest morsels have been removed.

The redactions made most of the documents unintelligible. Long ribbons of bowdlerizing black punctuated by abbreviations, acronyms, and the occasional noun. Witness statements were expurgated. Sources and methods were obscured. Proper names were deleted. Anything that might reveal a special agent's suspicion or conclusion was sanitized.

What remained was the silhouette of an investigation. But it was enough to make me take notice, because I specialize in what is self-importantly called complex commercial litigation—basically complicated business disputes involving lots of documents and lots of money. It is an area of the law in which the peculiarities of my personality are reinvented as virtues: a passion for mysteries, a memory for trivia, an obsessive attention to detail, and an annoying refusal to quit when both logic and good sense demand it.

Thus, by both trait and training, I was well suited to tease the truth out of the bits left by FBI censors. I took it as a personal challenge—to immerse myself in the minutiae of the Bureau documents and divine the content of the redactions. The project promised to be deliciously tedious.

The foundation of my reconstruction effort was a time line, a chronology of any intelligible data that could be squeezed from the

FBI documents. In order to make these un-redacted data fragments comprehensible, I had to teach myself the specialized language of Bureau investigators and censors. This had the happy and unexpected effect of making some of the redactions meaningful.

For example, an "FD 302" was a special agent's report on a witness interview and the marginal notation "b1" opposite a deletion was the censor's judgment that the blacked-out information was properly classified in order to protect national defense or foreign policy. Thus, a b1 redaction of an entire FD 302 told a story: The FBI had interviewed a witness and the evidence provided by that witness was classified for reasons of national security. The extent of the deletion gave a hint about the amount of relevant evidence elicited in the interview.

In addition, it was possible to derive information about both the witness and the interrogation based on where a document appeared in the chronology. For example, if the censored FD 302 was preceded by correspondence to FBI headquarters requesting "country clearance," then the special agents had traveled to a foreign country to conduct the interview. If one of the unnamed agents requesting such travel authorization was identified as a polygrapher, then the FBI deemed the prospective witness cooperative enough to voluntarily submit to a polygraph but unreliable enough to necessitate the use of a lie detector.

Further, an appreciation of the historical context in which a document was created could give insight into redacted content. For example, if an FD 302 indicated that special agents interrogated a witness in the days immediately following a newsworthy event—for example, the arrest of CIA traitor Aldrich Ames—then it could be deduced that the interview was informed by and perhaps related to that event. This logical inference is bolstered if the interview occurred during a flurry of classified Bureau activity that commenced immediately following the event.

Finally, my time line was organic. As I learned new information I added it to the chronology. Thus, if I interviewed a witness who said that he or she had been previously interrogated by the FBI,

I would search for the corresponding FD 302 and identify the prior interview on the time line. If the witness gave me details regarding the evidence he provided to the special agents, I would attempt to identify that evidence in the redactions and to carry the thread of that evidence forward into subsequent documents.

My first step was to put the FBI documents in date order. When I did so, it became apparent that there had been two *completely separate* FBI investigations into the murder of Freddie Woodruff. The first investigation began immediately after the shooting and ended when the Georgian authorities convicted Anzor Sharmaidze six months later. The second investigation started eight days later—two days after the FBI arrested Aldrich Ames for espionage.

According to the documents, the Bureau's first concern was for the safety of its investigators. As recommended in the Shukin memo, the FBI demanded that the Georgian government give written assurances that it would provide adequate security. The issue of lawlessness in Georgia had been raised the day after the murder by George Shukin. In his report to FBI headquarters Shukin recommended that any other FBI personnel sent to Tbilisi "be accompanied by an appropriate number of fully-armed HRT personnel." The need for the Bureau's elite hostage response team was not hypothetical. By the summer of 1993, Georgia had devolved into a state of almost perfect anarchy. The only recognized authority was the gun.

However, some of those guns were in the hands of American commandos.

In 1979 the newly mobilized US Army Delta Force agreed to provide operators to train and lead local bodyguards at the State Department's most threatened embassies. This arrangement gave Delta a permanent covert presence in some of the most unstable places in the world. A month before Woodruff's death, the *Washington Times* reported that these Special Forces soldiers had been sent to Georgia in a secret mission to protect Eduard Shevardnadze. The Georgian-speaking Delta operators provided the chairman's bodyguards with antiterrorism training, equipment, and weapons. In addition, they brought two squads of Georgian paramilitary to the United States for training at Fort Bragg, North Carolina.

The CIA had proposed the program and Bill Clinton had approved it in a presidential directive. It was the first operation of its kind on the soil of the former Soviet Union and it did not go unnoticed in Moscow.

After his murder, Woodruff was quickly identified as the CIA officer in charge of this covert operation. Journalists speculated that this US security initiative (or Clinton's recent offer to mediate armed conflicts between former Soviet states) might have provoked a violent response from revanchist elements in Russia. Nevertheless, on August 12—the same day the FBI team arrived in Georgia—US ambassador Kent Brown told the press that he expected the investigation to show two things: that the killing was not premeditated and that Woodruff had not been targeted because he was an American.

Brown's statement seemed to be a none-too-subtle message from the State Department to the FBI: It was politically unacceptable for Woodruff's death to be anything other than a senseless tragedy. If the facts suggested otherwise, the facts would have to be adjusted.

While in Tbilisi the special agents were billeted at the Sheraton Metechi Palace—an outpost of Western comfort and a hub of social activity for newly prosperous Georgians. "Unfortunately numerous Georgians who visit the Metechi carry handguns," said the embassy's understated security guidelines for Tbilisi. "There have been several instances where these firearms have been discharged in the hotel. While there are no absolutes in gun play, there seem to be two recurring characteristics when these incidents have occurred: the gun wielders have been drinking heavily and/or have been engaged in arguments with other Georgians. If you observe obviously drunken and/or angered Georgians, avoid them."

But in the summer of 1993, it was very hard to avoid drunken or angry Georgians. There was a lot to be angry about. And some good reasons to drink. The government had failed to obtain a monopoly on violence. As a result, Georgia was governed not by the rule of law but by each local strongman's will to power. It was perfect anarchy: a society dominated by criminals and warlords. Crime was not the exception; it was the rule.

In order for the FBI to operate officially in a foreign country, it is required to obtain advance approval from the host government. Shevardnadze had granted this approval on behalf of Georgia; however, in 1993 the real power of government lay with another member of the four-person State Council, a mafia warlord named Jaba Ioseliani. It was perhaps for this reason that the scope of the first FBI investigation was limited to providing laboratory support and interviewing embassy staff. Alternatively, the State Department may have requested that the Georgians restrict Bureau activities in order to minimize the possibility that US investigators would discover politically inconvenient evidence. In either event, the special agents were allowed to examine the crime scene and the physical evidence but were not permitted to interrogate Georgian witnesses or perform independent investigation.

The first piece of physical evidence examined by the forensic team was Gogoladze's white Niva hatchback—the same vehicle that had been inspected by Special Agent Shukin on the day after the murder. In his report Shukin had said he "saw no indication of glass or other part of the vehicle having been damaged by gunfire." However, the newly arrived FBI documents stated that the forensic team had identified an obvious bullet hole in the upper right corner of the rear hatch.

There were only two explanations for the appearance of this previously undiscovered evidence. Either Shukin had missed the bullet hole or it had been placed there after his inspection. But if there was no bullet hole in the Niva at the time of the special agent's inspection, then the fatal shot either originated inside the car or entered the passenger compartment through an open door or window. I studied the documents carefully to come up with less damning alternatives and in the process noticed that Shukin's three-page memo had a different file number from the 356 pages I had just received. I called the FBI's FOIA office to inquire why.

"You have file number 185A?" asked the information officer.

"Yes," I said. "It's a three-page memo saying that there wasn't a bullet hole in the car."

She laughed nervously. "You weren't supposed to get that," she said. Apparently, this was information the FBI had intended to keep from me.

The FBI forensic team measured the diameter of the hole to determine the caliber of bullet that made it and took scrapings from the lip of the puncture. One agent sat in the dead man's seat—turning left and right, looking up and down—as his colleagues calculated angles and computed trajectories. They analyzed spatter patterns, sifted through dried pools of blood, and collected minuscule bone fragments. They tested for gunpowder residue and searched for evidence of more exotic accelerants. They checked the car's operating condition and diagnosed a malfunction in the driver's window crank. They removed the headliner, the seats, the carpet, and the interior panels. They catalogued and photographed everything.

At the end of this fourteen-hour examination the special agents drew four conclusions: Freddie Woodruff had been shot while sitting in the back seat of this automobile; the path of the bullet was from the back-right to the front-left of the passenger compartment; there was no gunpowder residue in the vehicle; and the bullet was not in the car. How and when the lead-and-steel bullet core had exited the vehicle remained a mystery.

The special agents spent the next day with Eldar Gogoladze, the car's driver and head of Shevardnadze's personal protection force. He spoke idiomatic English with an American accent. He volunteered to lead the forensic team to the crime scene and the special agents used the opportunity to conduct an informal interrogation.

The agents' armored SUV crossed the Mtkvari River and traveled along the right embankment through Tbilisi. Georgian paramilitary and HRT personnel followed closely in chase cars. Just outside the city the highway veered west. The convoy passed through Mtskheta and two miles on the other side turned north onto the Old Military Road. Gogoladze signaled the driver to stop.

"Here," he said. "This is where Freddie was shot."

It was an unremarkable spot on the road between the turnoff and the village of Natakhtari. The agents had traveled eighteen miles from the Sheraton Metechi Palace. The trip had taken twenty-eight minutes.

The forensic team did a ground survey and photogrammetric analysis from which they produced a crime scene sketch. They performed a grid search and discovered two brass shell casings. This evidence was marked for purposes of identification and chain of custody; its location was plotted on the sketch; and the casings were transmitted to the FBI lab for analysis.

As the agents worked, Gogoladze described the shooting: It was dark. There was a cluster of men standing on the side of the road. They were dressed in military uniforms and one of them held an automatic weapon. The man with the gun tried to stop the car and Gogoladze accelerated to evade him. He heard a single shot when the car was fifteen to twenty meters past the men. That shot killed Woodruff.

"It's highly unlikely that there could have been a plan to kill me," he said. "I am, after all, highly trained in countersurveillance and security matters. And I didn't detect any hostile or suspicious activities directed toward me or Woodruff."

However, it was difficult for the special agents to credit this declaration of professional excellence in light of Gogoladze's actions. First, he did not shoot at or immediately attempt to arrest the would-be assassin. Instead, his first act after delivering Woodruff's dead body to the Kamo Street Hospital was to go home for fifteen minutes.

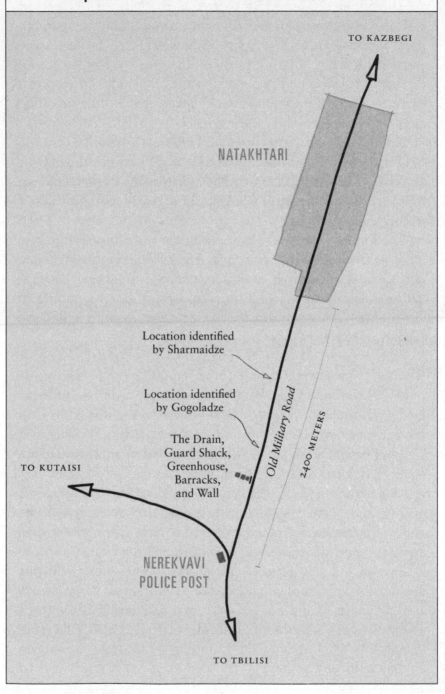

Disputed Location of Freddie Woodruff's Murder

TO KAZBEGI

NATAKHTARI

Location identified by Sharmaidze

Location identified by Gogoladze

The Drain, Guard Shack, Greenhouse, Barracks, and Wall

Old Military Road

2400 METERS

TO KUTAISI

NEREKVAVI POLICE POST

TO TBILISI

Second, he did not order the police to close the road. If the police had blockaded the road they would have trapped the shooter between the Tbilisi turnoff and the Russian border.

Third, he did not know which of the area hospitals were currently open and operational. As the head of Shevardnadze's bodyguards he would be expected always to know the nearest working trauma facility in the event of injury to the chairman. Instead, Gogoladze raced fecklessly from one closed hospital to another while Freddie expired in his back seat.

And fourth, he did not correctly identify the place where Woodruff had been shot eight days earlier. Gogoladze, a self-proclaimed expert in security matters, had misidentified the location of a crime to which he was allegedly an eyewitness.

On August 17 the Prosecutor General's Office organized a reenactment of the shooting, by the confessed killer, Anzor Sharmaidze. The FBI team participated. As the caravan of investigators approached the location previously searched by the FBI forensic team, Gogoladze asked Sharmaidze whether he wanted the cars to stop.

"No," said the prisoner. "Further down."

According to a special agent riding in the car with them, Gogoladze became visibly angry and might have killed Sharmaidze but for the presence of the American.

Sharmaidze said that the location of the shooting was a nondescript spot five hundred meters beyond the featureless site identified by Gogoladze. The prisoner showed where he had stood and demonstrated how he had fired his rifle. The special agents searched through the nearby grass and found *another* spent shell casing. Unlike the brass casings discovered with Gogoladze the day before, this newest evidence was later confirmed by the FBI lab as having been fired from Sharmaidze's rifle.

Thus, there was undeniable physical evidence connecting Sharmaidze's rifle to this location. But the FBI forensic team was not persuaded. They considered it improbable that the casing would have lain in the grass undiscovered for nine days despite multiple searches by the Georgian investigators. It appeared to be a theatrical presentation for the benefit of foreign visitors.

"Do they think we're idiots?" asked one of the special agents.

I was pondering one of the several excuses given by Sharmaidze for firing his weapon—anger that the thoughtless driver had not dimmed his bright headlights—when I came across the murder site coordinates. The FBI had helpfully identified the exact location by plotting its latitude and longitude.

I wondered how dark it was at the time of the shooting, so I consulted the US Naval Observatory website regarding sunset in that location on the day of the murder. On August 8, 1993, the sun set over the village of Natakhtari at 8:29 p.m. and civil twilight ended at 9:02 p.m. News reports and FBI documents stated that the murder occurred at approximately 9 p.m. Thus—at the time Anzor Sharmaidze was allegedly blinded by Eldar Gogoladze's bright headlights—it was not yet dark.

The official version of Anzor Sharmaidze's guilt depended, at least in part, on Gogoladze's demonstrably false claim that it was dark at the time of the shooting. It was difficult to believe that he could make such a fundamental mistake without malicious intent. Nevertheless, embassy personnel told the special agents that the Georgian's affection for Woodruff was sincere. They described the two men as "true friends" who met every day for coffee and hunted or fished together during their off-hours. Gogoladze was, they said, "visibly and genuinely upset" over the shooting.

So how could Gogoladze make such a basic error about the circumstances surrounding the death of his "true friend"? Like the location of the bullet that had crushed Woodruff's skull then disappeared, that was a mystery.

At least one US intelligence professional thought that the mystery led back to Russia. An embassy-based military attaché told the FBI investigators that he believed the shooting was a deliberate assassination. The attaché suspected that Woodruff had been killed by the GRU—the Russian military intelligence service—and that the Georgians may have been involved. According to the attaché, the GRU had remained largely unchanged by the collapse of the Soviet Union. It was possessive of the erstwhile Soviet empire and, he believed, had murdered Woodruff to warn Washington not to run intelligence operations in the territories of the former USSR. As for Georgian involvement, the attaché pointed out that its intelligence service was controlled by Jaba Ioseliani. The mafia warlord was known to have GRU affiliations and had been informed that Woodruff was CIA.

The issue of Georgian treachery came up again when a special agent interviewed a member of the American embassy staff. The staffer had breakfasted with Woodruff on the morning of August 8. Woodruff had needed to borrow the staffer's camera for a day trip to Kazbegi with Marina Kapanadze, an English-speaking waitress in the hotel's Piano Bar. "Freddie told me that he thought Marina was an officer in Mkhedrioni," he said. "They're a local mafia group controlled by Jaba Ioseliani." In the evening three days after the murder the staffer was having drinks with colleagues. Marina had returned to her work and served their table. The staffer reported that as he rose to leave Marina approached him. "I'm sorry for Freddie," she said, "but, you know . . . I am a spy." The staffer thought she'd stepped closer and said something else, but he couldn't remember. He'd been dumbstruck by the unexpected admission.

These interviews appeared to offer potentially fruitful lines of inquiry. However, I could find nothing in the record of the first investigation to indicate that the Bureau had pursued any of them. As I tried to imagine the motivations for such intentional indifference I realized that there was an Agency-sized omission in the FBI investigations at the Tbilisi embassy: There was no indication that the special agents had interviewed any of Woodruff's CIA colleagues or examined any documents relating to the work he was doing in Georgia.

The FBI is a law enforcement agency. It is tasked with identifying and arresting criminals. When an American diplomat is murdered, the Bureau will almost always investigate what the dead man was doing that made someone want to kill him.

The CIA is an intelligence agency. It is tasked with collecting and keeping secrets. When a covert officer is murdered, the Agency will almost never reveal the officer's clandestine activities.

Criminal investigator versus intelligence officer: different goals, different rules, different cultures. And in the absence of truly extraordinary circumstances, the need for secrecy will always trump the desire for justice.

This was my first lesson about the world of Realpolitik inhabited by spies. If avenging Woodruff's murder in the courts meant that the CIA had to reveal national security secrets, then Woodruff's murder would not be avenged in the courts. As I later learned, professional intelligence officers understood this as one of the unforgiving rules of an unforgiving game.

The FBI special agents departed Tbilisi on August 26, 1993. They took with them the rifle, cartridges, and magazine confiscated from Sharmaidze; the shell casings found during both roadside searches; the bullet fragments recovered during the Georgian autopsy; multiple crime scene sketches; dozens of laboratory samples; hundreds of photographs; a videotaped recording of Sharmaidze's confession; and Woodruff's clothes including his ball cap. In addition, the agents had a portion of the Georgian investigation file (which was still in the process of being translated). But what the agents did not have were FD 302s regarding Bureau interviews of Georgian citizens. With the exception of limited conversations with Gogoladze and Sharmaidze, the American investigators had not been permitted to interview any of the Georgian eyewitnesses.

Meanwhile, the Bethesda-based Armed Forces Institute of Pathology (AFIP) was completing a second autopsy of Woodruff. The first autopsy had been performed in Tbilisi by Georgian pathologists. American officials had given strict instructions that the Georgians were not to "touch the head" during their procedure. Nevertheless, when the body arrived in the United States the brain was missing and the skull was packed with cotton.

The body presented with a small circular wound above the right eye and a hand-sized wound above and behind the right ear. Georgian pathologists had concluded that the small wound was the point of entry and the large wound was the point of exit. However, using a scanning electron microscope, the AFIP pathologists reconstructed the bone fragments from around the wounds. Based on the fracture patterns of these fragments the AFIP experts concluded with 100 percent certainty that the bones at the back of the skull had broken *inward* and the bone above the eye had broken *outward*. The trajectory of the bullet was from *back to front*, slightly left to right and downward. There was no gunpowder or gunshot residue on Woodruff's body or clothes.

Woodruff had been shot in the back of the head and a bullet fragment had exploded out of his forehead.

The AFIP pathologists X-rayed the cotton with which Woodruff's skull had been packed and discovered a few minuscule metal fragments. These fragments, together with the splinters collected during the Georgian autopsy and the shell casing found during the reenactment, were delivered to the Firearms and Toolmarks Unit at the FBI Laboratory. The lab made two conclusions: First, the shell casing was fired from Sharmaidze's rifle; and second, the bullet fragments taken from Woodruff's skull were not sufficient to identify the caliber of the bullet or to establish a connection to Sharmaidze's gun.

I considered the results of this forensic analysis. Woodruff's brain and the bullet that scrambled it were missing. It was impossible to prove (or disprove) the caliber of the fatal bullet and it was impossible to prove (or disprove) that the fatal bullet had been fired from Sharmaidze's weapon. However, it was possible to prove that a shell casing from Sharmaidze's weapon had been found at the alleged murder site nine days after the murder. Thus, it looked to me like someone was working hard to eliminate any scientific evidence that would exonerate Sharmaidze while manufacturing circumstantial evidence that would convict him.

The special agents returned the weapon, cartridge, bullets, and shell casing to the Georgians for use by them in the murder trial. In addition, they provided selected photos (conveniently mounted on foam core), diagrams made at the time of the reenactment, and the report from the FBI Firearms and Toolmark Unit linking the shell casing to Sharmaidze's weapon. But they did not furnish to the Georgians the AFIP autopsy report, the evidence of Gogoladze's unreliability, or the results of their interviews with US embassy personnel.

If the government of Georgia was going to judicially murder Anzor Sharmaidze, the FBI wasn't going to get in the way.

CHAPTER 3

THE TESTIMONY OF TWO SPIES
AND A HOUSEWIFE

The trial of Anzor Sharmaidze began in Tbilisi at noon on December 30, 1993. The timing guaranteed that the press and public would be distracted with celebrations of the New Year and Orthodox Christmas. As a lawyer accustomed to the holiday rhythms of the American courts, I found this scheduling decision odd. The Georgian court clearly intended to do its business with a minimum of public scrutiny.

Sharmaidze was charged with three crimes: robbery of a house in April 1992; illegal acquisition and possession of a weapon and bullets; and the intentional murder of Freddie Woodruff on August 8, 1993. He pleaded guilty to the first charge and not guilty to the other two. He explained that as a soldier he was allowed to carry the weapon, and that although he had killed Woodruff it had not been deliberate.

The penalty for intentional murder was imprisonment from eight to fifteen years or death.

The Georgian court was presided over by a panel of three magistrates: Chief Judge Djemal Leonidze and two junior judges. This panel would decide the law, the facts, and the punishment. As was traditional in Georgia, there would be no impartial jury of Sharmaidze's peers. The government was represented by an experienced trial attorney from the Prosecutor General's Office. Sharmaidze was represented by a young lawyer named Tamaz Inashvili.

Inashvili had been appointed to represent the defendant by Chief Judge Leonidze. It was a strange choice for such an important case. Inashvili suffered from a crippling stutter that made him painful to hear and impossible to understand. And this was his very first case. It appeared to me that the chief judge did not intend to leave anything to chance in his march toward conviction.

Sharmaidze sat in a metal cage by the wall. He was twenty-two years old and had an eighth-grade education. Like everyone else in the room, he was wearing a heavy winter coat. There was no heat in the courthouse and it was bitterly cold. The room seemed an unlikely setting in which to decide whether a man should live or die.

Notwithstanding the holidays, a few people were sitting in the gallery. One of them was Lynn Whitlock, the Georgian-speaking vice consul at the US embassy. She had been assigned to monitor the case for the United States. Her twenty-page memorandum recounting the day-by-day proceedings was provided to me by the Department of State in response to my FOIA request.

Curiously, the FBI did not send an investigator to observe the trial. Perhaps Georgia was still too dangerous for the intrepid special agents. Or perhaps the FBI did not believe that the testimony of the so-called eyewitnesses was worth the price of a plane ticket. In any event, the Bureau's professional indifference to the trial suggested a certain lack of confidence in the Georgian legal process.

The chief judge conducted the questioning of Sharmaidze. The defendant had trouble speaking and could not remember details, but was generally calm. He told the chief judge that he was a machine gunner in the White Eagle Brigade and had been fighting in Abkhazia for ten months. While at the front he had two weapons: his official rifle and an AK-74 (an updated version of the infamous AK-47) that he'd found on the battlefield. When his battalion returned to Tbilisi, he delivered his official rifle to the quartermaster but kept the unofficial AK-74. It was with this weapon that he had allegedly killed Woodruff.

Sharmaidze testified that, on the morning of August 8, he invited his friends Genadi Berbitchashvili and Gela Bedoidze to accompany him to his family home near Mount Kazbek. Before leaving Tbilisi, the trio visited the grave of a fallen White Eagle comrade. They drank three or four bottles of vodka at the cemetery and several bottles of wine at the home of the dead soldier. Sharmaidze told the chief judge that he was too drunk to know the time when they finally left the city for his village.

Sharmaidze was uncertain whether they ran out of gas or simply realized they wouldn't have enough to make the trip. In any event, Bedoidze stopped the car on an isolated patch of road close to the village of Natakhtari and Sharmaidze began trying to wave down passing cars to ask for fuel. He was holding the AK-74.

Several cars went by without stopping. Sharmaidze said he was standing in the road as Gogoladze's Niva approached and that the speeding car almost hit him. The near miss made him angry. He raised his rifle and fired one shot.

At first he said that he shot into the air. Then he said he shot in the general direction of the car. However, he denied that he had aimed at anyone in particular or that he had intentionally shot in any specific direction. He estimated that the Niva was about thirty meters past him at the time when he fired his weapon.

He did not remember much about what happened next, except that his friends were upset with him for firing the rifle. Two hours later he and his companions were arrested by the police.

The chief judge passed the witness to the prosecutor, who asked about a cut bullet in the AK-74 magazine. According the FBI lab, the tip of the top bullet in the gun's magazine had been sliced off, effectively turning the round into a dum-dum or expanding bullet. Flattening the nose of a 5.45×39 mm round makes the bullet more likely to deform and fragment upon impact with soft tissue—something that the high-velocity AK-74 round typically does not do. This tendency to fragment increased the projectile's wounding effectiveness and formed the basis for the official explanation of the missing bullet: Sharmaidze fired a cut bullet at Woodruff and it disintegrated when it struck the victim's hard head.

But to me there was an obvious flaw in the logic of the official explanation: Freddie's head was not the first hard thing that the bullet hit. In order to reach the victim's skull the bullet first had to penetrate the metal skin of the Niva. It seemed unlikely that a deformed bullet would retain its physical integrity when it passed through steel but fragment when it encountered bone.

"Was Woodruff's skull harder than steel?" I wondered.

However, Sharmaidze's lawyer did not pose this common-sense question. Instead, he asked his client about the unofficial AK-74 and whether he was aware of an obligation to report it. And that was all.

It troubled me that the court-appointed defense lawyer did not ask about the circumstances of Sharmaidze's confession. This was the central piece of evidence in the case, and Inashvili did not attempt to impeach it by raising the specter of coercion. Even the American witnesses acknowledged the excesses of Georgian interrogations. In her daily summary Vice Consul Whitlock wrote, "We would not rule out that the defendant was beaten while under detention. Such abuse is a common phenomenon in the Georgian criminal justice system."

If the Americans could see it, why couldn't Sharmaidze's lawyer?

Eldar Gogoladze, the driver of the car, was the next person called to testify. The chief of Shevardnadze's personal protection force was relaxed and aloof, clearly not intimidated by the process.

He said that the quartet of two men and two women had traveled to the village of Arsha on August 8 for lunch at the home of his relative. None of the four consumed alcohol during the meal. Freddie wasn't feeling well and the group left during daylight. They stopped several times on the way back to take photographs.

By the time they reached the village of Natakhtari, it was dark. He observed three men in the glare of his headlights. Although one of the men was holding a rifle, the security officer did not accelerate or slow down. He heard a shot when the Niva was fifteen or twenty meters past the men. That shot struck Woodruff.

He took the wounded American first to the hospital in Mtskheta and then to the Kamo Street Hospital. It was 9:30 p.m. when they arrived in Tbilisi.

He had radioed the ministry duty officer while on the way, and members of the bodyguard service were waiting for him when he arrived. Accompanied by these men, he returned to the scene and arrested Sharmaidze.

The chief judge again asked Gogoladze whether Woodruff had drunk any wine at lunch and then excused the witness.

It was the kind of performance that makes a real trial lawyer itchy. The questions were general and the answers were vague. And there was no cross-examination.

No comparison of the witness's current testimony to prior inconsistent statements. No exploration of Gogoladze's failure to shoot back or close the road. No inquiry about his unexplained trip home after off-loading Woodruff's body. No interrogation concerning his failure to preserve his own bloody clothes for spatter analysis. No questions regarding his five-hundred-meter error in identifying the location of the murder. No impeachment of his claim of "no drinking" when the Georgian pathology report said that Woodruff had a .07 blood alcohol level. No examination about the weapons he was carrying on the day of the murder. No consideration of security protocols violated by traveling alone with a US diplomat. No scrutiny of the reasons why he had been fired as head of Shevardnadze's personal protection force.

And most important, there was no detailed development of the time line. In order for Anzor Sharmaidze to have killed Freddie Woodruff, the shooter and the victim would have had to be at the same place on the Old Military Road at precisely the same time. If Inashvili could prove that Woodruff arrived earlier or that Sharmaidze arrived later, then his client had to be innocent.

But the court-appointed defense counsel did not ask the witness any of these questions. Instead, Gogoladze was permitted to leave the courtroom with his testimony unchallenged and his aura of professional competence intact.

The depth of analysis did not improve in the direct examination and cross-examination of the female passengers. Elena Darchiash-vili, a married woman, testified that she had been invited on the outing by Gogoladze and that she sat in the front passenger's seat next to him. The court was tactfully disinterested in the nature of her relationship with the security chief but did ask about her association with Woodruff. It was the first time she'd met the American, she said. He sat in the back seat directly behind her. She thought he looked a little pale at lunch but did recall that he drank wine with the meal. She claimed that her eyesight was weak and as a consequence, she couldn't tell the court anything about the shooting.

Marina Kapanadze, the English-speaking barmaid also in the car, was similarly unhelpful. She was sitting in the back seat of the Niva, behind Gogoladze and next to Woodruff. She admitted that she saw a group of men standing on the side of the road and that one of them had a gun. But she claimed to have become hysterical when Freddie was shot and so could offer no useful evidence.

This was the core of the prosecution's case: a suspect confession and the testimony of two spies and a seemingly adulterous housewife. It would have been red meat to a vigorous advocate. But Inashvili ended the day as tamely as he had begun. I was beginning to get frustrated.

The trial adjourned for the long holiday weekend and reconvened the following Tuesday. The panel turned its attention to witnesses whose testimony was peripheral to the issue of guilt. The father of the dead White Eagle comrade testified that he met Sharmaidze at his son's grave. The defendant and his companions were drunk and the witness invited them home for food and more alcohol. The mother of the dead comrade could not specifically recall Sharmaidze; however, she did recollect that three people had come to her house for wine on August 8. She denied that her son had been a member of any military unit. He died, she said, when he was hit in the head by a stone.

The cross-examination of these witnesses was again disappointing. The defense lawyer did not attempt to use them to establish exactly when Sharmaidze left the family's house or exactly how long it would take to drive from their house to Natakhtari. The assumption that the defendant had departed in time to shoot Freddie Woodruff was allowed to stand without critical examination.

The deputy chief of Sharmaidze's battalion was summoned to testify. He said that the defendant was a good soldier during the fighting in Abkhazia but that he had broken army regulations by failing to register a weapon found on the battlefield. Predictably, the commander was not asked how an alleged violation of military law came to be prosecuted in a civilian court.

The panel called three of the presidential bodyguards to testify. They had been in the ministry offices on the night of August 8 and heard Gogoladze's radio report of the shooting. They raced to intercept their commander's car but missed him along the way. He had already unloaded Woodruff's body by the time the subordinates caught up with him at the Kamo Street Hospital. The assembled contingent of security men drove to the scene of the murder. They stopped at the Nerekvavi police post, near the turnoff to the Old Military Road, where the authorities had detained three drunken men for extorting gasoline from passing cars. Gogoladze recognized the men immediately and they were arrested. One of them was armed with an AK-74 assault rifle.

It was an admirable account of professional competence, but the devil (along with the truth) is in the details. And Inashvili did nothing to expose either one.

He did not fix the time of Gogoladze's radio message or his arrival at the Kamo Street Hospital. He did not inquire whether the bodyguards inspected the Niva or Woodruff's corpse and (if so) whether they found a bullet hole in one and rigor mortis in the other. He did not explore Gogoladze's furtive trip home or confirm that the security chief had showered and changed clothes. He did not inquire if Gogoladze appeared drunk or if he correctly identified the murder site. He did not confirm which of the three young men was holding the AK-74 at the time of their arrest. And he did not establish that on the night of the murder the bodyguards considered Gogoladze to be a legitimate suspect in the crime.

It was a less than inspiring performance.

On the fourth day of trial the panel called a ballistics expert from Georgia's Ministry of Internal Affairs. He testified that the fatal shot was fired from outside the car and at a distance greater than two meters. He could not identify the caliber of the bullet; however, he opined that the tip end of the unknown bullet had been cut off, causing it to explode on impact with Woodruff's skull. He claimed that this cut bullet had penetrated the car through the rubber molding around the rear window; that the hot projectile had melted the rubber on contact; and that after the bullet had passed through the molding the melted rubber had resealed with no obvious scar.

I paused to consider the foundation for this fantastic explanation. A bullet of unknown size, shape, weight, speed, and temperature strikes a molding of undetermined width, depth, density, and composition, causing the molding to instantly melt. This molding—which seals the interface between the body of the metal hatch and the rear window glass—is presumed to be the only thing that the bullet must pass through in order to reach the victim. It is simply assumed that the molding does not overlap glass or steel. So the first "hard" thing the cut bullet encounters is the victim's skull, at which point the blunted projectile shatters into numerous infinitesimal (and unidentifiable) pieces. The mechanics of this theoretical process were never reproduced in a laboratory, nor were they ever observed in practice. The witness simply speculated the theory into existence and then proclaimed it to be a fact.

I fantasized how this so-called expert would have responded to a methodical series of simple questions from a Texas lawyer. The exercise made me depressed.

The fragment of bullet recovered from Woodruff's head was too small to allow the expert to definitively associate it with Sharmaidze's weapon. However, according to the expert, the fragment had deformed in the manner characteristic of a cut bullet striking a hard object. And, the expert noted, at the time it was confiscated the AK-74 had a cut bullet in the chamber and twenty-three uncut bullets in the magazine.

Twenty-four bullets in all.

I felt like I'd been shot with a Taser. The number ricocheted through me like an electric pulse. I quickly searched the trial testimony and found independent confirmation from the security officer who had taken possession of the weapon at the time of the arrest: one bullet in the chamber and twenty-three in the magazine.

The FBI is very good at many things. One of them is keeping an accurate inventory of evidence. I had read the Bureau receipt several months before and tucked it away in my mind as an extraneous detail of no immediate importance. Now it mattered. The AK-74 received by the special agents and examined by the FBI lab had one cut bullet in the chamber and twenty uncut bullets in the magazine.

Twenty-one bullets.

Three bullets had disappeared from the AK-74 between the time the authorities seized the rifle and the time they delivered it to the FBI. This was direct proof that the Georgians had tampered with the physical evidence. And it was compelling circumstantial proof that they were responsible for the bullet hole in the Niva and the shell casing at the (alleged) murder site. But Inashvili did not ask about it.

The next day Sharmaidze's parents hired a new lawyer to represent their son.

A court-appointed lawyer could only be removed for cause, and the panel of judges could see no reason to terminate Inashvili's services. Nevertheless, the chief judge permitted Sharmaidze to engage the second lawyer. The case would go forward with two attorneys representing the defendant: the court-appointed Tamaz Inashvili and the privately retained Avtandil Sakvarelidze.

I was excited. Sakvarelidze was more experienced, more aggressive, and not beholden to the chief judge for his employment. The cavalry had finally arrived.

The new lawyer was given six days to familiarize himself with the case. When the trial reconvened, the panel called the Georgian pathologist who had performed the first autopsy. He testified that a bullet entered Woodruff's body on the right-hand side of the forehead and exited the body from the back of the head. He testified that the wound canal ran from front to back, slightly from bottom to top, and slightly from right to left. He testified that the nature of the damage indicated that, at the moment of penetrating the body, the ballistics of the bullet had been altered, and as a result the massive exit wound was caused by the side surface of the bullet.

And he was wrong about everything.

Lynn Whitlock noted the error in her summary of the daily trial proceedings. "As the embassy is aware," she wrote, "according to the FBI autopsy, the bullet entered the rear/top of the skull and a small fragment exited the forehead area." Nevertheless, neither the vice consul nor the government she represented informed the Georgian court of the mistake. Apparently, the United States was content to see Sharmaidze convicted on the basis of false evidence and inaccurate conclusions.

The next witness, an expert in juridical psychiatry, testified that Sharmaidze was cognizant of his actions and competent to stand trial. Although the defendant did exhibit some psychopathic traits, he did not have a mental disease that would excuse him from the legal consequences of his acts. In response to questions from the new defense lawyer, the expert admitted that Sharmaidze's participation in the Abkhaz war could have influenced his psychology. However, the witness said, the effects were not sufficient to allow the defendant to avoid accountability.

Defense attorney Sakvarelidze was making his presence felt. He asked the chief judge for permission to reexamine the defendant. Sharmaidze told the panel that he had planned to surrender the AK-74 to the army quartermaster, but since he'd intended to return to Abkhazia in a few days he decided to keep it. He denied that he had cut the bullets. They were, he said, given to him during the terrible battle for Sukhumi, the bloody first engagement in Georgia's war with Abkhaz separatists.

The new lawyer was subtly focusing the court on the difficulty of judging a military man by civilian standards. Would the court really convict a soldier for carrying an unregistered rifle and cut bullets to a battle for Georgian sovereignty?

Sharmaidze told the panel that on the night of the shooting he was afraid that the Niva was going to hit him. He got angry, lost control, and fired his weapon. But he did not intend to shoot the car or its occupants. Otherwise, he said, he would have fired more than one shot and not lingered at the scene.

The new lawyer was only nibbling at the edges of the prosecution's case. Nevertheless, it was encouraging to me. This was advocacy.

The panel called three roadway policemen from the Nerekvavi police post, a defunct railway car planted three hundred meters past the turnoff to the Old Military Road. They had been on duty the evening of August 8 when, a few minutes after 11 p.m., three drunk young men arrived in a Soviet-made compact car. All three were wearing military uniforms and one was holding a Kalashnikov assault rifle. They asked for gasoline and, because the police had none to share, for permission to stop cars to get some. A short while later a carload of military police arrived. They demanded to see the ersatz soldiers' identification papers and proof that they were authorized to carry the weapon. An argument ensued. Just then Gogoladze appeared with two cars full of security officials. He accused the three young men of shooting an American and arrested them for murder.

In addition, he arrested one Officer Agsabadze for failing to close the highway.

According to the witnesses, Gogoladze claimed that he had driven by the Nerekvavi police post on his way to Tbilisi and had told a policeman standing outside that a man had been killed in his car. The chief bodyguard was certain that the policeman to whom he had spoken was Agsabadze. However, Officer Agsabadze could prove that he was not at the post when Gogoladze allegedly drove by. He and a colleague had been in western Georgia all day on official business and had only returned at 11 p.m.

It was a stunning revelation. The arresting officer could not identify a policeman to whom he had spoken face-to-face two hours earlier, but could (allegedly) identify Sharmaidze, a nondescript young man he had seen in his headlights as he raced by at fifty miles per hour. The statements were completely incongruous. But neither of Sharmaidze's lawyers seized on the discrepancy.

According to one of the roadway policemen, investigators fired a test shot at the alleged murder site to see if anyone could hear it at the post. They could. However, none of the policemen remembered hearing a shot earlier in the night. This fact suggested three different possibilities to me: first, that the policemen simply missed the sound of the shot; second, that the shooting occurred at a different location; and third, that the weapon used to kill Freddie Woodruff had a silencer.

One of the young men arrested with Sharmaidze was Genadi Berbitchashvili. He was a municipal policeman in the Chugureti District, a section of Tbilisi that included the Sheraton Metechi Palace. He testified that (with no prior arrangement) Sharmaidze and Gela Bedoidze had come to his house on August 8. Bedoidze put on one of Berbitchashvili's military uniforms and the trio drove to the home of a friend named Baia.

"Why did Bedoidze put on a uniform?" I wondered.

After drinking for a while the foursome decided to visit the grave of Baia's cousin. They were joined there by some guardsmen with whom they drank more alcohol and fired off an automatic weapon. Berbitchashvili was not pressed to explain where the weapon had come from; however, he was emphatic that Sharmaidze did not have a rifle when he first arrived at the house.

The group adjourned to the home of Baia's dead cousin, where they continued drinking. After a while, Sharmaidze suggested they visit his family. He was from Arakhveti, a ramshackle roadside village perched on the side of Mount Kazbek. The only way to get there was via the Old Military Road.

I checked a map. Freddie Woodruff would have driven directly by the defendant's home on his way to and from the village of Arsha. It was a curious irony.

The intoxicated trio set out for the Sharmaidze family home in Bedoidze's Jiguli sedan. Along the way they gave twenty liters of gasoline to an acquaintance. It was an unfortunate decision. Five hundred meters past the Nerekvavi police post they ran out of fuel. Bedoidze made a U-turn and pulled the car to the side of the road. He and Sharmaidze got out to flag down passing cars. Berbitchashvili stayed in the back seat of the Jiguli.

The witness saw Sharmaidze fire a shot in the air and demanded to know why he had done it. According to Berbitchashvili, Sharmaidze said that a white Niva came close to hitting him so he got angry and fired the weapon.

When no cars stopped to help, the young men drove five hundred meters to the Nerekvavi police post. A few minutes later the military police arrived and (after them) Gogoladze and the security officers. Berbitchashvili, Bedoidze, and Sharmaidze were arrested and taken to Tbilisi.

"If they ran out of gas on the Old Military Road, how did they drive to the Nerekvavi police post?" I wondered. Apparently, this paradox did not trouble the court.

Notwithstanding his accusation that the defendant had fired the rifle, Berbitchashvili gave testimony potentially helpful to Sharmaidze. The witness had described a very busy day. However, the defense lawyers made no attempt to establish the exact time when each of the identified activities had occurred. In the absence of those details, it was impossible to prove that Sharmaidze had not arrived at the murder site in time to kill Woodruff. The impression had been created, but the fact had not been established.

At the conclusion of this testimony the chief judge read a jailhouse letter from the witness to Sharmaidze. In it Berbitchashvili begged the defendant to confess. "It is pointless for you to hide the facts and it will get us all killed," he wrote. "You must tell them that you alone fired the gun. You must tell them that I was asleep in the back seat and that I was not involved."

The chief judge noted that the letter had been confiscated from Sharmaidze in jail; that he had sewn it into the waistband of his trousers; and that it had been discovered by vigilant policemen. But to me it all seemed highly improbable. Where did the imprisoned Berbitchashvili get pen and paper? How did he smuggle the correspondence from his cell to Sharmaidze's? How did Sharmaidze sew the letter into his waistband? And why did he retain such a damning letter?

These were basic authentication and chain of custody questions. Regrettably, no one asked.

The new defense lawyer requested that the panel recall the ballistics expert. His reexamination focused on the distance between where Sharmaidze was allegedly standing and the location where the FBI found a shell casing linked to Sharmaidze's rifle.

"How far would an empty shell casing fly upon ejection from an AK-74?" the lawyer asked.

It was a shrewd question. The distance between the shell casing and Sharmaidze's alleged location had been measured by the FBI. It was 12.8 meters or about 42 feet.

The ballistics expert equivocated. Distance could depend on a number of factors—the type of steel in the bullet, the angle of the shot, the terrain, the weather conditions.

But Sakvarelidze persisted. "How far?"

"Between three and eleven meters," the expert said.

Sakvarelidze now had a specific opinion that could be objectively tested with a simple demonstration. Investigators could fire the rifle (repeatedly and in different conditions) and see how far each shell casing traveled. If the ejected casings flew a distance substantially shorter than forty-two feet, then Sakvarelidze would have circumstantial proof that the shell casing in evidence had been planted.

And the shell casing found by the FBI was the only physical evidence tying Sharmaidze to the murder.

But the chief judge refused to permit the demonstration. He claimed that there were too many variables and it would be impossible to get an accurate result.

It was a disturbing decision.

Ordinarily the existence of variables affects the weight that is given to a result and not a defendant's right to perform a demonstration. The defendant performs the demonstration, and then the parties argue whether the circumstances of the test were sufficiently similar to the original event to make the results meaningful. In this case, the chief judge refused to allow any attempt to compensate for the variables. He was taking sides, protecting the prosecution from potentially embarrassing evidence. It was unfair.

I felt a cold and unfamiliar chill. What's a smart Texas trial lawyer supposed to do when the whole judicial process is a charade?

Gogoladze, the driver of the car, was recalled to the stand. Sakvarelidze quizzed him about the clothes he was wearing on the night of the murder. According to the security chief, his jacket was bloodstained but none of the investigators inspected it. The testimony highlighted a significant deficiency in the official investigation: Examination of the spatter patterns could prove whether Gogoladze was sitting in the front seat at the time of the shooting. If the spatter did not confirm it, then the murder did not happen in the manner claimed by the government.

It was an astute attack on the heart of the prosecution's case. But it didn't seem to matter to the panel. I began to suspect that this trial was little more than theater. Sakvarelidze could go off script, but it would not change the final act.

On the eighth day of trial Gela Bedoidze was called to testify and the drama veered dangerously close to farce. The witness confirmed Berbitchashvili's account of the day's activities and was then interrogated regarding his exact location when Sharmaidze fired at the Niva.

"Can you show us on this photograph exactly where you were standing at the moment the defendant fired his rifle?" asked the chief judge.

"There," said Bedoidze, pointing to a nondescript stretch of roadside in the photograph.

"And how do you know that's where you were standing?" asked the chief judge.

"Because that's where I was told to say I was standing," said Bedoidze.

It was a blunder. The chief judge had violated a basic rule of cross-examination—he asked a question to which he did not already know the answer. Bedoidze's childlike candor had revealed a conspiracy to manufacture evidence of guilt. However, instead of vigorously exploring this prosecutorial corruption, the chief judge ruled the testimony inadmissible. It was improper and impossible for a witness to suggest that the authorities had instructed him what to say.

I paused to consider the implications of the court's ruling. How could I hope to reverse Sharmaidze's conviction if proof of fabricated evidence and official misconduct were *per se* inadmissible?

This was the beginning of my Georgian education. It was not enough to be a good lawyer and it was not enough to be right. Something more would be required.

The trial was drawing to a close, and Sakvarelidze played his last cards. He reexamined Sharmaidze, and this time the defendant told a different story. He completely repudiated his confession. He did not run out of gas on the Old Military Road, he did not fire his rifle, he did not kill Freddie Woodruff. He told the panel that he had been brutally tortured several times and that the police had threatened to kill his entire family. The chief judge asked why he had waited until the end of the trial to tell the truth.

"Because I was beaten every time I tried to speak up," said the defendant.

Sharmaidze said that the trio stopped at the Jvari Monastery, and while they were there, people in two cars asked them for gasoline. An acquaintance, Tamaz Zakaidze, was a passenger in one of the cars and suggested that they all drive to Natakhtari to get fuel. When they arrived, Sharmaidze met another old friend, a military policeman named Gia Chokheli. They drank vodka together, and after a while, Chokheli advised them to drive to the Nerekvavi police post because it was easier to get gasoline there. At the Nerekvavi police post they were immediately confronted by the military police and (a little while later) arrested by Gogoladze.

Sakvarelidze reinterrogated Berbitchashvili. The witness confirmed Sharmaidze's new chronology and the identities of his alibi witnesses. The defense lawyer attempted to establish the timing of specific events and the distances between the locations at which they occurred. I was elated that finally someone was trying to prove that Sharmaidze could not have arrived on time to fire the fatal shot. He asked the court to order a reinvestigation or (at the very least) to interview the alibi witnesses. He claimed that the prosecution had failed to disclose that someone *else* had been arrested for the murder, a drug addict and car thief named Inaurai.

It was a startling allegation. Nevertheless, the chief judge rejected the accusation and denied the request. Instead, the panel permitted the prosecution to present rebuttal evidence—the videotape of Sharmaidze's original confession. Although it was obvious in the video, neither the prosecutor nor the chief judge mentioned the bruise on the side of the prisoner's face. It was the size and shape of a rifle butt.

And with that, the prosecution and defense rested their cases. There had been ten days of trial and nineteen witnesses. Oral argument was scheduled for February 2, 1994.

The prosecutor's summation was perfunctory. He reviewed the relevant statutes and reread the official chronology. He argued that testimony by Berbitchashvili and Bedoidze confirmed testimony by Gogoladze and the women (and vice versa). He insisted that the shell casing found at the scene proved that Sharmaidze had fired his weapon at that location. And he concluded by asking the panel to sentence Sharmaidze to fifteen years, five years in prison and ten years in a work colony.

I was surprised by the restraint manifested in the sentencing request. "Why didn't he ask for the death penalty?" I wondered. If he believed his evidence, then it would have been an appropriate remedy.

Inashvili, the court-appointed defense lawyer, argued for acquittal or reinvestigation of the murder charge. He focused on the key fact that there was no evidence that the bullet that killed Woodruff had been fired from Sharmaidze's weapon. Admittedly, a shell casing from Sharmaidze's rifle was found at the scene; however, the fact that a shell came from the defendant's weapon did not prove that Sharmaidze fired the shot *or* that the shot killed Woodruff. And none of the other evidence presented filled this important gap in the prosecution's proof. The witness testimony was unreliable, and there was good reason to believe that Sharmaidze had been tortured and made to confess falsely.

It was a credible performance—clever, nuanced, and insightful. Inashvili had given the panel a legitimate basis to exonerate Sharmaidze without having to adjudge the police and prosecutor guilty of misconduct. He had invited them to do justice in half steps: If they could not stretch themselves to find the defendant not guilty, then they could at least order a reinvestigation and revisit the case in the future.

I was forced to reevaluate Tamaz Inashvili. It was clear that he understood better than anyone the panel's agenda and its limited tolerance for justice. A good lawyer knows the law, a great lawyer knows the judge. And Inashvili had revealed himself as a great lawyer.

By contrast, Sakvarelidze, the new defense lawyer, showed himself to be a competent journeyman. He claimed that Sharmaidze had been tortured and that he had confessed only after the police threatened to kill his family. He argued that the timing of Sharmaidze's activities on August 8 proved that it was impossible for him to have arrived at Natakhtari in time to kill Woodruff. He contended that the investigators and the court had violated Sharmaidze's rights and that the defendant should be found not guilty.

It was an all-or-nothing approach: Sharmaidze was innocent and the panel should say so. But if the panel of judges accepted his arguments then they would implicitly accuse the police and prosecutor of serious crimes and gross violations of human rights—and they were never going to do that. They would kill Sharmaidze before they would let that happen.

Meanwhile, attorney Sakvarelidze had spoken the truth, but not in a way that would help his client. It was sobering and more than a little deflating to realize that I would have done exactly the same thing, and thereby assured my young client's execution. I was going to have to learn a whole new set of skills if I wanted to succeed in my quixotic quest without getting someone killed.

On February 7, 1994, the panel returned with a verdict. Sharmaidze was guilty of murder. He was sentenced to fifteen years in a labor camp and confiscation of all property. Pursuant to court order, the defendant was denied the right to appeal.

Eight days later the FBI issued its final report regarding the murder: Freddie Woodruff was killed "by person or persons unknown." The report did not implicate or accuse Anzor Sharmaidze and did not recommend that he be extradicted to the United States to stand trial. The case would remain open but unassigned pending new developments.

And it didn't take long for something new to develop. On February 21, 1994, the FBI arrested Aldrich Hazen Ames on suspicion of spying for the Soviet Union and Russia.

The follow-up investigation of Ames's espionage would lead the Bureau straight back to Tbilisi and the murder of Freddie Woodruff.

CHAPTER 4

AN OBSCURE HINT

In 1985, eight years before the murder of Freddie Woodruff, the CIA suffered an unprecedented loss of human intelligence assets related to the Soviet Union and Eastern Europe. As one CIA officer put it, the KGB was wrapping up American intelligence operations "with reckless abandon." Forty-five cases and two technical operations were compromised or developing problems. Each of these cases represented a foreign national who, at the risk of his or her life, was providing useful information to the United States. The loss of these human sources resulted in a virtual collapse of CIA Soviet operations.

Initially, the Agency suspected that the KGB had penetrated its communications with the field, using either technical means or a human source. To determine whether this hypothesis was accurate, the CIA ran a series of probes; however, none of these tests elicited any discernible response from the Soviets. There was no evidence that CIA communications had been breached.

William Casey, then the director of Central Intelligence, requested a review of the compromised cases and an analysis of the reasons for the failures. In a ten-page memorandum, the reviewer concluded that each of the compromised operations could be attributed to problems evident in that operation. This myopic deduction was due in part to a reluctance to think the unthinkable—that one of the elite professionals in the Directorate of Operations (DO) was engaged in espionage.

The Soviet–East European (SE) Division put in place "draconian measures" to limit access to its ongoing operations and to ensure that communications from the field were accessible only to the employees working on those operations. The results of this heightened security were encouraging: SE Division initiated new Soviet operations that appeared to survive.

The success of these post-1985 Soviet operations led some to suspect that Edward Lee Howard was the original source of the compromise. A former SE Division trainee, Howard had been hired by the DO in 1981. As part of his training for an initial assignment in Moscow, he had been given access to details about certain Agency operations in the Soviet Union. In 1983, after he made damaging admissions during a polygraph examination, the CIA abruptly terminated his employment. Embittered by what he thought was unfair treatment, Howard decided to retaliate by selling CIA secrets. Subsequent investigation revealed that he had begun talking to the KGB in 1985 and escaped to the Soviet Union in 1986.

But the 1985 losses could not be attributed to Edward Lee Howard alone. The young trainee simply did not have access to information about most of the compromised cases. In light of this fact, there appeared to be only one plausible explanation: There was a traitor in the Soviet–East European Division of the Directorate of Operations.

In October 1986 the chief of the CIA Counterintelligence Staff created a four-person "special task force" (STF) to investigate the 1985 losses. The STF was directed to analyze the compromised cases and to identify commonalities among them. In particular, the STF attempted to determine which CIA employees had access to the compartmentalized information about those cases.

That same month the CIA and FBI learned that two Soviet sources who had worked closely with the FBI had been arrested by the KGB and were about to be executed. The FBI responded by creating its own six-person analytical team (code-named ANLACE) that worked full-time to analyze the compromise of its two sources.

The STF and ANLACE investigations continued in tandem for eight years, until the FBI arrested Aldrich Hazen Ames for espionage on February 21, 1994. At the time of his arrest, Ames worked at CIA headquarters, in the Counternarcotics Center. He was chief of an Agency task force that monitored drug traffic in the former Soviet Union.

While in this position Ames had established the "Black Sea initiative"—a pet project intended to develop intelligence sharing and antinarcotics cooperation among countries in the region. Tbilisi had been chosen as headquarters for the initiative and Ames had traveled there in July 1993 for the start-up conference. However, that meeting was called off when at the last minute DCI James Woolsey canceled his plan to attend.

The *New York Times* reported on March 14, 1994, that the CIA intended to investigate whether there was any connection between Ames's treachery and the murder of Freddie Woodruff. Apparently, the proposed inquiry struck a nerve in Moscow. Two weeks later, TASS, the official Russian news service, declared, "Ames Case, Woodruff's Murder Not Linked." The article said that some American intelligence officers suspected that Woodruff had been murdered by the GRU because he was providing Shevardnadze (who was at the time chairman of the Georgian State Council) with intelligence on Russian military support for separatists in Georgia. Although the Russians rejected any connection between Ames and Woodruff's death, they did not deny that Freddie had been killed by Russian military intelligence.

It was the first time I realized that spies sometimes use newsprint to talk to each other.

I searched for details about Ames's professional involvement with Woodruff and found them in the Congressional Record. Three weeks after the TASS article Senator Jesse Helms disclosed that, in addition to facilitating US training of Shevardnadze's security forces, Woodruff was investigating Georgia's role as a conduit for heroin being smuggled to the West. "Some informed Georgians think Mr. Woodruff had come to believe that the men Washington had sent him to cooperate with were in fact involved in the heroin shipments," said Helms. "Had Mr. Woodruff reported this, Mr. Ames would have been the first man in the CIA to receive his report."

Although Ames had not yet been debriefed by the CIA or FBI, following his arrest it was assumed that he had given the Russians everything that crossed his desk, including Woodruff's reports from Georgia. If the Russians were reading Freddie's dispatches in real time, it might provide a motive for his execution.

Helms called on the Clinton administration to "clear up any connection between Mr. Ames's visit to Georgia last year and the murder of CIA station chief Woodruff." However, according to my heavily censored stack of FBI documents, by the time Helms made his speech on the Senate floor the Bureau was already hard at work investigating the connection.

Although the name Aldrich Hazen Ames did not appear anywhere in the redacted FBI production, his presence was pervasive. Responsibility for the post-Ames investigation was transferred to the counterintelligence specialists in the Bureau's National Security Division, the same special agents who had unmasked and arrested the CIA traitor. These elite investigators had the resources, security clearance, and will to accomplish the FBI's redefined task: "to determine the person or persons responsible for the death of Fred R. Woodruff."

The FBI was no longer simply providing laboratory services. It was fully involved in the hunt for Woodruff's killer. My document chronology revealed that the agents' initial step was a thorough review of the first FBI investigation. The newly assigned investigators pored over the first case file and identified specific topics and witnesses that required further attention. The FOIA censors had expurgated any statement of these conclusions; however, the context of the redactions allowed me to make certain deductions.

First, there was a series of transmittal memoranda to and from the FBI Language Services Unit. These memos described the receipt and return of Georgian language materials that were translated into English. One of the translated items was a VHS videocassette tape—probably the recorded confession of Anzor Sharmaidze. The other items were Georgian-language documents that "served to give WMFO (Washington Metropolitan Field Office) a better understanding of the events that occurred on August 8, 1993." Based on the fact that the agents considered the documents sufficiently reliable to affect their understanding of the murder, I deduced that those documents were investigation materials from a Georgian-speaking professional source—possibly the police or security service.

I made a note for my wish list. If the FBI could get a copy of the Georgian investigation file, maybe I could too.

Second, there was a bureaucratic paper trail of travel authorizations. These documents allowed me to see the international destinations that the agents deemed relevant to their investigation—Tbilisi, Baku, Moscow. It was the trail I would follow in the ensuing years.

In addition, each request included a redacted list of identifiers for the people who would be traveling. Information related to an individual traveler's technical skills gave me insight into the purpose of the trip. For example, if the request sought approval for a Class 3 Georgian linguist and a Bureau polygrapher to travel to Tbilisi, I could reasonably infer that the agents intended to interview Georgian speakers and to polygraph at least one obliging witness. This kind of extraterritorial FBI investigation implied broad cooperation from the Georgian authorities and hinted that there might be Georgian security officers with detailed knowledge of FBI activities in the country.

I added another item to my wish list: find a knowledgeable Georgian security officer and convince him to tell me what the FBI special agents did in Tbilisi.

Each travel authorization included an abbreviated statement about the purpose of the proposed trip. These statements were so thoroughly censored that it was almost impossible to divine any meaningful information from them. However, in the process of analyzing the statements, I learned about FBI protocols for international travel.

In order to operate in a foreign country, a special agent must obtain approval from the US Department of State. This approval is called "country clearance." The Bureau maintains liaison officers at the DOS Office of Foreign Missions to coordinate State's processing of FBI travel applications. The traveling special agent briefs the liaison officer, and the liaison officer helps the agent obtain the necessary country clearance.

Insight into this procedure led me to discover one of the singular ironies of this case. During the Bureau's reinvestigation of Woodruff's murder, the senior FBI liaison at the DOS Office of Foreign Missions was Robert Hanssen. In 2001, Hanssen was arrested and pled guilty to fifteen counts of espionage committed on behalf of the Russians. It was later revealed that his KGB handler was Victor Cherkashin, the same DC-based spymaster who supervised Aldrich Ames. Thus, as a precondition to their international investigation of the Woodruff murder, the FBI special agents were required to brief one Cherkashin-run Soviet spy regarding the status of their investigation of another Cherkashin-run Soviet spy.

But before undertaking any international travel, the special agents interviewed the people in America with knowledge of the relevant facts about Woodruff's murder. This included Aldrich Ames. On April 28, 1994—sixty-six days after his arrest—Ames pled guilty to two counts of conspiracy to commit espionage and two counts of conspiracy to commit tax fraud. He was sentenced to life in prison with no possibility of parole. In order to avoid the death penalty, he agreed to forfeit all of his assets; to forgo any profits from book, movie, or television deals; and most importantly to fully cooperate with the CIA and FBI.

I pondered the utility of Ames's commitment to cooperate. After all, he was a confessed traitor with a long history of deceit and a demonstrated ability to beat the CIA's periodic polygraphs. "How do you learn to trust someone that you know is a liar?" I wondered.

One area of interest to the FBI was Ames's reaction when he first learned of Woodruff's murder. Eyewitnesses who were with him in a hallway at CIA headquarters reported that when he heard the news he began sobbing and fell to his knees. This tearful exhibition seemed out of character for a man whose blithe treachery had murdered more than a dozen foreign agents.

The FBI wanted to know the origin of this extravagant emotional display: Was it grief or remorse? Sadness or guilt?

I looked into the history of the personal association of the two men and discovered that while Ames was posted to New York, he had rented his house in Reston, Virginia, to Woodruff. The transaction appeared to be arm's-length and one of mutual convenience. I could find nothing to indicate that Ames and Woodruff had the kind of intimate relationship that would provoke such an intense display of grief.

Perhaps the explanation lay in Ames's July 1993 trip to Tbilisi. The FBI interviewed the CIA analysts and officers who had traveled from the US to attend the start-up conference for the Black Sea initiative. Several CIA employees reported that Ames and Woodruff had a loud and angry exchange in the Piano Bar at the Sheraton Metechi Palace. The argument occurred in the evening after the DCI announced his decision to cancel the conference. The witnesses confirmed that Marina Kapanadze, the English-speaking barmaid and confessed spy, was on duty and observed the clash.

One analyst described a happier interaction: She, Ames, and Woodruff spent a free day touring Mount Kazbek and sampling local wine. It was vaguely disconcerting to learn that Ames and Woodruff had traveled the same route on which Woodruff would later be assassinated. Then a darker question occurred to me: Did the CIA suspect Ames of espionage at the time they authorized his trip to Tbilisi?

Several months later I put this question to the man who had been CIA Moscow station chief at the time of the murder.

"No way," he said. "If the Agency suspected Ames of being a spy for the Soviets, they wouldn't permit him to get within walking distance of Russia. If he got across the border, the United States wouldn't be able to touch him. Everyone at the Agency knew what had happened with Edward Lee Howard—and nobody was going to let that happen again."

He was right, of course. Edward Lee Howard had rolled out of a moving car in Santa Fe, New Mexico, and eluded his FBI tail. He traveled to Finland, crossed the frontier into Russia, and began a new life in Moscow. He lived there until 2002, when (according to the *Washington Post*) he broke his neck falling down stairs at his dacha. However, the official Russian news service quoted an unnamed Russian intelligence officer who enigmatically denied "this version of Howard's death." Perhaps it wasn't an accident. Perhaps it was the CIA settling accounts.

Documents that I received from the Department of State indicated that US ambassador Kent Brown met with then-chairman Eduard Shevardnadze to brief him on the purpose of the FBI's return trip to Georgia. The ambassador explained that the Woodruff case had continued to attract public attention and was frequently the subject of rumors in Tbilisi. As an example, he cited the recurring reports that Anzor Sharmaidze had recanted his confession and that he was receiving special treatment in prison. In addition, he pointed out that the timing of Ames's visit to Georgia fueled speculation that Woodruff's death was part of a broader conspiracy.

"The US Government continues to believe that the Georgian investigative and legal processes worked well," the ambassador told the local press. "We remain satisfied with the results."

Nevertheless, given the recurring rumors and speculations, the US government requested permission from the Georgian government for FBI special agents to return to Tbilisi in order to review the findings of the original investigators.

It was artful duplicity. The US wasn't investigating the worst intelligence breach in its national history; it was simply trying to quash the Tbilisi rumor mill. Notwithstanding the transparency of this diplomatic fig leaf, the Georgians consented and the special agents were granted country clearance.

About the same time, a small intelligence newsletter reported one of the Bureau's working theories: that Woodruff was killed because he had discovered Ames's role in a Russian drug-smuggling operation. This reference to illicit narcotics reminded me of statements made by Senator Helms. "It is public knowledge in Georgia that the security forces of Edward Shevardnadze's regime are involved in the republic's rampant drug business," he said. "So severe has the problem become that even Mr. Shevardnadze recently felt obliged to undergo a heroin test to prove his credibility."

This was the state of governance in Georgia in August 1994 when the FBI special agents arrived to reinvestigate the murder of Freddie Woodruff. It was very difficult for the Americans to tell the good guys from the bad guys.

The purpose of the agents' trip was to interview Georgian witnesses and to perform a polygraph examination on Anzor Sharmaidze. The agents summarized the results of this initial investigation in a twenty-five-page letterhead memorandum— an FBI report that is prepared with the intention that it will be disclosed to people outside the Bureau. A thoroughly redacted version of this report was produced by the FBI in response to my FOIA request.

According to the memo, the agents met with Sharmaidze on two occasions. As he had done at trial, he denied any involvement in the murder and claimed that his confession was the result of torture. Nevertheless, he refused to submit to a polygraph. He had been warned that once he was hooked up to the machine the Georgian police would ask him about other crimes and use the results to prosecute him.

This third-party interference seemed to be a calculated disruption of the FBI investigation. It made me think that someone didn't want the Bureau to prove that Sharmaidze was telling the truth when he said he was innocent.

The FBI's interviews with chief bodyguard Eldar Gogoladze were not much better. Armed with translations of the Georgian investigation file, the special agents quizzed Gogoladze about previously undisclosed details. He acknowledged that between the time he delivered Woodruff's body to the Kamo Street Hospital and the time he arrested Sharmaidze he went home to take a shower and change his clothes. In addition, he admitted that he did not preserve the clothes he'd been wearing for later inspection by investigating officers.

I could only imagine one motivation for this audacious act of personal hygiene: Gogoladze had an urgent need to eliminate evidence. But what was that evidence? Was it something on the clothes that shouldn't have been (such as gunpowder residue)? Or was it something that should have been on the clothes but wasn't (such as blood spatter)?

Another curiosity was Gogoladze's choice of vehicle. He typically drove a large green four-door American sedan, a car that proclaimed both his importance and (perhaps) his insecurity. However, for the long trip to Kazbegi he chose a Niva 1600, a cramped and uncomfortable Russian-made two-door hatchback jeep. No one from the embassy had ever seen him in this car before.

I studied photographs of the Niva and deduced a possible reason for the choice: There was no quick and easy egress for passengers sitting in the back seat. Whether intentionally or not, once Woodruff was in the back seat he was essentially contained and controlled in a box. This would not have been true if Gogoladze had driven the four-door sedan.

The special agents also interrogated the chief bodyguard about his failure to comply with Georgian security protocols. Ministry regulations required that any transport of foreign diplomats outside the city be guarded by a chase car. Gogoladze's violation of this rule was one of the reasons cited for his (curiously temporary) termination from the security service.

It seemed likely that the effective use of a chase car would have prevented Woodruff being shot by a drunken soldier standing on the side of the road. But this fact *alone* did not mean that Gogoladze was involved in a plot to kill Woodruff. It was equally plausible that Woodruff, an operations officer who (according to a colleague) had a reputation as a cowboy, persuaded the security chief to disregard the chase car requirement. After all, it is difficult to be inconspicuous when you're being followed by an SUV bristling with armed men.

The FBI censors had redacted Gogoladze's statements about how the shooting occurred; however, they left a tantalizing suggestion that the Bureau suspected the chief bodyguard's account might be false. "The fact of the matter," said the memo, "is that there is a variance in information reported to the FBI concerning ▆▆▆▆▆▆."

"A variance in information" was a delicate phrase to describe different people telling inconsistent stories. It was an explicit acknowledgment by FBI special agents that there were other witnesses to the murder. Given the limitations imposed on the Americans investigating in Georgia, it seemed probable that the identities of these witnesses had been provided to the agents by Georgian investigators.

The half-redacted phrase wasn't exculpatory evidence, but it was proof that exculpatory evidence existed. If I wanted to find those witnesses, I would need to establish a relationship with someone inside the Georgian security services.

The discussion of the Gogoladze interviews concluded with an examination of his failure to obtain prompt medical care for Woodruff. The first FBI investigation had already raised the issue of his professional incompetence—racing wildly from one closed hospital to another when (as the head of Shevardnadze's bodyguards) he was expected always to know the nearest available trauma facility. The second investigation hinted at a darker explanation.

"The first hospital was closed," said the memo. "The second hospital had no electricity, but a doctor offered medical assistance ▆▆▆▆▆▆."

This was new information to me: A doctor had offered medical assistance to Freddie Woodruff. I focused on the verb. The memo said that the doctor *offered* the assistance, not that the doctor *provided* the assistance. This suggested that the offer was not accepted.

I felt a cold chill. Was it possible that a doctor had offered to ride to Tbilisi with Woodruff and that Gogoladze had refused? If so, what was Gogoladze's motive? Did he simply want to minimize Woodruff's chances of survival or was it something more ghoulish? Did he need to be alone with the body in order to fish the bullet out of Woodruff's skull? If so, did this explain his need to shower and change clothes?

It was all very confusing. The only thing I knew for sure was that Gogoladze was hiding something.

The memo focused next on Woodruff's camera and five canisters of film. These items had been inventoried among the meager possessions returned with his body. I inferred from the discussion that some or all of his five rolls of film had been pulled from their canisters and exposed. It was a fairly simple deduction, really. If the agents had the photos, they'd have been discussing the photos. Instead, they were talking about the camera and the film. And besides, there were no cover memos among the FBI documents requesting that the film be developed or the photos be printed.

The pictures would have provided a photographic chronology of Woodruff's last day. However, in the frantic minutes after the shooting, someone destroyed this evidence. Logically this spoliation had to have occurred after Woodruff was shot but before his body was delivered to the Kamo Street Hospital. Before the shooting, Woodruff was alive to protect his film; after the body arrived at the hospital, American security officers, alerted to the murder of a colleague by Georgian authorities, were on hand to protect the integrity of his possessions.

But why would one of Woodruff's companions do this? It seemed safe to assume that the spoliator did not want the authorities (Georgian or American) to see the photographs. As far as I could tell, possible motivations for this act fell into one of two broad categories: motives related to the murder and motives unrelated to the murder.

If the motive for destroying the photographs was *unrelated* to the murder, then it was probable that the purpose of the quartet's Sunday outing was something more than mere tourism. For example, Woodruff could have used the trip as a cover to investigate drug trafficking, and Marina Kapanadze (an operative for the mafia group Mkhedrioni) could have taken advantage of Woodruff's death to destroy the photographic fruits of that investigation. In that case, the destruction of the photographs would not necessarily implicate the spoliator in the killing. However, it seemed unlikely that Woodruff would invite Marina to join him if he intended to spy on her criminal gang without her cooperation.

But if the motive for destroying the photographs was *related* to the murder, then the spoliator was almost certainly complicit in a plot to kill Freddie Woodruff. For example, it was possible that Woodruff was taking photographs at or near the time he was shot. If so, it was conceivable that he photographed the shooter. In that event, the spoliator could have protected the shooter's identity simply by exposing the film in the camera. But the FBI memo seemed to indicate that all five canisters of film had been exposed. This suggested that the spoliator believed there might be relevant damning evidence in photographs taken earlier in the day.

I could think of only one reason why photographs from earlier in the day might contain evidence relevant to the murder: Woodruff had inadvertently photographed his assassin. It seemed absurd, but the probability of such a close encounter was not as unlikely as I initially thought. My research into the arcane priesthood of the professional assassin revealed that it is standard operating procedure for a shooter to personally observe a victim prior to execution of the contract. This process—called "showcasing"—involves a co-conspirator using a prearranged signal to identify the target while the shooter watches. It is a gambit of betrayal as old as the Judas kiss.

If the shooter could see Woodruff, then it was possible that Woodruff could see the shooter. And if Woodruff could see the shooter, he could take his picture—or at least the spoliator might fear that he had.

It was time to take a deep breath. I had started with a hint about exposed film and ended with a conclusion about showcasing for a contract killer. I felt ridiculous. But ridiculous or not, the FBI memo strongly implied that its author had reached exactly the same conclusion.

The agents were fully attuned to the deficiencies and absurdities of the official version—the Georgian pathologist's erroneous opinion that Woodruff had been shot just above the right eye; the orchestrated discovery of a bullet casing linked to Sharmaidze's rifle; the jailer's fortuitous finding of a smuggled letter sewn into the defendant's pants; the retracted confession and the probability of torture. However, the matter of greatest concern to the special agents was the fact that "it had never been determined what type of round killed Fred Woodruff." According to the occupants of the Niva, the vehicle was almost entirely sealed up at the time of the shooting. Nevertheless, no bullet was ever found inside the body or inside the car. And in the absence of both the shooter's bullet and the victim's brain, it was impossible for the FBI to link Woodruff's murder to any particular weapon.

The special agents hypothesized that Woodruff had been the target of an assassination. The investigators consulted members of the US Army Special Forces and were advised that—at a distance of ten to twenty meters—firing at an individual in a vehicle that has slowed its pace does not present a difficult shot for a trained sniper.

But Anzor Sharmaidze was no trained sniper—and he had been drinking.

Citing a potential threat to national security, the FBI refused to disclose the factual and analytical link between the investigators' hypothesis and their conclusion. However, the censors left just enough of the explanatory detail that I could deduce that conclusion: The special agents believed that Woodruff had been assassinated by a former member of Spetsnaz Group Alpha.

Group Alpha was the KGB's elite counterterrorism force—the operational equivalent of the US Delta Force. The FBI memo strongly suggested that the shooter was a former member of Group Alpha and that he had been assisted in the assassination by active-duty members. "Group Alpha is a highly trained group of individuals who form bonds that are deep and long-lasting even after separation from the group," said the memo. "They have been trained to lean on each other for support and trust each other for discretion. The adage former Special Forces rather than ex–Special Forces is as applicable to the Russian Special Forces as it is to any Western Special Forces group. It is not unthinkable to rationalize that a former Group Alpha member would have the assistance and support of a current Group Alpha member ▮▮▮▮▮▮▮."

The censors left an obscure hint regarding something that happened shortly after the killing: "▮▮▮▮▮▮ was ▮▮▮▮▮▮ days after the shooting death of Fred Woodruff." Based on the context, this snippet appeared to relate to the alleged assassin. However, the text was so vague that I could make nothing of it. Little did I know that finding out what happened in the days after the shooting would be the key to unraveling the mystery of the murder.

It is an axiom among investigators that the person responsible for a crime may be found among those who have something to gain from it. Accordingly, the special agents concluded their letterhead memorandum by analyzing who would benefit from the assassination of Freddie Woodruff. The un-redacted portion of this discussion focused on only one potential beneficiary—Russia. The agents reasoned that the murder was detrimental to Russian reformists and (therefore) beneficial to Russian revanchists. American accusations of Russian complicity would put Yeltsin on the horns of an intolerable dilemma: cooperate in the investigation and risk a coup by the perpetrators or resist the investigation and risk the loss of Western support. "Most, if not all, ██████████ oppose the breakup of the Soviet Union and see the undermining of Boris Yeltsin as a way to strengthen Russia and begin a return to the old ways," said the memo.

But this rationalization seemed superficial to me. The murder itself had no direct effect on Yeltsin. The only way the Russian president would be weakened by the assassination was if the Americans reacted by diminishing their support for reform—and the revanchists could not be certain that killing Woodruff would make that happen. As far as I could tell, destabilization of Yeltsin was not probable enough to justify the risks attendant to killing a CIA branch chief. After all, the US could always find another branch chief.

The motive seemed more personal than political. Whoever killed Freddie Woodruff did so because of something unique about Freddie Woodruff.

By April 1995 the special agents believed that they knew the identity of the shooter. "Information received at WMFO has determined that Woodruff may have ██████████. This individual has been tentatively identified as ██████████." Armed with a provisional identification of the assassin, the investigators obtained travel authorization and country clearance for additional interviews in Baku, Vienna, and Tbilisi.

I could not guess why the special agents chose Baku as their first stop. The capital of Azerbaijan, the city sits 350 miles east of Tbilisi, atop an ocean of oil. By 1995 it was already the crossroads of intense competition between Russia, Iran, and the West. Whatever the special agents did in Azerbaijan was so sensitive that the FBI censors did not disclose a single word about Baku.

The stated purpose of the Vienna trip was to follow up on leads provided by the FBI legal attaché in that city. The resident legat had identified a man matching the shooter's description who lived in Austria. "WMFO is aware that Legat Vienna has information concerning an individual whose last name is ██████████, was allegedly born ██████████, and was the approximate age of ███████." Upon review of the legat's file, however, the investigators determined that the local individual was not the suspect.

Notes of a witness interview conducted in Tbilisi were more ambiguous—and more intriguing. "██████ gave an unusually good appearance," the teletype said. "He was clean and clean shaven."

It was an odd observation. "Why would FBI agents comment on a person's cleanliness?" I wondered.

The remark suggested that the agents expected the witness to be dirty and were surprised to discover that he was clean. As far as I could tell, an expectation that a person will be unwashed is ordinarily based on preconceptions about his character or his circumstances. Did the investigators expect the witness to be dirty because he was uneducated or did they expect him to be dirty because he was in a place where he would not be able to wash himself?

"██████ was bright and obviously well educated," the teletype said. In light of this comment, it seemed improbable that the agents expected the witness to be dirty because of poor socialization. But if it wasn't a matter of socialization, then what were the circumstances of the interview that caused the agents to expect the witness to show up soiled?

"WMFO opines at this point that the production of ██████ for interview by the FBI is ██████ intended to mislead the US Government into believing ██████."

It took me a little while to digest the full implications of this judgment: The FBI believed that the entire interview of an unexpectedly clean witness was a charade staged by a third party to deceive the US government.

I could think of only one entity in Georgia with both the ability and audacity to perpetrate such a hoax on the FBI: the Georgian government. And I could imagine only one place from which the special agents would expect the Georgian government to produce an unwashed witness—a Georgian prison. For some unknown reason the Georgians wanted the Americans to believe that the witness was being held in prison.

"Who was this witness?" I wondered. "And why was he worth all this trouble?"

I briefly considered the possibility that the witness might be the shooter and that the Georgians were pretending to imprison him on other charges. But that would mean that the FBI met face-to-face with Woodruff's killer and left the encounter with nothing except their impression of him as clean, bright, and well educated.

"That can't be right," I thought. But I was wrong.

Shortly after their return to the US, the special agents reported the results of their trip to FBI director Louis Freeh. Although this communication was censored, its two principal points remained clear. First, the witness had told the investigators that *he knew Woodruff had been shot in the back of the head*. This fact had been discovered by the Armed Forces Institute of Pathology using a scanning electron microscope. But most important, it was unknown to anyone except the US government and the shooter.

Second, after the interview the investigators had traveled to Baku where they obtained a copy of a statement provided to a third party by the witness. In that document *the witness claimed to be part of a group that was responsible for Woodruff's death*. He said there were several reasons for the assassination: "One was to send a message to the United States to refrain from actions in countries that border Russia that might be considered threatening to Russians."

An embassy-based military attaché had told the first FBI investigators that the assassination was a Russian warning to the Americans. Then two Georgian security service chiefs had publicly declared that Woodruff had been murdered by the Russian SVR. Now a mysterious witness had claimed credit for the killing on behalf of Russia.

The bread crumbs of evidence had begun to turn toward Moscow.

So in July 1994, five months after the arrest of Aldrich Ames, the special agents requested travel authorization and country clearance for Russia. The FBI documents did not disclose whether the investigators ever made it to Russia. But one teletype did reveal a curiously timed Bureau personnel decision: The case agent responsible for reexamination of Woodruff's murder was replaced shortly after he steered the investigation toward Moscow.

The successor case agent did not share his predecessor's suspicions about a Russian conspiracy to assassinate Woodruff. Instead, he limited the focus of his investigation to a single issue: whether—when hooked up to a polygraph machine—any of three witnesses presented recordable evidence of deception in response to a predetermined "relevant question" that the case agent intended to ask. The FBI documents were silent as to the topic of this relevant question; however, as far as I could see there wasn't any single question-and-answer that would resolve all the mysteries that clustered around the Woodruff murder.

One of the witnesses refused to be polygraphed. The other two passed the exam without incident. Whatever the agent's silver-bullet question, the witnesses answered with no physiological indication of deceit. Based on this finding, the successor case agent closed the Bureau's investigation into the connection between Aldrich Ames and the murder of Freddie Woodruff. His judgment was final and unequivocal: "Exhaustive interviews ▮▮▮▮▮▮▮ have left nothing to suggest something other than an accidental shooting. . . . Any further investigation or polygraph examination would be non-productive."

This seemed to be an awfully big step to take on the basis of polygraph results alone. After all, the machine only measures physiological manifestations of shame attendant to lying. And I knew from life experience that not all lies cause shame and not all cultures are ashamed of lying.

But that was it. The FBI investigation of a possible link between the treachery of Aldrich Ames and the murder of Freddie Woodruff was over. And all because of polygraph results recorded in response to a single question.

All this made me wonder if there was any scientific evidence to support the use of polygraphs on people who weren't from the West. It would be a few years before I found the answer to this query. In the meantime, I would need to do a little investigating of my own.

CHAPTER 5

MR. AMERICAN LAWYER

I was afraid to go to Georgia. After all, someone had already murdered a CIA branch chief, and he was a lot more important than a meddlesome lawyer from Texas. The stakes were high and the players were ruthless—serious people who wielded weapons far more lethal than my subpoenas and legal motions. I comforted myself with the belief that it was pointless to make the journey. The people who had arrested and convicted Anzor Sharmaidze were still in power. They already knew he was innocent and so were unlikely to be moved by my time line and logical inferences.

But I was burdened by a desire to console the Woodruff family. It had now been ten years since Freddie's murder. If I intended to find evidence that he had not died in a botched robbery, I would need to do it soon. Memories were fading; documents were being lost or destroyed; witnesses were dying. The inexorable passage of time was rendering my theories irrelevant.

So I decided to disregard my trepidation and fly to Tbilisi. I would visit the (alleged) murder site and meet discreetly with a few of the relevant participants. It would be a fact-finding mission only. I would not agitate for Sharmaidze's release. If all went well, I would be in and out of the country before the government noticed me. I would report my findings to the Woodruff family and then end my quirky crusade.

I began searching for on-the-ground resources in Georgia and remembered having read about CEELI—the American Bar Association's Central and Eastern European Law Initiative. It was a kind of legal Peace Corps created to assist emerging democracies in establishing structures essential to the rule of law. I contacted ABA headquarters and discovered that CEELI had an office and a liaison attorney in Tbilisi.

The CEELI liaison was Carolyn Clark Campbell, a Harvard-educated lawyer whose easy charm belied her prodigious competence.

"You'll need a translator," she said. "You should hire Lali Kereselidze." I didn't know it at the time, but Carolyn had just given me the most important advice I would receive regarding my project. "Yes," she repeated, "you're definitely going to need Lali."

I arrived in Tbilisi from Prague. The airport terminal was a Soviet-era relic built with no expectation of business travel or tourism. It had a concrete floor and a makeshift conveyor belt for luggage. Passport control was two plywood desks staffed by severe-looking women in uniform. There was a scrum of sweaty men offering to drive me to my hotel for $20. I waited a little while and got the same ride for $5.

I stayed at the Sheraton Metechi Palace. A relentlessly functional looking building, it sat on a hill overlooking the old part of the city. For me the hotel had two attractions: first, it had been home to Freddie Woodruff and the US embassy; and second, it had its own generator and was (in theory) immune to the city's frequent power outages.

There was an airport-style metal detector by the front door. It reminded me of the embassy's security guidelines warning of frequent gunplay in the lobby. I walked outside to watch the sunset. Tbilisi is nestled in a valley on the banks of the Mtkvari River. A city of 1.5 million, it is geologically and politically unstable. There was evidence everywhere of periodic quakes—both acts of God and acts of men.

I waited for lights to flicker on but they didn't. The city simply faded into darkness. In the distance I heard the hotel generator kick on. The Metechi Palace lit up like a beacon, a visible reminder to the people below of the power they did not have.

Lali Kereselidze arrived in the morning, and I understood immediately why the local CEELI liaison had recommended her. First, she had a genius—not simply for simultaneous translation of English, Georgian, and Russian—but for navigating the treacherous minefields of intercultural relationships. Second, she was amazingly well connected. When she wasn't teaching Shakespeare at Tbilisi State University or tutoring English language students in her home, Lali served as President Shevardnadze's personal interpreter. And third, she was gracious beyond anything I could have anticipated.

To whatever extent I succeeded in Georgia, it would be because of Lali Kereselidze. I told her my goals for the visit: I wanted to see the crime scene, talk with Anzor's defense lawyers, and then interview Eldar Gogoladze, the former chief bodyguard who was driving the Niva in which Freddie died.

"We can do that," she said.

In a country with no central telephone directory, Lali could still find anybody. She dove into her oversized purse, came out with a few scraps of paper, made one or two calls, and then announced that we had an appointment with Avtandil Sakvarelidze.

The private attorney hired by the Sharmaidze family had an office roughly the size of a closet. He sat at a small metal desk by the window; his secretary sat at a smaller table by the door. The office telephone occupied about one-third of her tabletop. If a call came for the advocate, she would hand him the receiver.

I sat across from him—my back touching the wall, my knees pressed against his desk—and explained the purpose of my visit. I was fairly sure he didn't believe me. Nevertheless, he said, "I am available for a consultation."

I told him that I had studied the US consul's daily summary of the murder trial but was still confused: The description seemed to raise more questions than answers. He dismissed my observation with a wave of his beefy hand.

"The trial was for show," he said. "It was not in the government's interest to discover the true facts."

According to the advocate, there was never any question of Sharmaidze's innocence. After being arrested, he had been offered the same deal as his companions—freedom in exchange for testimony against one of the other two boys. The police had beaten all three until the other two, Berbitchashvili and Bedoidze, gave up and accused Sharmaidze.

"Anzor was simply too strong," said the advocate.

I puzzled about the comment for a moment. It described a perverse natural selection in which the weakest and most craven survive.

"What about the letter?" I asked. Berbitchashvili had written to Sharmaidze implicating him in the shooting and encouraging him to confess. The authorities had found the letter in Sharmaidze's possession and offered it as evidence at the trial.

The advocate grunted his disdain. "Fraud," he said.

Sharmaidze had described the process to him. Several days after his arrest the guards told him that his pants were dirty and needed to be washed.

"It was true," said the advocate, "his pants were filthy, but so were the rest of his clothes. Nevertheless, the guards only wanted his pants."

They returned the poorly laundered garment, insisting that he dress himself immediately. A few minutes later they rushed back into the cell and accused him of hiding something (in his pants, of course). They stripped off his camouflaged fatigues, ripped open the stitching around the waistband, and pulled out a piece of paper.

"It was your letter from Berbitchashvili," said the advocate.

I sat silent as I tried to grasp the motivation for such a hamhanded farce. "Why would they go through this charade?" I asked.

"It was for Sharmaidze's benefit," he said. "Torture wasn't working. They had to break his will. And in order to do that, they needed to show him that his situation was hopeless. Once he realized that Berbitchashvili had betrayed him, he confessed and it was over."

I had never before encountered such systematic prosecutorial abuse and so did not immediately comprehend what the advocate was describing: a form of legal process that existed without any substance of justice.

"Did you object to the letter on this basis?" I asked. "Did you try to show that it was manufactured evidence?"

The advocate looked at me blankly. I felt like a schoolboy who had just said something particularly stupid.

"To what end?" he sighed.

He lit a cigarette and looked out the window. I could see that he was struggling to decide whether I was worth the effort of explanation.

Finally he spoke. Lali was staring at him blankly, allowing his Georgian words to flow through her and magically emerge as English. I was making notes as fast as I could.

"I cross-examined Bedoidze," he said. "During his direct examination, he had pointed to a spot on a photograph and said it was the place where the murder occurred. I got him to acknowledge that there were no distinctive landmarks in that area. Then I asked him to explain how, in the absence of such landmarks, he was able to identify the location so precisely. He didn't know how to answer the question and became quite agitated. The judge told him to calm down and answer truthfully—so the witness said, 'I pointed at the place where I was told to point. The police and prosecutor told me that this is the spot where the murder occurred.'

"As you might imagine, there was a big reaction in the courtroom," he said. "Bedoidze had done the unthinkable: He had told the truth. But in the end the judge simply struck his answer from the official record. The judge said that the answer suggested that the police and prosecutor had manipulated the testimony '—and since we know that cannot happen, the answer must be wrong and must be stricken.' "

The advocate paused to let me process the implications of such institutionalized tyranny.

"Sharmaidze was terrified," he said. "He cried for three hours, begging me not to raise the issues of torture or manufactured evidence. He'd been warned by the police that if he talked about those things, they would kill him and his whole family. So you see, Mr. American Lawyer, there wasn't really much point in objecting to the letter."

And with that, the consultation was over.

I paid the advocate $50—but would have paid much more. He had given me an invaluable insight into the central issue facing lawyers in Georgia: If the government isn't required to obey its own laws and procedures, how do you get it to do something it doesn't want to do?

I didn't know it at the time, but I would spend the next five years of my life trying to answer this question.

We stopped for sweet Turkish coffee while Lali fished through her bag to find our next appointment. After only two telephone calls she had a meeting scheduled with Tamaz Inashvili. Sharmaidze's court-appointed lawyer was working as an in-house general counsel at the government's Ministry of Electricity. He agreed to see us in the afternoon.

Inashvili ushered us into a tidy little office. He was a trim and starched young man. His handshake was firm but his smile seemed awkward, as though he wasn't completely comfortable with human contact.

I had been forewarned about his speech impediment but was not prepared for what I encountered. His stutter was a spasm that battered and mauled every word before letting it escape. Nevertheless, I did not have to struggle in order to understand him. I had Lali, and she translated his Georgian stammers into fluent English.

I explained the purpose of my visit and he consented to talk to me. He began by describing the circumstances of his court appointment. Anzor's murder trial was the very first case he ever handled as a lawyer. It was clear to him that he had been chosen because of his inexperience, his lack of political connections, and his stutter.

He got word of his court appointment shortly before the trial began. There wasn't much time to prepare. He needed to review the official investigation file as soon as possible and that was kept at the courthouse. It was winter and the Russians had choked off the flow of natural gas to independent Georgia. The temperature was bitter cold, and Chief Judge Leonidze's office was the only room in the courthouse that had a fireplace. The judge permitted Inashvili to work there while he reviewed the case materials.

He sat opposite the judge and quietly studied the investigation reports, witness statements, and confession. The more he read, he told us, the more troubled he became.

He saw no evidence that established Sharmaidze's guilt with a certainty sufficient to justify his execution. For Inashvili, it was one thing to participate in a courtroom charade that resulted in his client's imprisonment; it was quite another for him to play a knowing part in the client's judicially sanctioned murder. He simply wasn't willing to do that.

Inashvili knew that once the trial began he would be powerless to influence the outcome. But before the trial he had something the government wanted and needed: his continued participation as defense counsel. The government was eager to resolve the case during the holidays when no one was paying attention. If Inashvili quit, the case would be delayed beyond the Christmas camouflage.

And so he decided to bargain privately with the judge—to trade the prospect of a prompt resolution of the case for the life of Anzor Sharmaidze. But talking to the judge outside the presence of the prosecutor was a risky strategy. Leonidze could report this ex parte communication to the bar association and Inashvili could lose his law license. Nevertheless, the young lawyer considered disbarment preferable to participating in his own client's extermination.

He collected himself and began talking. At first Leonidze didn't understand, so Inashvili tried again. ". . . new lawyer . . . first case . . . death penalty . . . withdraw . . ." The judge's eyes suddenly lightened with comprehension, he told us.

"Oh—don't worry about that, Mr. Inashvili," said Leonidze. "That's already been decided. We're not going to execute him. He's going to be sentenced to fifteen years in prison. Hard labor, but he'll be alive."

So what appeared to be a life-and-death drama was actually a sham. The outcome of Sharmaidze's trial was known before the proceeding ever began.

At that point, Inashvili's principal concern became making sure that the judge kept his word. He decided that the best way to do that was to present a minimal defense: If the judge broke his promise and imposed the death penalty, he could cite his own meager performance as evidence of the secret agreement with the judge. It would destroy his career but it would save an innocent man's life.

But in the end Leonidze kept his word. Sharmaidze was found guilty and sentenced to fifteen years hard labor.

"It's eighteen years now," said Inashvili. A few years previous the authorities had released Sharmaidze from prison and then arrested him a few days later. They tacked on three more years of hard labor for having allegedly escaped when they pushed him out the front door.

I was thinking about the brutality of a system that would add a three-year insult to Sharmaidze's many injuries, when Inashvili interrupted with a question.

"Does the Woodruff family plan to intervene in Sharmaidze's case?" he asked.

"I didn't know such a thing was possible," I said. After all, in US courts there is no procedure that will allow the family of a victim to intervene in a defendant's case ten years after his conviction.

"In Georgia the family of a victim has the right to participate in the criminal case," he said. "If they find new evidence—something suggesting that the defendant is innocent or that someone else committed the crime—they can ask the prosecutor to reopen the investigation."

He looked at my stack of FBI documents and then at me. I felt as though he was taking the measure of both of us. Finally, he spoke, this time quietly and without stutter. "That looks like new evidence," he said.

We exchanged our goodbyes and Lali drove me back to the hotel. Her little brown Lada bounced along the cobblestone streets while I sat in dejected silence. I had gotten involved in this Georgian escapade because I wanted to feel good about myself. I had budgeted a limited amount of time and money to establish my credentials as a humanitarian. And just as I was about to cross the finish line, this stammering lawyer had eloquently revealed that unless I took this case to the next level, my efforts would never be anything but narcissistic folly.

I rode the elevator to the top floor of the hotel. An English-language sign identified the room at the end of the hallway as the Piano Bar—the watering hole where Marina the barmaid worked and Freddie the spy caroused. There was a mirrored back bar, a plastic parquet dance floor, booths lining one wall, and randomly stacked chairs. The air was stale and the tables were dusty. Nobody had gotten drunk in this room for a long time.

The Piano Bar was indistinguishable from any cocktail lounge found in any Midwestern Holiday Inn. I thought about it for a moment and realized that perhaps that was the point: It was a place where lonely expatriates could drink and imagine they were somewhere else. The lingering smell of desperation didn't help my mood. I went to my room and waited for morning.

Lali pulled into the hotel parking lot promptly at 10 a.m. She had arranged an afternoon meeting with Eldar Gogoladze. We planned to spend the hours beforehand visiting the location where the murder had allegedly occurred.

Lali drove us along the left bank of the Mtkvari River until the road divided. Then she steered the car north onto the Old

Military Road. The tsar's gateway to the Caucasus was a two-lane asphalt ribbon that the Russian army started building in 1799.

Less than two miles from the turnoff the GPS announced that we had arrived at the FBI coordinates. This was the place identified by Sharmaidze as the scene of his crime. This was where he reenacted the shooting and where the FBI found the shell casing linked to his rifle.

What impressed me most about the location was how utterly unremarkable it was—a straight stretch of road with thirty feet of grassy apron extending out to a hedgerow of trees. The terrain was the same on either side. There were no prominent features to distinguish this place from the roadside a half mile in either direction. The idea that a blindly drunk man would be able to distinguish this exact spot from any other struck me as dubious at best.

There were, however, two noteworthy structures between the intersection and the village of Natakhtari: First, there was a small concrete kiosk near the turnoff. The building was slightly larger than a bus stop and appeared to have been abandoned for some time. Lali said that in 1993 it had been a roadway police post. Second, there was the Natakhtari Drain—the water power station for the Tbilisi water system—and its support buildings. A dirt road leading to the Drain intersected the highway about a half mile before the alleged murder site. The road was about fifty yards long and ran past a barracks, a greenhouse, a guard shack, and a water tower. A seven-foot wall separated the shack from the highway and a gated fence protected access to a barracks.

At the junction of the dirt road and the highway was a kind of ersatz parking area. At its edge there was a large oak tree to which some enterprising soul had nailed an automobile tire—a black "O" suspended about ten feet above the ground. Lali said it had been there as long as she could remember.

I tried to imagine its purpose and only one explanation made sense: It was a landmark. You could tell someone unfamiliar with the area that you'd be waiting for them at the oak tree with the tire on it. They couldn't miss it.

We drove back to the city for our meeting with Gogoladze. Lali said he'd been a detective at the police station near the train depot prior to being tapped in 1992 as the chairman's security chief. Later, he'd been arrested following a failed attempt to assassinate Shevardnadze. The prosecutor suspected that he had conspired with Igor Giorgadze and Jaba Ioseliani to murder the chairman. Gogoladze sat in jail for six months before being released in a general amnesty.

I was very curious to see how he had fared following this avalanche of disgrace.

We arrived at the nicest office building in Tbilisi, where several late-model Mercedes and BMWs sat in the parking lot. Obviously, this was home to a prosperous company.

"This is Cartu Group," Lali said. "It's the largest conglomerate in Georgia. They're in banking, insurance, manufacturing, construction, real estate, media—everything. It's owned by the billionaire Bidzina Ivanashvili. And Eldar Gogoladze is the vice president."

We rode the elevator to the executive suite and were shown into Gogoladze's office, a tastefully appointed room with European designer furnishings—subdued, understated, expensive. Gogoladze, a short, bald man about fifty, was wearing an Italian sports coat and Gucci loafers. He crossed the room with predatory grace. His eyes were passive but alert. Lali made the introductions in Georgian and he replied in idiomatic English. He dismissed the interpreter to the outer office and closed the door.

"I don't know what this interview is about," he said as he settled into his white leather sofa. "All the facts of Freddie's death are already well known to the Americans."

I explained that I was there to obtain information for the family, that I understood that many of the details of the investigation were classified and that I had no desire to expose any secrets. I apologized in advance if I inadvertently stumbled into matters that he as an intelligence professional deemed inappropriate, that I was after all just a lawyer.

I was being a little stiff, a little formal, a little solicitous, a little naive—that is, pretty much just being me. But my clumsy approach had its intended effect. It induced Gogoladze to feel superior to me. He did not perceive me as a threat and even allowed me to videotape the entire conversation.

Everything about Gogoladze proclaimed him to be an insecure bully, a man who believed that his talents and contributions had never been properly appreciated. So I settled into the role of enthusiastic admirer—and the more I listened, the more he talked.

It had been Freddie who organized the trip to the high mountains, he said. Gogoladze had been reluctant, but Freddie had insisted. He wanted to see the stunning nature, to drink the local wine, and to be with Marina Kapanadze.

"Freddie had feelings for this woman," said Gogoladze. "But I'm not sure she was the kind of woman who deserved such serious feelings."

This statement seemed an oddly aggressive way to start a conversation with a putative family representative: an unsubtle warning that—if I pushed too much—Gogoladze would be forced to tell some particularly embarrassing truth. It did not dissuade me from my inquiry, but it did make me curious about what he was hiding.

"I did not know her," he said. "It was the first time we'd met."

People who lie tend to litter their conversation with too many details and this was one detail too many. It seemed implausible that a Georgian intelligence officer wouldn't know every English-speaking waitress at the only Western hotel in the country—especially when that hotel housed the US embassy. I made a mental note to check on Gogoladze's relationship to Marina.

He skipped over the day's events and started his story with the shooting. It was nighttime. The highway was dark. His headlights were on. Just before the turnoff to Mtskheta he saw three men standing on the side of the road. One of them had a machine gun. That man stepped forward and signaled for the car to stop.

"My first reaction was to speed up," he said. "I don't know if it was the right decision."

He accelerated past the three men. He heard a gunshot and then Marina screamed.

"Freddie was hit in the forehead," he said. "I saw the wound. There was no chance of survival."

He didn't stop. He wanted to avoid a second shot and to get Freddie to a hospital as quickly as possible. Nevertheless, he paused briefly at the roadway police post and ordered the officers to block the highway. He then drove to the district hospital in Mtskheta, but they had no electricity. He contacted headquarters by radio, reported the shooting, asked for reinforcements, and requested that his colleagues find a working hospital. By the time he arrived at the Kamo Street Hospital in Tbilisi, Freddie was dead.

After he'd off-loaded Woodruff's body, he searched the car for evidence of a bullet hole, but found nothing. At first he suspected it was a sniper who had fired through the front passenger's window. "It was the only window that was open," he said. But a few days later a forensic investigator found a bullet hole in the hatchback.

"There's a resin strip around the hatchback window—a rubber gasket that holds the glass in place," he said. "The bullet was hot. It melted the resin and then the hole resealed. That's why we didn't see it."

I was familiar with this explanation but that didn't make it any less extraordinary. Sharmaidze was alleged to have killed Freddie with an AK-74 loaded with cut bullets. If that was true, then a blunt-nosed 5.45 mm bullet traveling at 2.6 times the speed of sound had struck a strip of silicone rubber and passed through the strip without leaving a trace. It sounded like a ballistic miracle. I was about to ask Gogoladze if anyone had actually calculated the temperature of the bullet or the melting point of the silicone rubber, but he changed the subject.

The FBI investigators had asked him whether the Niva had been followed on the day of the murder. So I asked him the same question.

"It was Sunday and I was relaxed," he told me, "but I was still checking. I absolutely exclude the possibility that we were followed. There was a gas crisis at the time. I saw only a dozen cars the entire day."

Gogoladze said he stayed at the Kamo Street Hospital for only fifteen minutes before returning to Natakhtari. He was accompanied by a dozen members of the presidential protection force. The group stopped at the Nerekvavi police post, a repurposed railroad car that had been marooned at the intersection of the Tbilisi Highway and the Old Military Road. A squad of military police were questioning three young men about an automatic rifle they carried. Gogoladze recognized the young men as the same ones he'd passed just before the shooting—the same clothes, the same machine gun. He arrested the trio and delivered them (and their AK-74) to the Tbilisi jail.

I tried to imagine this scene of professional efficiency, but reality kept intruding on my vision. Gogoladze's self-exculpatory account did not address any of the troubling details chronicled in the FBI investigation. For example, where was his quick trip home to take a shower? And there was something about the arrest that troubled me—but that was going to require a lot more thought.

"I resigned the next day," he said. "I wanted to distance myself so that no one could say I was trying to influence the investigation."

This claim of resignation was inconsistent with information I'd gotten from other sources. According to the FBI (and several newspapers) Gogoladze had been fired for malfeasance. However, not all inconsistencies are malicious. I decided to explore the issue obliquely.

"Why was there no chase car?" I asked.

The tiny muscles at the edge of his mouth twitched a little. His eyes seemed to narrow.

"It was Sunday," he said. "I wanted the men to have a day off with their families. And there was a gas crisis. There wasn't enough gasoline for a second car."

The easiest answer would have been to say that he or Freddie didn't want a chase car full of armed bodyguards. But that would have suggested that the trip had a goal other than recreation—and Gogoladze had already tried to deflect me from exploring the trip's purpose. So he told me a story. Not from shame or embarrassment, but to protect a secret.

And then he changed the subject again. "The chief investigator confirmed that these criminals also robbed a senior policeman that day. The deputy director was returning from his country house. The criminals beat him and stole a carton of cigarettes—and they tried to steal his car."

This was new information to me. There was no mention of this crime in the FBI documents or in the State Department summary of the trial. And none of the three young men had been charged with this robbery.

"One of the three boys confessed to a cellmate in the jail. He said that his friend—the one with the machine gun—had killed an ambassador. And Sharmaidze was wanted by the police for stealing and for desertion from the army."

Gogoladze was trying a new tactic: to persuade me that the accused was a bad man and that the evidence against him was far more substantial than had been placed in the official record. He apparently hoped I would think Sharmaidze unworthy of any serious effort.

"Two or three days after the shooting the FBI asked for help to find the crime scene," he said. "I missed the location by three hundred meters—but Sharmaidze found it."

The former chief bodyguard was contrasting his well-intentioned error with Sharmaidze's knowledge in order to prove that the defendant was guilty. It was both sad and cunning.

"There's still a lot of speculation and gossip about this case," he said. "People claim to be investigating but their only goal is to discredit Georgia, the intelligence service, or me. Even now—ten years later—there was a scandalous article in a Philadelphia newspaper."

I recognized the reference. A small Russian-language weekly

had printed a story linking Gogoladze and Woodruff's murder to the narcotics trade in Georgia. The publisher had circulated only three hundred copies of the newspaper; nevertheless, this retired intelligence officer living half a world away had found it and read it.

"Did you know that Freddie had heart problems?" he asked. It was an unexpected question. "He made me promise not to tell anyone. I took him to the best cardiological center—maybe ten days before he died. The doctor told him he was a candidate for death if he did not immediately stop drinking and start treatment. But he refused. Most CIA officers don't drink very much alcohol, you know. But for Freddie, that was a burden."

The conversation drifted away from the past and to the present. "I am now number two in the biggest company in Georgia," he boasted. "We are the top managers: the president and me."

He did not explain what part of his professional résumé had qualified him for this august position. And he did not discuss how he had navigated the path from prison to a vice presidency. But I knew enough about the former Soviet Bloc to realize that employment opportunities for retired warriors were a function of who you knew and what you had done for them.

Clearly, Gogoladze had a very powerful patron who believed that the former security chief was owed a substantial reward. If I was ever going to solve the mystery of Freddie's murder, I would need a deeper understanding of that relationship.

We exchanged a few pleasantries, talked about Gogoladze's role in the creation of Group Omega (the local CIA-sponsored special operations force), and the rise of financial crime in Georgia. After I received a bear hug and a hearty slap on the back from Gogoladze, Lali drove me to the hotel. I packed for a 4 a.m. flight and thought about what I had learned.

It seemed like the only thing I could trust about Gogoladze was the fact that he would try to deceive and mislead me. He had insinuated that an investigation would expose an immoral or unethical relationship between Freddie and Marina. He had implied that Sharmaidze was a bad man whose case did not deserve the benefit of careful scrutiny. And he had suggested that (even without an intervening bullet) Freddie's death had been imminent. Perhaps the key to understanding Gogoladze was to disregard his specific words and to focus instead on the direction those words were pushing me. If I could figure out what he wanted to accomplish, then I could trust that everything he said or did would be directed toward achieving that goal. And his immediate goal seemed fairly obvious: He wanted me to stop my investigation. The question I couldn't answer was why he was so concerned.

I flew home to Texas on the wings of self-satisfaction. Of course, I hadn't actually accomplished anything. But I had made a heroic gesture. Further effort was demonstrably pointless. I was confident that I had done all that could be done.

However, less than a month after I returned the people of Georgia swept away the basis for my confidence. In November 2003 tens of thousands of demonstrators took to the streets of Tbilisi to protest the flawed results of a parliamentary election. Citing the risk of civil war, President Shevardnadze deployed the army to confront the protesters. But in an elegantly theatrical response, the student demonstrators gave red roses to the soldiers. Many of the soldiers received the flowers, laid down their weapons, and embraced the protesters.

The Rose Revolution had begun. On November 23, a former justice minister named Mikheil Saakashvili led the demonstrators to the parliament building where Shevardnadze was giving a speech. Flanked by thousands of supporters, Saakashvili forced his way into the chamber and—waving a long-stemmed red rose in the president's face—shouted, "Resign!"

Shevardnadze's CIA-trained bodyguards hustled the seventy-five-year-old president out of the building and into history. It was the ignominious end of a spectacular career.

In his place stood a thirty-five-year-old US-trained lawyer known simply as Misha. In January 2004 Misha was elected president with 96 percent of the vote. In February the parliament amended the constitution to increase the powers of his office. In March his party won a landslide victory in parliamentary elections. He launched a vigorous anticorruption campaign and proposed that Georgia join both the EU and NATO. He sent Georgian troops to join America's war in Afghanistan. He promised to create an independent judiciary and to correct the excesses of the prior regime. He set about pardoning and rehabilitating political prisoners.

The United States welcomed him as a Georgian paragon of liberal democratic values. I saw him as a threat to my comfortable life.

Before Misha, I had a reasonable excuse for not carrying my evidence of Sharmaidze's innocence to the Georgian judicial system: The country was too chaotic and the government was too corrupt. After Misha, this no longer seemed to be a credible excuse for inaction.

But in the end it was the professional challenge that seduced me: Could I use my knowledge, skill, training, and experience to minimize the probability of danger while maximizing the possibility of success? I'd never done such a thing and was eager to find out if I could.

But if I was going to try, I would need a client—and the Woodruff family still lived in Searcy, Arkansas. It made me nervous to think of returning to the little town where I'd grown up. I'd done my best to get as far away from it as I could. The irony was almost comic. I was more reluctant to confront Bible-quoting zealots than gun-toting spies.

CHAPTER 6

HOMETOWN OF A SPY

When I was a little boy we would drive through towns like Searcy, Arkansas, and my mother would say, "My God, how can anyone live here?" But then came February 16, 1967, and a doorbell in the middle of the night. Three men in uniform standing on the porch looking embarrassed and saying they were sorry. I was ten years old and my father had just died trying to rescue a fighter pilot shot down over the Ho Chi Minh Trail.

After we'd buried him, my mother announced her intention to move our little family away from Lubbock, Texas. A leader in the local church counseled her to choose a city that was home to one of the Bible colleges associated with our fundamentalist sect. She could get her degree while my sister and I attended the affiliated parochial academy.

That's how the three of us came to find ourselves in Searcy, a little Arkansas town on the road between St. Louis and Texarkana. It was hot and humid when we arrived and there seemed to be a wind blowing in from a prior decade. We turned left off the incongruously named Main Street and circled the town square, past a granite Confederate soldier standing perpetual guard outside the antebellum courthouse—a stony reminder that we'd arrived in the Old South, where things changed very slowly.

A drugstore, a department store, a Sears Roebuck catalogue store—Searcy boasted all the products of American prosperity. There was a pool hall for the men, a baseball field for the children, and a fabric store for the women. A one-screen movie theater

offered family entertainment in air-conditioned and racially seg-
regated comfort. There was no place you could buy a beer but
lots of places you could save your soul.

And that was exactly why we'd come. Searcy was home to
Harding College—a four-year liberal arts institution associated
with the Churches of Christ. The school was proudly fundamentalist and passionately anticommunist. It was a Mecca for innocent, earnest, sincere believers who wanted to change the world.
They gladly embraced its regimen of self-discipline, self-denial,
deferred gratification, and personal responsibility. They viewed
themselves as a small army of holy warriors in the titanic battle
of Good against Evil.

The quality of education was by any measure used in Arkansas academically superior. The disciplines of the academy were
rigorously applied in a word-by-word study of the Bible. Students
were taught to debate obscure nuances of Greek and Hebrew.
Victory depended on careful analysis and a chapter-and-verse
knowledge of the holy text.

The same intellectual diligence employed in study of the sacred
was applied in study of the secular. Harding emphasized a Christian duty to do your best in all endeavors—to master a subject, to
examine it honestly and thoroughly, to make a judgment about
it, and to be prepared to defend that judgment. This made for
detail-oriented, highly verbal, stubbornly opinionated people.
Students were trained in a cunning (and manipulative) form of
persuasion: to identify a person's core values and to reframe the
gospel message in a way that was consistent with those core values. Success was defined in terms of conversion—and conversion
was evidenced by immersion baptism.

Fifteen hundred students marching to heaven in lockstep.
Young men with hair above the ears, collar, and eyebrows. Young
women with skirts not more than two inches above the knee.
No smoking, no drinking, no dancing, no sex. Chapel and Bible
class five days a week. Church twice on Sunday and again on
Wednesday. A Thursday-evening devotional by the lily pond.

A persistent and pervasive social pressure to conform to the appearances of piety.

Of course, enrollment at Harding did not repeal the rules of human nature. Some students became adept at surreptitiously feeding their animal appetites while maintaining the appearance of moral propriety. Others used the newly acquired tools of logic and analysis to deconstruct the assumptions of faith, all the while demonstrating their rhetorical skills in the pulpit. In order to survive in the dominant culture, these dissenters were required to master the delicate art of living multiple lives.

All in all it was an ideal education for would-be preachers, lawyers, and spies.

It was around that time that I first met Jill Woodruff. She was a fifth-grader, in the class behind mine, and the youngest of the three Woodruff sisters. Quiet, watchful, unpretentious, she seemed to glide outside the normal cliquish social circles. Somewhere around the eleventh grade Jill became a full-fledged member of my Class of '74. We were twenty-eight souls. The middle sister, Chery, was frumpy and cheerful. Although I was five years younger than her, we spent an entire semester together in study hall. I'd been banished from eighth-grade math class for impertinent questions and told to finish the textbook on my own. Chery was good-natured and gracious and seemed to take a special pleasure in calling me impudent. She was, I think, a good judge of character.

There were two other Woodruff siblings: Freddie and Georgia. They were older and outside the modest social network of a junior high student. I remember seeing Freddie play football for the college team but have no recollection of meeting Georgia. I knew only one thing about her: She'd been named after her father.

George Woodruff was a fireplug of a man with a thick neck and a bowling ball head. A bald, ruddy-complected, energetic biologist, he was an object of admiration in my provincial universe—an honest-to-goodness man of science who believed the Biblical account of creation. Dr. Woodruff was living proof of Harding's academic credibility, and as such, he was called upon regularly to teach young believers how to resolve the dissonance between ecclesiastical faith and evolutionary fact.

I used to sit in on those classes. A tie knotted around his too-small collar, his shirtsleeves rolled up—he was animated, inquisitive, clever, and infectiously positive. He delighted in unanswerable questions and prayed as though he was talking to someone he knew well. He was equal parts preacher, teacher, and coach. He had an impish sense of humor and an obviously unstinting love for his family.

George was the only boyfriend that his wife Dorothy ever had. Sweet-hearted, fun-loving, and playful, the homemaker was a lifelong participant in children's games. She rode bikes and jumped on pogo sticks well into her seventies. More obsessively religious than her husband, it was she who had pressed Freddie to become a preacher.

I lost touch with the Woodruff family when I left Searcy for law school and the big city. But I had been to Tbilisi and wanted to share the results of my investigation. The year was 2004.

I tracked down Chery Woodruff's telephone number. She was living in a clapboard house two blocks from the Harding campus. In the thirty years since our last conversation she had married, raised a family, and developed inoperable brain cancer. She lived just long enough to connect me with her older sister.

"You don't want me," she said. "You want to talk to Georgia. She's always been interested in that stuff."

Georgia answered my call on the first ring. Her pronounced Arkansas twang belied her education as a registered nurse. She seemed unpretentious, guileless, and emotionally brittle.

"Oh, my goodness," she said. "I want to see everything you've got. When can you come to Searcy? Meredith won't like it, but I don't care. When can you come?"

I didn't know who Meredith was or why she wouldn't like my visit; nevertheless, I made arrangements and rang off. Two weeks later I flew to Little Rock, rented a car, and drove fifty miles north to Searcy. I was headed for a two-bedroom house just outside of town. The door swung open as I reached the top step.

"Come in! Come in!" said a slightly disheveled fifty-year-old woman. "I want to know everything. Oh, I wish Daddy could see this."

This was Georgia Woodruff Alexander. Bubbling with energy and opinions, she was a bespectacled crusader in search of a next cause. She would prove to be the perfect partner in my quest.

"Did you know Freddie?" she asked. "Freddie was mean. He had this amazing ability to see your weaknesses and deepest desires—what you wanted and what you feared. And it gave him pleasure to torment you with them. He made my life miserable."

It occurred to me that she was unwittingly describing the ideal CIA case officer: someone with the sensitivity of a psychotherapist and the morals of a pimp. A valuable national security asset and an interpersonal train wreck. For the first time I began to comprehend the heartbreaking sacrifices made by spies and their families. The job cultivates behaviors that make normal relationships impossible.

I showed her my documents, described my analysis, and recounted my interviews. I walked her through my time line and demonstrated the improbability of Sharmaidze's guilt. I listed the unanswered questions and offered the seemingly obvious conclusion—that Freddie was a hero who had been assassinated in the line of duty.

This was what I had set out to do, to report to the family and provide the comfort of detailed information. And I was pretty pleased with myself. But only for a minute.

"This is terrible!" said Georgia. "Daddy worried about this to the day he died. Every night he would get on his knees and pray for that boy in prison. He was so afraid that Sharmaidze was innocent—and now you tell me that he is! What are we gonna do, Michael?"

It was not the response I had anticipated. The sister of the victim wanted to rescue the man who had confessed to murdering her brother. I looked at this rumpled redhead sitting at the kitchen table and realized that I was in the presence of greatness.

After a moment's hesitation I told her what Sharmaidze's court-appointed lawyer had told me—that the family of the victim could intervene in the criminal case to present new evidence.

"Well, are you gonna do that for me?" she asked. "I can't pay you, but we've got to do what we can."

I felt like a deer caught in headlights. I had come to offer solace and had instead sown disquiet. I had committed the sin of the busybody and was responsible for the mess I'd made. She was calling on me to deliver the comfort I had intended.

"I'll try," I answered. "It won't be easy, but I'll try."

"Do you think Freddie's murder had anything to do with Aldrich Ames?" she asked, making a sudden transition to a surprising question. I had mentioned Ames in my narrative but hadn't emphasized his role. He was one of those questions that had not yet been answered.

"I'm not sure," I said. "He was in Tbilisi just before the murder—and that does seem oddly coincidental."

"I met him the day of Freddie's memorial service," she said. "We had a reception at the house and Ames came over. He sat at Meredith's kitchen table laughing and telling stories all afternoon. I kept thinking how close they must have been—because Ames was really touched by Freddie's death."

It was the second time she'd mentioned Meredith.

"Yeah, Meredith was Freddie's second wife," she said. "His widow. She's in the CIA too. With all the publicity around Freddie's death, she had to stop being a covert operative. But she still works for the Agency."

Georgia paused. She seemed to be wrestling with an unseen opponent. I waited quietly to see who would win. Finally, she spoke—softly, almost a whisper.

"Meredith's not going to like this," she said. "After the funeral she got the family together and told us that we must never talk about Freddie—not to the press, not to a lawyer, not to anyone. If we do this it's gonna cause trouble . . . but it's the right thing to do."

There was steel in this woman from Arkansas. She was willing to risk a rupture in her family to save a man she did not know. Such generosity of spirit would require my very best efforts.

As I prepared to leave, she went into her bedroom and returned with a cardboard box of treasures. "This is my Freddie file," she said. "The DVD is an interview he gave at Harding. The cassette is his speech at the 1993 Stillwater high school graduation. And that stack of papers—that's an article published in a Georgian magazine a few months ago. I found it online and had it translated."

Georgia had given me a gold mine of context and clues. She let me take it home in my briefcase. The whole file was valuable, but the thing that made my heart race was the videos. In 2004—a decade after his death—I was about to meet Freddie Woodruff.

The DVD was a part of a series: "Is There Life After a Major in . . . ?" A representative of the alumni association interviewed graduates whose careers were considered interesting or impressive. The focus was on how education at a provincial faith-based college had prepared them for vocational success.

The interviewer was a diffident mathematics professor, Dean Priest. I recognized him from my time at Harding. He had copious notes, good intentions, and a naive expectation of candor. He was completely unprepared to deal with someone who lied for a living.

"With us today is Mr. Freddie Woodruff, a 1969 Bible major at Harding," said Priest. "We all know that there is definitely a great life after a major in Bible—eternal life! But we've asked Mr. Woodruff to talk about the secular life he's had since graduation. He's a foreign service officer with the Department of State and has been stationed all over the world."

Freddie showed no reaction as Priest proclaimed him to be someone that he was not: no tension in his body, no shifting in his seat, no fleeting micro expression on his face. He sat perfectly still, his legs crossed, his hands folded in his lap. A relaxed posture that suggested confidence bordering on arrogance.

He was bald and wore a mustache—a bushy extravagance

that had been forbidden at Harding when he attended. He had a square chin and gray eyes. The lines of his charcoal-gray suit testified to an athletic physique and the potential for physical power. The massive chronometer on his wrist and the oversized ring on his finger bespoke a certain tendency to flamboyance.

He was a man that women would want and that men would want to be.

"I always enjoy coming back here," he said. "Harding deserves a great deal of credit for what I am and where I am."

I smiled at the cryptic joke. Freddie was actually telling the truth—but not a truth that the interviewer could comprehend.

"My parents raised me in such a way that I probably knew the Bible better than anything else," he said. "When I was young I didn't know what I wanted to do with my life—except for one thing: I wanted to play football. So I chose to come to Harding because here I could do the two things I knew best: football and Bible."

I had a vague recollection of seeing him on the field. He was smaller then and played flanker. His first year he caught enough passes to earn an athletic scholarship. But after his second year he married Jacqueline Suella Braddock and was forced to give up both football and his dream of playing for the Pittsburgh Steelers.

In deference to Harding's religious objection to divorce, Freddie didn't mention either the making or the dissolving of this ill-fated union.

"I had no qualms about majoring in Bible," he said. "I had an idea that I might become a preacher."

Like all Bible majors at Harding, Freddie was required to study Koine Greek—the language in which the New Testament was written. "I did quite well in Greek," he said. "I don't know that one is necessarily born with a talent in languages, but that was something I discovered I could do."

The other ancient language offered at Harding was Hebrew, and Freddie's comments about it gave a subtle hint about a professional relationship with the Israeli Mossad. "I didn't study

Hebrew—to my constant regret. I deal with Israeli diplomats quite frequently in my life and it would be fun to have some Hebrew."

Freddie's other academic passion was English literature. "I had enough hours for a major in English except I didn't have the required modern foreign language credits," he said. Years later, at its 2012 ceremony to honor fallen colleagues, the CIA memorialized Freddie as "a gifted linguist who had mastered German, Turkish, Greek, and Russian." But he never got enough modern foreign language credits for a degree in English literature.

"One of the best things that happened to me is that I enrolled in a course called art appreciation," he said. "My instructor was Elizabeth Mason."

I laughed out loud at the symmetry. Mrs. Mason had been a Bohemian among Puritans, a splash of wild color in a world of monotonous gray. And she had been married to an officer in Wild Bill Donovan's OSS (the predecessor of the CIA).

It seemed ironic, and almost portentous, that this would be the person who most profoundly affected young Freddie. The future is always built on the past.

"I'll tell you a story," he said. "I used to live just down the street from the Hermitage in Leningrad. It is perhaps the grandest museum in the world. I had a Russian friend who worked there. One day he said he wanted to show me something but we had to be very careful. He took me down to the basement—quite literally the dungeon of an old castle—and opened a door. The room was damp and smelled of mildew. Inside there were several hundred paintings by the masters: Picasso and Chagall, Malevich and Klee. And they were all rotting. Mrs. Mason taught me to have a feeling about art—and that day in Leningrad I did: I felt just awful."

In the chaos that prevailed after the fall of the Soviet Union, the Hermitage disclosed that it had a trove of priceless art that had been stolen from the Nazis during World War II. I wondered if Freddie had been invited to a private showing of this booty. But more than that, I was curious why an American spy had cultivated a relationship with a Russian museum curator.

His first year after graduation Freddie took a job teaching Bible and English at Great Lakes Christian College. And he continued preaching on the weekends. "Eventually, for personal reasons, I decided that preaching was not the career for me," he said. "I wanted to go to graduate school and find a job in which I felt more comfortable."

But that didn't happen. Fate was about to intervene.

In December 1969 the Selective Service System conducted a lottery to determine the order in which men would be drafted for military service during the Vietnam War. The days of the year were represented by numbers and written on small slips of paper. The slips were placed in separate plastic capsules that were mixed in a shoebox and dumped into a deep glass jar. The capsules were then drawn from the jar one at a time. The first number drawn was 258, corresponding to September 14—Freddie Woodruff's birthday.

"To this day it's still the only thing I've won in my life," he said. "It was purely a question of fate."

The army gave him an aptitude test and assigned him to language school. "I did well in the Russian language," he said. "I was sent to West Berlin and worked there as a Russian interpreter for three years."

It was in Germany that Freddie was recruited by the CIA. "I met people who were involved in foreign policy and various aspects of international relations," he said. "I was able to talk to them about a lot of different things. I had an interesting story to tell and frankly they liked me."

By the time his tour of duty was over, he had earned a masters in psychology. "I've never practiced psychology as a professional discipline," he said, "but I think I probably use it every day in my job."

I was pretty sure that was true.

After discharge from the army he went home to Oklahoma, and again enrolled in graduate school, and waited for a call from the Agency. He took courses in international relations, international agricultural economics, and petroleum marketing.

Finally the call came—but Freddie couldn't tell the truth about who had actually placed it. "I was close to thirty years old before I became a career foreign service officer with the Department of State," he said. "My specialty is the Soviet Union. I deal with Soviets on a daily basis. I've had dinner in the Kremlin and talked to Leonid Brezhnev in his own language. I have a lot of pride in what's happened to me. And I wouldn't do it differently."

At the time of the interview Freddie was stationed in Turkey. "I'm living right in the middle of my freshman Western civilization course," he said, "right in the heart of the Apostle Paul's missionary journeys. Western Civ was probably the last history course I took, but somehow I was instilled with a hunger to keep learning—hopefully for the rest of my life."

In a subtle hint about the focus of Cold War espionage, he admitted two specific weaknesses in his formal education. "My life, my profession revolve around technology and economics," he said, "and I wish I had a little better understanding of them. Technology transfers, wealth transfers—these are matters of great interest to everybody. I probably should have paid a little more attention to my science and economics courses. I'm trying to teach myself, but I wish I'd started earlier."

The DVD had been made before the collapse of the Soviet Union. The VHS cassette had been recorded after. Freddie was giving the commencement address at his high school alma mater. It was May 1993.

"This is my school and my town," he said. "A few years ago I was back there in the 'W's' sitting where you are. And a lot of your parents who are here today were in that class with me. I'm sure you expect me to say that it's an honor to be here—and it is, indeed."

Stillwater High's favorite son had come home to give his valedictory just three months before his assassination.

I expected an inspiring oration challenging the graduates to seize the future. What Freddie delivered was far more personal and revealing.

"My dream for you is two things," he said, "that you always

remember where you came from and that you learn that there's a big world out there that needs you. Because I'm a guy that's seen it and I've come back to tell you."

The stories he told gave a hint about his peripatetic career after postings in Russia and Turkey. The first stop for the Russian-speaking Sovietologist was the Horn of Africa. The transfer put him on the front line of a proxy war with Moscow.

"I spent several years in Ethiopia," he said. "There was a war going on there for about thirty years. The government lost that war—but in a last desperate attempt to win they started pulling my daughter's Ethiopian classmates out of school. They would go to their houses at night and pull thirteen- and fourteen-year-old children out of bed and send them to the front. There's no way for you to know what that's like—but I've seen it and I've come back to tell you."

After his apparent success in Ethiopia, he returned to the Soviet Bloc.

"I was in Berlin on the day they started tearing down the Wall," he said. "They made a hole in the Wall and I just walked into East Berlin. It was unimaginable. The whole world changed that day."

After that, Freddie traveled extensively throughout the former Soviet Union: Russia, Siberia, Armenia, Azerbaijan, Kazakhstan, and ultimately Georgia. "Last year I was the first American invited to the old Soviet space center to watch the liftoff of a Russian rocket," he said. "Last month I saw grandmothers in Moscow selling their shoes to buy food. These are hard times in Russia—but I think the Russians are going to make it."

Freddie's concluding words would have made a fitting eulogy: "I've had dinner with kings and presidents. I've interpreted for ambassadors and secretaries of state. I've run into interesting people all over the world. And I would say I'm very happy with where I am and what I'm doing. I've had a good life. And I don't regret any of the choices I made."

I turned off the videos and thought about what I'd seen and heard. In both the interview and the graduation speech Freddie made attestations of being fulfilled by family and faith. But these statements seemed out of sync with the rest of his narrative. He was most alive when painting himself as a man on the move, disconnected from pedestrian commitments, utterly consumed with matters of consequence. His conversation was completely devoid of references to other people in his life. There was no team, there was only Freddie.

I pondered the utility of this particular insight. I wasn't sure, but I thought it might help explain how he ended up on the Old Military Road without backup.

CHAPTER 7

THE THIEF IN LAW

I now had a human client and a humanized victim. What I needed next was a deeper knowledge of Georgia's recent political history. I was pretty sure that without an adequate appreciation of the formal and informal forces struggling for control of Tbilisi, I would never solve the mystery of Freddie Woodruff's murder and might even get myself killed.

My education began in books and ended in admiration. The Georgians, I learned, are a hearty, passionate, extraordinary people. During the Soviet era, ideologues developed an elaborate mythology asserting that the Russian conquest of the Caucasus was both anti-imperialist and progressive: "anti-imperialist" because the Russians liberated the region from the Ottoman and Persian empires, and "progressive" because it opened the way for peoples of the region to develop their cultures and economies according to their own needs and desires. The culmination of this happy process was, allegedly, the Soviet system itself—a giant leap forward that bestowed on the region the blessings of brotherhood, peace, and prosperity.

While the conquerors congratulated themselves for their good intentions, the conquered experienced the occupation from a slightly different perspective. To the peoples of the Caucasus, the Soviet Union (and the Russian Empire before it) were colonial powers—outlanders who supplanted local power structures and economic models for their own benefit. Admittedly, their colonization of this multiethnic, multilinguistic, multireligious region did have some positive effects: It created more peaceful conditions and more orderly administration; it led to the development of infrastructure; and it promoted industrialization. However, by its nature the Russo-Soviet colonial model was more pernicious than that of other European colonial empires.

Unlike its British counterpart, the Soviet colonial system never sought to develop local institutions of self-government. The Communist Party did not cultivate colonial administrators and cadres of indigenous civil servants. Instead, local party officials were conditioned to obey and implement orders that emanated from a distant central government. As a consequence, the needs and desires of the local populace were always a lower priority than the dictates from Moscow.

Any government that persistently refuses to respond to the demands of the governed comes to be viewed by them as (at best) irrelevant and (at worst) illegitimate. To the average Georgian, the local administration was an utterly corrupt and self-serving bureaucracy that governed by terror and the promotion of ethnic rivalries and resentments. It was the newest in a long line of enemies to be evaded, exploited, manipulated, and cheated. In the absence of any proper government, people relied on family, clan, and ethnic group for social cohesion and basic survival. They bought and sold in the black market—and thereby became willingly complicit in officially illegal activity. As a result of this lifestyle of defiance, any generalized sense of civic responsibility atrophied and any basic respect for the rule of law was compromised.

There was, however, one Georgian institution that had not been undermined by Soviet colonial administration. It was the *Vory v Zakone*—the Thieves in Law. In Georgia, a thief in law is a professional criminal and respected member of society who operates an alternative government in the cracks and shadows of the established order. In addition to conducting illicit business activities, the thief's minions serve as neighborhood supervisors, judge-arbitrators, and private security. If your car is stolen, the thief can find it and tell you how much you have to pay to get it back. He can clear your building of homeless squatters that the police will not touch. But above all, the thief in law can provide reliable protection for businesses and fair arbitration of their commercial disputes. Of course, all these services come at a price—but the thief's process is incorruptible and he can be counted on to keep his agreements and to enforce his decisions.

A Georgian might ignore the laws passed by parliament, but he would never ignore a thief's law.

A thief in law is a gangster who—after proving himself repeatedly in the crucible of Soviet prison—has been chosen as a *vor*, a godfather, a leader with a demonstrated talent for organization and a proven résumé of violence. He has sworn to abide by the Thieves' Code, has been marked with the tattoos of his rank, and is utterly devoted to crime.

In the Soviet Union, where making a profit was an offense punishable by death, the thief in law was a practical dissident and a proto-capitalist. His violations of the colonizer's criminal code were secretly cheered as acts of civil disobedience and patriotic resistance. He was celebrated as a nationalist hero—a kind of racketeering Robin Hood with a merry band of psychopaths.

And when the Soviet Union disappeared from the Georgian stage, it was a larger-than-life criminal genius who filled the vacuum left by its implosion. Jaba Ioseliani was a playwright, bandit, entrepreneur, and killer. He was one part Arthur Miller and two parts Al Capone. A professor of theater science, he boasted a PhD and more than twenty-five years in prison. He had authored several successful plays and been elected "curator" of the mafia in Georgia. He was admired by intelligentsia and supported by bureaucrats. His network of relationships—both criminal and political—connected him to all corners of the Soviet Union. And when that union began to come apart, this amoral Renaissance man was ideally positioned to seize control.

Disintegration of the USSR started in 1988. The cool breeze of glasnost blew in from Moscow and whipped up a whirlwind of Georgian nationalism. There were nonstop political rallies in the Tbilisi city center. Students held hunger strikes demanding that the Soviet constitution be amended to allow Georgia to secede. The local patriarch led the crowd in the Lord's Prayer—a forbidden act of religiosity made militant because it was spoken in Georgian. And there were speeches by the rock stars of resistance: Georgian academics and artists who had made a life in the USSR as professional dissidents. They seized center stage and demanded national independence.

Soviet soldiers kept an uneasy watch from the periphery, unsure how to react to protest in the age of perestroika. They did nothing until April 9, 1989, when—buttressed by shock troops from outside Georgia—the soldiers attacked a candlelight vigil with nightsticks, shovels, and tear gas.

"I have just been told that the danger is real," the patriarch announced in the darkness. "We may have only a few minutes left before they start."

"Long live Georgia!" cried someone in the crowd. "Lift up your souls because God is on our side!"

When it was over, twenty people were dead and four thousand wounded. The show of force had been intended to frighten the Georgians into submission. Instead, it incited them to revolution. They sloughed off the last vestiges of Moscow's central control and began an inexorable march toward secession. This wildly destabilizing process was led by an ultranationalist literature professor from Tbilisi State University.

Zviad Gamsakhurdia was a virulent anticommunist with no practical experience as a politician. He was an urbane chauvinist whom the US Congress once nominated for a Nobel Peace Prize. His principal qualifications for leadership were intolerance of opposition and contempt for compromise. These traits would propel him to the presidency and assure the catastrophic failure of his administration.

In the aftermath of the April 9 massacre Gamsakhurdia formed a coalition of nationalist parties and a militia to protect it. This political movement—called the Round Table/Free Georgia bloc—was united around two propositions: total independence for Georgia and complete transition to a market economy. These populist themes inspired a previously disenfranchised electorate. The newly aroused common man wanted to redefine both Georgia's relationship to Russia and Russian influence within Georgia. It was a comprehensive revolution: a threat to Moscow and a threat to the Georgian elite who drew their power and prestige from Moscow. This nationalist political platform guaranteed the formation of a powerful fifth column intent on maintaining Georgia's connection to Russia.

A man of ideas, Gamsakhurdia had little appreciation for the practical mechanics of power. He created an armed "national guard" to protect the politicians and then delegated its leadership to a friend with no military experience. This newly minted general—a sculptor named Tengiz Kitovani—began immediately to acquire weapons and matériel from Soviet armories scattered throughout Georgia. Regrettably, his accumulation of lethal firepower was not subject to any official civilian control. Gamsakhurdia had naively established Kitovani as an authentic warlord and legitimate competitor for supremacy.

Nevertheless, Kitovani and his national guard were neither the largest nor the most menacing independent army marauding through Georgia. That distinction belonged to mafia godfather Jaba Ioseliani and his Horsemen.

As Soviet control of Georgia collapsed, there was a sharp increase in ethnic clashes. Some of this violence was a natural product of long-simmering tensions; some a direct result of Soviet mischief. Ioseliani used these conflicts as an excuse to form a private army called *Mkhedrioni*. The name (translated in English as "the Horsemen") had deep cultural resonance for Georgians: it conjured images of Cossacks riding to the rescue of persecuted Christians. However, unlike those fifteenth-century knights, the freebooters in Mkhedrioni did not swear allegiance to state or church. Instead, their oath was to obey Ioseliani alone. In return for this absolute obedience, the Thief in Law agreed to be their benefactor, guaranteeing the profit of their adventure.

Within a few months the mafia chieftain was commanding a heavily armed corps of five thousand opportunists. Weapons for this brigade-sized force—including heavy artillery, tanks, armored personnel carriers, and helicopters—were supplied by Soviet military units stationed in Georgia. Moscow was building a proxy army and expanding a long-standing partnership with the mafia.

In the meantime, as a result of intense pressure from the opposition, Georgia held the USSR's first democratic multiparty election. The Round Table/Free Georgia bloc won a convincing 64 percent of the votes cast. The Communist Party—also running on a platform of Georgian independence and free market reforms—won 30 percent of the votes cast. However, Gamsakhurdia used his authority as leader of parliament to prevent any of the Communist delegates from participating in the legislative body. His commitment to democracy did not extend to those with whom he disagreed.

On April 9, 1991—the second anniversary of the Tbilisi massacre—the nationalist-dominated parliament declared Georgian independence from the USSR. This was the first time in history that a Soviet republic had left the Union. Secession was an unprecedented event with unpredictable consequences. But the world took little notice. Public attention was (at the time) distracted by Saddam Hussein's invasion of Kuwait and his subsequent eviction.

A month later Gamsakhurdia was elected president of "independent" Georgia. Ninety percent of the adult population voted and 86 percent of them voted for Gamsakhurdia. Armed with this mandate, the new president began immediately to sever ties with Moscow. He was openly hostile to both Soviet president Mikhail Gorbachev and his Georgian-born foreign secretary, Eduard Shevardnadze. These two unelected Communist functionaries enjoyed near saintlike status in the West. It was an article of faith among the liberal democracies that anyone who opposed Gorby was by definition bad. Even President George

Bush denounced Gamsakhurdia as a man "swimming against the tide." As a result, the first democratically elected president of Georgia—a political dissident who had been imprisoned by Shevardnadze—was disqualified from Western support because he refused to recognize the virtues of his former jailers.

Gamsakhurdia moved aggressively to check Moscow's influence in Georgia. He banned the local Communist Party and suspended the process for establishing new political organizations. He prohibited public criticism offending the "honor and dignity" of the president. He dispatched the national guard to South Ossetia to suppress a Russian-backed independence movement. And he stripped Mkhedrioni of its official status as a benevolent rescue corps and declared illegal its private ownership of military-style weapons.

All of this was carefully chronicled and criticized in the West. Politicians and press described Gamsakhurdia as authoritarian, dictatorial, and insane. The NGO Helsinki Watch adjudged his government guilty of "severe violations of human rights." One of the principal indictments was his arrest of warlord Jaba Ioseliani. The mafia godfather—in jail on weapons charges—had reinvented himself as a political dissident and prisoner of conscience. When Gamsakhurdia declared the mafia chief ineligible to run for president, liberals everywhere were righteously apoplectic.

Two things were becoming apparent: The West would spend no blood or treasure to defend Georgia's popularly elected president from subversion; and Ioseliani intended to take control of the new republic's legitimate government.

Gamsakhurdia's political isolation became more acute after the failed putsch against Gorbachev in 1991. Russian premier Boris Yeltsin proposed that Georgia join a Commonwealth of Independent States. Gamsakhurdia's vehement refusal provoked crippling economic sanctions by Russia and demonstrations by Tbilisi intellectuals. They accused Gamsakhurdia of fascism. To these formerly privileged members of the One Party elite, the Georgian president's application of majority rule was just a little too much democracy.

Fearing that a victory by Soviet hardliners would be followed by an attack on Georgia, Gamsakhurdia moved to consolidate his power. He ordered the national guard to turn in its weapons and subordinate itself to the Ministry of Internal Affairs. But it was too late. Kitovani liked being a warlord and did not want to surrender his prerogatives. He defied the government and together with about half his troops joined the opposition. Soon an internecine war was raging in the center of Tbilisi. The government and opposition forces were evenly matched until Kitovani liberated Ioseliani from jail. The Mkhedrioni warlord was immediately given leadership of the movement to oust Gamsakhurdia. He ordered his Horsemen to surround the parliament building, where the president was hiding in a Cold War–era bunker. For two weeks they hammered away with cannons, tanks, and bombs. The West—which had been scandalized by Gamsakhurdia's nonviolent dispersals of illegal demonstrations—said nothing as Mkhedrioni laid waste to the city and killed more than two hundred people.

Georgia's first democratically elected president was removed by coup d'état on January 6, 1992. After barely eight months in office, Gamsakhurdia fled the country and was replaced by an unholy trinity—Mkhedrioni warlord Jaba Ioseliani; national guard warlord Tengiz Kitovani; and prime minister Tengiz Sigua. However, there was no ambiguity about who sat at the pinnacle of this triumvirate. As Ioseliani said in a frank assessment of his relationship to Kitovani, "In Georgia there came into authority a known Thief over an unknown sculptor."

Moscow had equipped and funded this counterrevolution, and it was an apparent success. They had ejected an uncooperative nationalist irritant and replaced him with an obliging mafia godfather. And they had done it without the United States raising even the hint of an objection. The ruling junta made overtures to the international community, but no one was willing to bestow recognition on the thinly veiled military dictatorship. Fortunately, there was a recently unemployed Georgian with impeccable diplomatic credentials. Eduard Shevardnadze had been out of a job ever since resigning as Soviet foreign minister. Nevertheless, this shrewd political operator—a man Gamsakhurdia had called "an international spider"—was already preparing himself for the next call to service: The lifelong atheist had been baptized into the Georgian Orthodox Church.

Ioseliani and Kitovani needed legitimacy; the West needed a reliable interlocutor; and Shevardnadze needed rescue from political oblivion. It was a compromise of mutual convenience: If the warlords would bring Shevardnadze into their government, the West would recognize Georgia as a sovereign nation. The perceived benefits appeared to outweigh the apparent risks.

The heads of Mkhedrioni and the national guard ordered their soldiers to sign petitions begging Shevardnadze to return to Tbilisi. The former first secretary of Georgia's Communist Party wept at this sincere display of political theater. After suitable protestations and delay, Shevardnadze humbly accepted appointment as acting chairman of the Georgian State Council. International recognition of the unelected government quickly followed.

However, there were some critics of this Faustian bargain. A reporter from the *Moscow News* challenged Shevardnadze to explain his alliance with gangsters.

"Discussing the criminal records of certain people who are now my partners is embarrassing to me," he said. "One should not be reminded of sins committed in youth. On the contrary, I admire these people who've had enough strength, willpower, and courage to overcome all and make a new start in life. Now they are great statesmen."

Shevardnadze arrived in Tbilisi on March 2, 1992. He was met at the airport by the warlords. The rivals had already divided the "power ministries" between them: Kitovani would run the Ministry of Defense (and the illegal arms trade) and Ioseliani would control both the Ministry of Internal Affairs and the Ministry of State Security (and have a monopoly on distribution of fuel). They assigned Shevardnadze a largely ceremonial portfolio. After all, he was the only one of the three who didn't have his own private army.

However, Freddie Woodruff was coming to Georgia and all that was about to change. Prior to returning to Tbilisi, Shevardnadze had called former Secretary of State James Baker with an intriguing inquiry: If he accepted the warlords' invitation and became the junior member of the Georgian State Council, would the United States train and equip his bodyguards? It was a practical question from an astute political survivor. Shevardnadze knew that whoever controlled his personal security held his life in their hands. Throughout his career as a Soviet functionary he had entrusted himself to the care of the KGB's mighty Ninth Directorate, the section of the civilian spy agency responsible for providing bodyguards to the apparatchik. However, the post-Soviet intelligence services were not necessarily a trustworthy guarantor of Georgian independence.

So the Silver Fox turned to America. It was a triumph of irony: Gorbachev's foreign minister had ushered in a new era in which his most trustworthy ally was his former principal adversary.

Baker and Shevardnadze had been well matched as their nations' chief negotiators—they were two wily horse traders accustomed to using power and people, but they trusted each other. And in this case they both wanted the same thing: an independent Georgia free of Russian domination.

Shevardnadze's question presented breathtaking possibilities, and Baker knew just who to call. In his mind, the mission to train and equip Shevardnadze's personal security force was an ideal assignment for America's elite Delta Force. Pursuant to a 1979 agreement, Delta operators were already providing bodyguard training at the State Department's most threatened embassies. But this operation would be different: 1st Special Forces Operational Detachment Delta was a Tier One national security asset and its deployment inside the former Soviet Union required and received written approval by President Clinton.

Shevardnadze's request and America's response were observed in Moscow with interest and concern. An editorial in *Izvestia* complained about the implicit insult to the KGB Ninth Directorate. "Was the previous protection really so bad?" it asked ironically.

In addition to provoking Russian discomfort, the operation also served the broader interests of the new CIA. Since its founding in 1947 the Agency had existed primarily to monitor and frustrate Soviet ambitions. As a result, the implosion of the Evil Empire represented a mortal threat to the CIA. It had lost its raison d'être. Overnight the Agency had become an anachronism: a huge bureaucracy in search of an enemy big enough to justify its budget. The Company was in crisis. How would it re-task its enormous resources in order to convince Congress to continue its $40-billion-a-year appropriation? In order to accomplish this goal, it would need to present itself as the solution to a critical national security problem. Among the issues considered for pride of place were nuclear proliferation, global terrorism, narcotics production and trafficking, illegal arms sales, money laundering, and economic espionage.

With the possible exception of economic espionage, the nascent Republic of Georgia stood at a crossroads of all these threats. The Georgia operation was a working partnership with a Machiavellian genius who could influence events far outside the borders of his own small country. Shevardnadze was a person of extraordinary accomplishment and his stature demanded an Agency liaison of equally high status. Accordingly, the CIA assigned Freddie Woodruff to interface with the Great Man. The Agency's assignment of such a senior officer was a compliment to Shevardnadze and a warning to Ioscliani and Kitovani.

Working together with Delta operators, Woodruff began the process of building a protection force for Shevardnadze. In addition to a bodyguard service, the CIA branch chief created an elite stand-alone special operations force. With a nod to Group Alpha (the KGB's premier antiterrorist battalion) Woodruff called his company-sized unit "Group Omega." It was trained, equipped, and intended to give Shevardnadze a military option that he alone could control.

However, both Shevardnadze's and Woodruff's authority over the force was initially limited. Normally, bodyguard services for Georgian officials were provided by a division of the Ministry of State Security, the secretive organization tasked with protecting Georgia from both internal and external threats. But the traditional structure of that ministry had disintegrated when (pursuant to his power sharing agreement with Kitovani) Ioseliani attempted to seize control. Roughly half the professional personnel at the ministry had refused to work under the Mkhedrioni warlord. And so—led by one Igor Giorgadze—they had decamped en masse to Kitovani's Ministry of Defense.

The fragmented ministry remained under Ioseliani's control. However, Ioseliani (unlike Kitovani) did not officially designate himself as head of this agency. His acceptance of such a job would have been a violation of the fourth law in the Thieves' Code: "A thief must never under any circumstances have a legitimate job."

Accordingly, Ioseliani named Irakli Batiashvili—a lieutenant in Mkhedrioni—as chief of the remaining intelligence and information services. In addition, Ioseliani appointed two deputy chiefs under Batiashvili: Shota Kviraya (a former KGB general and Mkhedrioni's partner in the drug cartel) and the unrelated Avtandil Ioseliani (a longtime security professional).

Finally, the mafia chief promoted a little-known detective from a minor police substation to be head of Shevardnadze's personal protection force. As a result, Eldar Gogoladze was not beholden to Shevardnadze for his job. Instead, he belonged to Jaba Ioseliani or to whoever had imposed their will on the mafia godfather.

Although he was titular head of an operational unit, Gogoladze was not an operator. He was more in the nature of commissar—a political functionary in a military unit. He was there to assure the loyalty of the officers and the obedience of the troops.

Woodruff brought Gogoladze and Group Omega to the United States for training. The CIA operations officer and the former KGB colonel appeared to be close friends. They worked together during the week and played together during the weekends. The unpopular commissar's Georgian colleagues generally assumed that Gogoladze was being recruited as an American spy.

Around that same time, supporters of Gamsakhurdia kidnapped some high-ranking government officials and were holding them in the western Georgian province of Abkhazia. Kitovani and Ioseliani responded by sending national guard and Mkhedrioni troops to (allegedly) rescue the officials. However, after the hostages had been released, the warlords turned their attention to violent suppression of the Abkhaz independence movement. One of the volunteers who went to Abkhazia was a twenty-year-old Georgian named Anzor Sharmaidze.

After a month of fratricidal fighting, ethnic cleansing, and appalling atrocities by all combatants, the Georgians seized control of most of the restive region. But in the process of reasserting central government authority, Kitovani and Ioseliani threatened Russian interests in Abkhazia. The Black Sea province was home to Russian military bases and (perhaps more importantly) beachside spas, sanatoriums, hotels, and vacation homes owned by the Russian army and Russian intelligence services.

A ceasefire was negotiated in Moscow but soon violated by the Abkhaz. Foreign fighters (including Russian military and Chechen special forces) entered the fray on the side of the separatists and—over a period of eight months—swept both the Georgian irregulars and the resident Georgian population out of Abkhazia.

It was an unmitigated disaster. And Shevardnadze used it to consolidate his power.

In the aftermath of the Abkhaz debacle, Shevardnadze forced Ioseliani's minister of internal affairs to resign and took direct control of the security portfolio. A conveniently timed parliamentary election allowed him to mobilize popular hatred of the paramilitaries and to force Kitovani to resign as minister of defense.

Shevardnadze publicly blamed the warlords for the loss in Abkhazia and demanded that both Mkhedrioni and the national guard surrender their weapons. When Ioseliani responded with a fusillade of vulgar insults, Shevardnadze tendered his resignation.

Thousands of Georgians poured into the streets and demanded that the government support the chairman. In response, the newly elected parliament formed a unity government, declared a state of emergency, and granted the sly Silver Fox authority to rule by decree.

He immediately made private militias illegal.

Kitovani fled to Moscow and his national guard began to disintegrate. Some parts of the organization were folded into official state agencies and other parts simply faded away. Mkhedrioni, meanwhile, attempted to exploit a loophole in the law and rechartered itself as a heavily armed charitable organization. Nevertheless, Ioseliani was becoming isolated. He had originally taken the suite of offices above Shevardnadze to symbolize his dominance over the chairman. But the metaphor had changed: Now the mafia warlord was trapped between Shevardnadze and the sky.

Under Shevardnadze, the Ministry of Internal Affairs was getting stronger by the day. It controlled remnants of the national guard and welcomed any Mkhedrioni soldier willing to swear loyalty to Shevardnadze. Using Group Omega and a newly trained police force, the government began targeting smaller, more localized paramilitaries. By early 1995 (a year and a half after Woodruff's murder) the balance of power had swung enough in the government's favor that the ministry could move directly against Mkhedrioni. Police in eastern Georgia arrested forty-five Horsemen and confiscated a large quantity of automatic rifles.

On the same day, Shevardnadze issued a decree ordering Mkhedrioni soldiers to hand in their weapons. Ioseliani reluctantly instructed his troops to surrender their guns to the government as a "gesture of good will." However, he did so only after extensive consultations with Igor Giorgadze—the man who had transferred out of the Ministry of State Security (allegedly) because he refused to work under the mafia chief.

Meanwhile, Shevardnadze was driving the Russians to distraction by his on-again, off-again commitment to their Commonwealth of Independent States. The Kremlin had conceived the CIS as an economic and security bloc of former Soviet republics—a kind of USSR-lite. But Shevardnadze's closeness with America threatened that dream of empire redux.

The Russians attempted to cow him into submission by creating an energy crisis and by provoking two separatist conflicts (i.e., Abkhazia and South Ossetia). But instead of bending Shevardnadze to their will, Moscow's decision to turn off the flow of Russian oil and gas had an opposite (and wholly unexpected) effect.

Disintegration of the Soviet Union had created several new oil-rich countries. One of these—landlocked Azerbaijan—had been producing oil in commercial quantities since the ninth century. Its reserves represented a strategically important alternative to Russian and Middle Eastern production. However, at the time of the Georgian energy crisis, the only practical way to access that Azerbaijani oil was via Russian or Iranian railroads or pipelines. In order to break this chokehold, a consortium of Western oil companies undertook to build two pipelines (one oil and one gas) from Baku, Azerbaijan (on the west coast of the Caspian Sea), to Ceyhan, Turkey (on the east coast of the Mediterranean Sea).

The easiest and most efficient route for these pipelines was due west from Baku through Armenia and the Kurdish region of Turkey. But this was a political impossibility: The Azerbaijanis hated and distrusted the Armenians, and the Turks hated and distrusted the Kurds. Thus, as a practical matter, the only available route (that didn't pass through any of the politically disqualified geography) looped northwest through Georgia and then southwest through Turkey.

Planning for the Baku-Ceyhan Pipeline began in 1992. Two years later, Shevardnadze negotiated construction of a third line—a pipeline to carry oil from Baku to the Georgian port city of Supsa on the Black Sea.

The Baku-Ceyhan and Baku-Supsa pipeline projects assured the destitute Republic of Georgia $71.5 million per year in oil transit fees and the right to take in kind up to 5 percent of the pipelines' annual natural gas throughput. Thanks to Shevardnadze's political finesse and America's diplomatic muscle, the little country was obtaining both a secure revenue stream and energy independence from Moscow. This energy alliance with the West was a threat to Russia's control of its near abroad. And that threat became palpable when (on March 23, 1994) the former Soviet republic joined the NATO-run Partnership for Peace.

It was a stinging repudiation of the Soviet colonial system and it did not go unnoticed in the Kremlin. Shevardnadze was moving quickly to create the formal institutions of government. He drafted and the parliament approved a new constitution—a compact that among other things restored the office of president and invested it with strong executive powers. Both Ioseliani and Shevardnadze announced their intention to run for this new office.

Five days later—on August 29, 1995—someone tried to assassinate Eduard Shevardnadze. It happened just as he was leaving the parliament building. The sixty-seven-year-old chairman was on his way to the formal signing of the new constitution when a platter charge was detonated near his limousine. But on this occasion, the chairman's driver had made an uncharacteristically wide right turn and driven Shevardnadze's vehicle closer to the horizontally mounted explosive device than the assassins had anticipated. As a result, when the directional mine was command-detonated, the cone of shrapnel was narrower than it would have been if the car had been farther away from the device. Ballistic projectiles ripped the trunk off the car but did not penetrate the passenger cabin. The evening news carried video of Shevardnadze sitting on a hospital chair in his undershirt and looking slightly dazed. His hands, face, and eyelids were cut and spotted with blood. And he was angry.

"They are cowards," he said. "They want to turn Georgia into a country where the mafia rules. But I won't allow it as long as I'm alive."

The day after the bombing the police arrested two of Ioseliani's lieutenants for attempting to assassinate the chairman.

Three weeks later the prosecutor general announced that the two Horsemen had confessed their involvement.

Shevardnadze immediately declared Mkhedrioni to be an illegal mafia organization. Its membership was decimated by arrest and prosecution. And (according to Igor Giorgadze) after Mkhedrioni was eliminated, its former partner in the drug cartel (Shota Kviraya) doubled his profit-sharing payments to the Shevardnadze family.

Ioseliani withdrew as a candidate for president to protest what he called Shevardnadze's rule of terror. He announced that he would, instead, run for parliament. The prosecutor general issued a warrant for his arrest, but did not execute it until after the mafia chief had been defeated in the October election. Ioseliani was found guilty of terrorism and sentenced to eleven years in prison. He was seventy-two years old.

As with almost everything of importance that happened in Tbilisi, suspicion quickly focused on Russia as the prime mover behind the attack. At a press conference, Shevardnadze was asked if he thought the assassination attempt might be related to the pipeline projects.

"Now you're asking the right question!" he said.

Suspicions about Russian involvement were fueled in part by the fact that Igor Giorgadze—the man that Shevardnadze had appointed minister of information and intelligence after the resignation of Irakli Batiashvili—had made a secret trip to Moscow immediately before the attack. When he refused to explain the purpose of this trip, Shevardnadze removed him from his post. Three days later, at a hastily called press conference, Giorgadze denounced the Shevardnadze regime as a "Mafia State" and announced his intention to move to Moscow. A warrant was quickly issued for his arrest, but he'd already fled the country in a Russian military plane.

Russia refused to extradite Giorgadze and his name was added to the list of Interpol's most wanted fugitives. During his tenure as minister, Giorgadze had worked to dismantle Group Omega.

He delivered much of their American high-tech gear to Georgian Group Alpha—a pro-Russian antiterrorist unit he had formed around a nucleus of Georgian veterans of Soviet Group Alpha.

Notwithstanding the obvious rivalry between the two units, Shevardnadze accused Group Alpha and Group Omega of having conspired together in the assassination plot. Government police arrested operators from both units and government courts imprisoned them. By the time he was finished, Shevardnadze had used the defeat in Abkhazia, the Russian energy embargo, and his own attempted assassination to eliminate all of his principal rivals. The anarchy of paramilitaries had been checked by legitimate police power. The dictatorship of warlords had been toppled by democratic elections. And Georgia's vulnerability to Russian domination had been offset by new alliances and new pipelines.

Shevardnadze had done the impossible: In less than four years, he had built a government.

By 1999, that government's monopoly on violence was sufficiently secure that Shevardnadze was able to be magnanimous. He pardoned hundreds of people convicted of offenses related to the civil war and the assassination attempt—including the sculptor Tengiz Kitovani and the mafia chief Jaba Ioseliani.

But Anzor Sharmaidze was still in jail.

CHAPTER 8

"THE AMERICANS KNEW EVERYTHING"

Early on in any representation a lawyer must identify the various outcomes that will constitute victory or defeat for his or her cause. This process will form the foundation of the lawyer's strategy and the measure of his or her success.

My client had given me a general statement of her objective—to get Anzor Sharmaidze out of jail. To accomplish this goal I would need to file a legal proceeding in Georgia alleging the existence of new evidence, which could be proof that Anzor was innocent or proof that someone else was guilty.

Both of these were dangerous claims. A lot of people had invested a lot of effort to make sure that Anzor went to prison, and I was fairly sure they would not take kindly to being called torturers and perjurers. At the same time there was a very real murderer on the loose who would most likely take umbrage at the prospect of being publicly accused.

I concluded that the single-minded pursuit of either claim could end with Anzor or me being killed. Such an outcome would indeed be a strategic defeat for my cause.

Accordingly, I would argue that new evidence proved Anzor's innocence. But I would demand *on behalf of the Woodruff family* that no additional prosecutions be undertaken—either for Freddie's murder or for Anzor's wrongful incarceration. In this way, I hoped to diminish the sting of Anzor's eventual exoneration and to placate the guilty parties' legitimate fears of impending retribution.

It was a tenable game plan; nevertheless, when I was making arrangements to return to Tbilisi I asked Lali if I could sleep on the couch in her spare room. Strategy is one thing, but physical safety is something else altogether. I hoped that the stringent obligations of Georgian hospitality would provide me with some small measure of protection.

But it was, at best, a token gesture. The mystery I was trying to unravel was important enough to someone that they'd murdered Freddie Woodruff to keep it secret. I would need to tread very carefully if I did not want to be that person's next victim.

I arrived to find the Rose Revolution in full bloom. President Saakashvili was doing everything he could to show that the old regime had been completely demolished. Every day commandos dressed in black fatigues raced around the city arresting corrupt former ministers. Every night the local news broadcast video of soldiers with automatic weapons bravely subduing potbellied middle-aged men. The downtrodden cheered to see the elite face swift and certain justice. It was political theater of the first order.

However, the principal objective appeared to be practical. The venal former ministers were able to secure their release in exchange for forfeiture of ill-gotten gains. The government—which did not have any effective taxation system—was accumulating much-needed capital while trying to teach a civics lesson.

I was encouraged by the young president's pragmatism, but could not help wondering how Georgia funded its government operations without any tax revenues. How Saakashvili was running a government with no visible means of support presented an intriguing question; however, my immediate concerns were more pedestrian. I needed to interview the witnesses whose testimony had convicted Anzor of murder.

The US embassy's twenty-page summary of the trial provided a road map of the evidence linking Anzor to the crime. The proof described in the memo fell into three broad categories: eyewitness testimony, forensic evidence, and Anzor's confession.

Eyewitnesses are notoriously unreliable. They misperceive, misremember, misreport, and lie. By contrast, forensic evidence is objective and verifiable. It is derived using scientific methods and unlike a human witness cannot be bribed or bullied.

Because of this, I wanted to start my examination with the autopsy and ballistics.

Lali arranged a meeting with medical examiner Levan Chachuria and translated our conversation. Chachuria had testified that Freddie was shot in the forehead just above the right eyebrow and that the bullet had exited the back of his skull above and behind the right ear. I was curious to know how this man of science had arrived at a conclusion directly opposite from that reached by the US Armed Forces Institute of Pathology.

We met in the morgue at the Kamo Street Hospital—the same facility to which Gogoladze had delivered Freddie's body. Chachuria was having morning tea with two colleagues. He introduced them as doctors who had assisted him in the autopsy. And he made a point to tell me how many decades each of them had been practicing.

I looked around the lab and noted a distinct absence of sophisticated scientific equipment. There was a microscope, a scale, a few surgical instruments—but none of the technology that defines modern pathology. I asked about the protocols for conducting an autopsy in Georgia.

"It's the same as in the US," Chachuria said. "But in this case we did not examine the thorax or abdomen. At the specific request of the Americans, we limited our procedures to the head."

This contradicted completely FBI reports confirming American requests that no autopsy be performed on the victim's head. However, Chachuria assured me that he had been given unfettered discretion to dissect Freddie's brain.

He opened the file on his desk and began reciting the principal findings from the autopsy. There was a 1.2 × 0.4 cm puncture wound above the right eye and a gaping 15 × 9 cm compound wound above and behind the right ear.

"I remember I could see bone fragments and brain matter through the larger wound," he said. "But I never found the bullet. It wasn't in the body and wasn't in the car."

Based on this visual examination Chachuria had concluded that a projectile entered Woodruff's skull in the front and exited from the rear.

"I saw a thousand of these during the war in Abkhazia," he said. "There is no doubt."

He was absolutely certain. And absolutely wrong.

This was the expert opinion he had offered at Anzor's trial—and it appeared to have the credibility of scientific method; however, it was nothing more than the subjective observations of an unreliable eyewitness. Chachuria had misperceived and therefore had misreported. This was not forensic evidence at all.

I told him that American pathologists had examined the bone fragments using a scanning electron microscope and that (based on the beveling of the fractures) they had concluded with 100 percent certainty that Freddie was shot in the back of the head.

He laughed. "These Americans depend too much on their toys," he said. "Even a beginner could tell that this man was shot from the front."

I asked him if he had measured the diameter of the bullets used in Sharmaidze's rifle to determine whether they would make a hole the size of the alleged entry wound. He dismissed the question as irrelevant.

"The bullet began to break up as soon as it struck the car," he said. "Only a fragment of the bullet struck the victim. The remaining parts of the bullet did not enter the victim's body."

Several seconds passed before I grasped the significance of what I'd just heard. At Sharmaidze's trial the ballistics expert had testified that the blunted bullet had passed intact through a rubber gasket and fragmented *upon impact* with Freddie's skull. However, Chachuria had now opined that the bullet had fragmented *before impacting* Freddie's skull. The two prosecution experts did not agree about a fundamental fact in the government's case.

I wondered aloud whether Chachuria was unfamiliar with the design details of the Niva 1600 or unaware of the location of alleged penetration. He grunted and led me to the parking lot where we inspected his own Niva 1600. He told me that he had seen Gogoladze's identical vehicle a few days after the murder and that he had actually put his finger in the bullet hole.

He showed me the exact location: the upper right-hand corner of the hatch, just above and behind the gasket that ringed the window. I pulled back the black rubber strip and saw that the glass overlapped the metal frame by a few centimeters and that the rubber gasket extended beyond the upper edge of the glass. I knew from the FBI investigation that none of the glass in the Niva had been cracked or broken by bullet penetration. That meant that if the murder occurred in the manner alleged by the prosecutor the bullet had to have penetrated *both* rubber *and* metal before striking Freddie. Thus, the ballistics expert was wrong when he said that Freddie's head was the first hard thing that the bullet hit.

This was no mere academic exercise. If the bullet fragmented upon impact with Freddie's skull, then the shrapnel would have been (at least initially) contained in his body. If the bullet fragmented upon impact with the car, and only a single fragment struck Freddie's skull, then there had been unaccounted-for fragments flying around the passenger compartment at supersonic speeds. What happened to that shrapnel? And why was there no other evidence of injury or damage?

I had always assumed that if a prosecutor was going to invent a story to frame an innocent man, good manners and professionalism required that the invented story be at the very least consistent. But this one wasn't. The more I pulled at it, the more it unraveled.

We left the hospital (and the resolutely amiable Chachuria) and drove to the offices of a local magazine that had published an exposé on Freddie's murder—the same article that Georgia Woodruff Alexander had found and given to me. I was eager to meet the authors because they clearly had access to evidence I'd never seen.

Sopiko Chkhaidze and Inga Alavidze were among a handful of reporters who were inventing journalism in post-Soviet Georgia. Their youthful appearance belied their serious professional competence. With help from a Western NGO the pair had submitted a FOIA request to the FBI. I thumbed through their stack of documents and quickly realized that they were not identical to the ones that I had received from the Bureau: There were subtle and not-so-subtle differences in the redactions. I could not tell if the variations were intentional or accidental; nevertheless, they did provide an insight into the censor's agenda: In its production to me the FBI had been careful to delete any reference to the political implications of either Freddie's murder or the subsequent investigations. The Bureau had been less scrupulous about these things in its production to Sopiko and Inga.

Of far more interest were documents the journalists had obtained directly from Georgian government files. One was a thirty-page report prepared by Woodruff regarding narcotics trafficking in the Caucasus. It had been written in English for submission to the CIA, but somehow a copy had ended up in the files of the Georgian intelligence service. In the report Woodruff described two routes used by an Iranian drug baron to truck Afghan heroin from the Caspian Sea to the Black Sea. One route began in Baku, transited near the Pankisi Gorge, and ended at Sarpi, a Georgian village on the border with Turkey. The other route began in Iran, passed through the Georgian port of Poti, and disappeared in the chaos of Abkhazia. The report identified by name the Georgian officials and Russian generals who were providing protection to this multimillion-dollar illicit enterprise.

I wondered if this was one of the Agency papers that Aldrich Ames had delivered to his Russian masters. It was very dangerous information. And knowing it could get a man killed.

Sopiko and Inga peppered me with questions: What was the Woodruff family's goal? Why were they motivated to help a

Georgian man they'd never met? Who was paying for all this? I answered as best I could—but no matter what I said or did, I wasn't going to be able to explain it to them. For the average Georgian, it was impossible to imagine the family of the victim wanting justice for the alleged perpetrator.

On the way home we stopped at a neighbor's kitchen for Georgian takeout—chicken salad with walnuts and pomegranates. This was embryonic capitalism: a woman making a business using her stove, a scrawny bird, and a half-dozen recycled plastic trays. Lali promised to return our tray when we came for the next day's meal.

In the morning I unfolded my six-foot-one-inch body from Lali's five-foot-ten-inch couch. There was a shower stall made of cinder blocks at the far end of the kitchen. Following instructions given the night before, I opened the water shut-off valve, turned on the gas flow, and lit the pilot in the tankless water heater. I climbed inside the circular shower curtain and tried to figure out how I was going to wash my feet in a space that was too small to bend over. It required both flexibility and a certain amount of shameless daring.

Lali sent me to the corner bakery for *tonis puri*—a canoe-shaped Georgian bread baked on the inner wall of a tandoor oven. I bought two loaves for about four cents. We ate it with butter and leftover chicken salad as she planned our day.

Our first stop was the ballistics expert. We met at his office in a police substation. Zaza Altunashvili had an open smile, a firm handshake, a blue button-down shirt, and khaki pants. He had attended an international program at the FBI Academy and returned to Tbilisi affecting the mien and manner of a special agent—like a college student who spends a year studying at Oxford and returns to West Texas wearing a tweed jacket and drinking tea with milk. Altunashvili was eager to talk about the Woodruff case. It was, he said, one of his proudest moments.

In 1993 he was young, enthusiastic, and inexperienced—but had been singled out to work on the murder of the American diplomat. The chief of police had asked him to reinspect the Niva. It was his first important assignment; the first time he'd been asked for by name; and the first time he'd been invited to participate on a high-profile case.

The older investigators thought the assignment was both an insult and a waste of time. They had gone over the Niva carefully and had reached a unanimous conclusion: There was no bullet hole in that car. They were convinced that the fatal bullet had come in through the open front passenger window. And they were annoyed that the chief had sent an unseasoned boy to check their work.

Gogoladze's car was parked inside the fence that surrounded the old Parliament Building. The minister of internal affairs had moved it there for safekeeping on the night of the murder, and it had been there ever since—doors and windows shut, baking in the August sun.

Altunashvili walked out of the ministry offices to begin his reexamination just after lunch, he told us. He pressed the button on the Niva tailgate, lifted the hatch, and was immediately drenched in the putrid smell of decayed human flesh. Superheated air belched out of the open car and into his lungs. His head spun, his knees buckled, he almost fainted. He stumbled blindly to a nearby tree and vomited.

"I could hear the older investigators laughing inside the office," he said. It was an inauspicious beginning.

After several minutes he steeled himself and returned to the car. The back seat and floorboard were painted in blood, a modern-art spatter on the ceiling and front seats. The pattern suggested that the bullet had come from behind the victim. A tear in the headliner—tracing from the back right toward the left front—seemed to confirm this observation. Altunashvili then turned his attention to the section of the hatch that aligned with the tear. There, in the upper corner just behind the victim's head, was a bullet hole. He followed it through to the external ply of metal and found a corresponding entry hole.

"The holes were close to the rubber gasket that ringed the hatchback window," he said, "but they were clearly visible to the naked eye."

He measured the diameter of the holes and calculated the caliber of weapon that had made them. He plotted the trajectory of the bullet and searched for the lead slug. He didn't find it—it wasn't in the corpse and it wasn't in the car—and he had no real idea where it had gone.

"It probably flew out the open passenger window," he said.

When he had finished, Altunashvili closed up the Niva and walked into the ministry offices to announce his discovery. The older investigators were incredulous. "Little boy, little boy," they said. "You don't know what the hell you're talking about."

He could feel the wet heat of embarrassment climbing up his neck—but he persisted.

"There is a bullet hole," he said. "And I found it."

Determined to put down the insolent upstart, the older investigators trooped en masse out the door and across the gravel parking lot.

"I will never forget the feeling I had when the laughter suddenly stopped," he said.

Later that day he was given the honor of reporting his findings directly to the deputy chief investigator. "The bullet hole had a diameter of approximately 5.62 millimeters," he said. "The same diameter as the bullet fired by the defendant's AK-74 assault rifle."

"What about fragmentation?" I asked. "Did you do any studies to determine what happened to the bullet on impact?"

"No," he answered. "We didn't do any studies—but we didn't have to. It was obvious that the bullet fragmented after impact with Woodruff's skull."

As a trial lawyer I had learned to be suspicious of phrases like "it is obvious that. . . ." Experts routinely use such phrases to excuse their sins of scientific omission: their failure to test a basic assumption or their inability to prove a fundamental fact. In this case, the pathologist had assumed that the bullet broke up on impact with the car, and the ballistics expert had assumed that it broke up on impact with the victim. Each of these prosecution experts then proceeded to construct an opinion on the basis of an assumption denied by the other expert.

They couldn't both be right. But they could both be wrong.

I now knew that Altunashvili's expert testimony contained only one verifiable observation: that the diameter of the bullet hole in the hatch matched the diameter of the bullets fired from the defendant's rifle. However, there was no scientific test that would allow me (or anyone else) to prove whether the hole was created *before or after* the arrest of Anzor Sharmaidze. For this issue, I had to rely on eyewitnesses—and those witnesses appeared to be uniformly consistent: In the days immediately after the murder a number of experts inspected the Niva in search of a bullet hole and none of them found it.

This fact was suspicious but not conclusive. The shell casing found at the scene of the crime was circumstantial evidence that Anzor's rifle had fired a bullet that *could have* made the hole and killed Freddie Woodruff. I needed to find someone who could talk to me about the provenance of that casing.

Once again, Lali found just the right person.

Irakli Batiashvili was a handsome and urbane child of privilege. The son of a celebrated movie director, he had been an early leader in the Liberation Movement. He was almost killed in 1989 when Soviet shock troops violently suppressed a nationalist candlelight vigil. His injuries established him as a genuine Georgian hero and sealed his place among the new leaders. In 1992 he was appointed chief of intelligence and information services.

He was thirty-one years old and had no prior professional experience.

We met in the parlor of his family's fifth-floor apartment. The walls were covered with portraits of long-dead Batiashvilis—a visual history of the clan's social and political prominence. The ancestors seemed to look down on Irakli with benign approval.

He rose from an overstuffed chair to shake my hand.

"I am very happy today," he said. "I just received a PhD in philosophy from Tbilisi State University."

Obtaining this degree in the current climate was a daunting achievement. According to Lali, the Georgian educational system had ceased to function during the revolution. Classes seldom met. Grades and graduation were a product of financial negotiation.

"You're here about the Woodruff murder," he said. "I was in charge of our intelligence service at the time of the killing. As you probably know, I didn't trust the official investigation: The prosecutor and police were not interested in finding the truth. That's why I had the ministry do its own separate investigation."

His statements were simple, direct, and strangely collegial—as though he viewed me as a professional colleague. I was just beginning to enjoy the idea of this unexpected efficiency when I had a chilling realization: Irakli believed I was a CIA officer.

Up to this point I had given very little thought as to how the Georgians (or Russians) would perceive me. After all, I was doing things that were fairly routine for lawyers in America. But I wasn't in America. And if these people thought I was a spy they would feel justified in treating me as an enemy combatant.

For a fleeting second I considered exploiting the misperception. If he thought I was an intelligence professional, Irakli might tell me things that he would not tell a civilian. But the cost of such duplicity would be my credibility and (possibly) my life.

"I'm a lawyer," I said. "I'm just a lawyer."

Irakli seemed oddly encouraged by my response—as though my overt denial had somehow confirmed my covert affiliation. This refusal to believe the true nature of my status was a maddening (and dangerous) non sequitur that would be repeated throughout my Georgian odyssey: The more emphatically I protested, the more confidently they assumed.

"I don't know how I can help you," he said. "I've already told the world what I think happened."

He was referring to a 1995 press conference in which he had publicly accused the Russian special services of complicity in

Woodruff's death and an attempt to assassinate Eduard Shevard-nadze. At the time his statements were dismissed as an unsubtle bid to incriminate Igor Giorgadze—the man who had replaced Irakli as director of the Georgian intelligence service.

"But you weren't very specific," I said. "I was hoping to get a few more details."

The conversation paused as Irakli served cognac. He was play-ing the consummate host and in the same gesture controlling the rhythm of our talk. I had the uncomfortable impression that he was estimating my value as a pawn in a chess match of political ambition.

"It was GRU," he said. "Woodruff was murdered by Russian military intelligence."

This was the same thing that the embassy-based military attaché had told FBI investigators—Woodruff was assassinated by the GRU. But the attaché had added a titillating wrinkle: He suggested that Georgians may have been involved in the killing.

I asked Irakli if this was accurate.

"Yes," he said. "Eldar Gogoladze was instrumental in the murder."

This was an astonishing accusation—not simply because he blamed his subordinate for the murder of an American diplomat, but because he implicitly confessed that he had been powerless to do anything about it.

I had arrived in Tbilisi thinking that (with a combination of charm and enthusiasm) I could navigate the labyrinth of Georgian political culture. I now realized I had been audaciously naive. Nothing was as it seemed. A government title was no sign of influence or authority. A subordinate position was no indication of subservience or accountability.

Power was a function of who you were and who you knew.

This disorienting insight left me with two very troubling ques-tions: Who was Eldar Gogoladze? And why was he untouchable?

I had already begun making organization charts detailing the formal relationships among the people with relevant knowledge.

My conversation with Irakli made me see that if I was to have any hope of understanding the true power dynamic I would need to chart the informal relationships among the players. This was much more difficult but potentially much more rewarding.

"I fired Gogoladze right after the murder," said Irakli. "Shevardnadze called four times asking me to leave him in his position—but I'm pretty sure someone was pressing him to do that."

Irakli's suggestion that the chairman of the State Council could be compelled to lobby for Gogoladze's retention was inconsistent with my preconceived notion of Shevardnadze's status. I had it in my head that he was in charge and that made it difficult for me to imagine that someone could press him about a personnel decision.

Clearly, I was still thinking like an American.

"But wasn't Gogoladze reinstated as chief of the protection force?" I asked. "How could that happen if neither you nor Shevardnadze wanted him?"

Irakli shrugged and raised an eyebrow. Then, as though changing the subject, he said, "Gogoladze was GRU."

For a moment I thought Irakli had exposed a lie by Gogoladze. "During our meeting he told me that he had retired as a KGB colonel," I said.

"It's true," said Irakli. "He was KGB. And GRU. Soviet military intelligence placed him inside Soviet KGB to spy on their sister service. After the revolution, Gogoladze went from officially working for Soviet KGB to officially working for Georgian KGB—but the whole time he was also working for GRU."

I was speechless.

Gogoladze was a KGB officer, a GRU agent, and the administrative head of Group Omega—the CIA-sponsored special operations unit that Freddie Woodruff and Delta Force had created in the former Soviet Republic of Georgia.

It seemed inconceivable.

But if Gogoladze had *in fact* enlisted to serve these three irreconcilable masters, to which of them, if any, had he given his ultimate allegiance? And how could I ever find out?

"When I realized that the prosecutor's investigation was corrupted," said Irakli, "I assigned my deputy, Shota Kviraya, the task of conducting a separate inquiry on behalf of the intelligence and information service. But it was never completed."

"Why not?" I asked.

"A month later—September 1993—Georgia suffered a humiliating defeat at the hands of the Russians," he said. "We lost the battle for the regional capital of Sukhumi and eventually all of Abkhazia. I resigned as minister and was replaced by Igor Giorgadze. He had no interest in the investigation and terminated it immediately."

I knew from my research that Giorgadze—a general in the USSR's Group Alpha—had continued to serve as head of Georgia's intelligence and information service until he was implicated in a 1995 attempt to assassinate Shevardnadze. He fled to Russia and was replaced as minister by Shota Kviraya. A year later, in 1996, Kviraya issued a public statement accusing Giorgadze of arranging Woodruff's murder on orders from Moscow and accusing Eldar Gogoladze of participating in the plot.

"Kviraya was lifetime KGB," said Irakli. "He hated Eldar. And vice versa."

I copied down Irakli's comment verbatim and wondered about this unexplained antipathy. Was he describing an irreconcilable personality conflict or giving me a hint about Gogoladze's ultimate loyalty?

"What about the shell casing?" I asked. "The FBI lab confirmed that it had been fired by Sharmaidze's rifle—and that would appear to tie him to the murder."

"The police planted it," he said matter-of-factly. "They fired the defendant's rifle and left the spent shell on the roadside so that your FBI could find it. Kviraya witnessed the whole thing and confirmed it in his reports."

My heart was racing. Irakli had discredited the last piece of forensic evidence and (at the same time) offered compelling proof of both police misconduct and a government conspiracy to frame Anzor Sharmaidze. If he was willing to confirm this under oath then I would have new evidence of the defendant's innocence from an unimpeachable source.

"Would you be willing to sign an affidavit?" I asked.

"I will," he said. "After all, it is the truth. The murder was thoroughly planned and professionally executed. It is simply absurd to suggest that it was done by a peasant."

We sat in silence for a few seconds. I was having trouble processing the torrent of revelations. I was (I believe) hobbled by my preconceptions. It was very hard for me to imagine that a legitimate government would willingly participate in such a calculated miscarriage of justice.

"What about the Americans?" I asked. "Did they know about all this?"

Irakli's expression changed. He looked at me as though I might really be *just a lawyer*.

"Of course," he said. "The Americans knew everything."

For the first time I began to doubt Irakli. It seemed impossible to me that the US would not expend every reasonable effort to expose and prosecute the person who murdered Freddie Woodruff. To do otherwise would have been to disavow a man who had died in service to his country and to repudiate the core ethos of the American warrior: that no man is ever left behind.

Irakli must have sensed my incredulity.

"Let me tell you a story," he said. "I was with Chairman Shevardnadze when he delivered Woodruff's body to your director of central intelligence. The chairman was very concerned that this crime was going to interfere in Georgia's strategic relationship with the United States. He offered a carefully prepared statement of condolence and then Director Woolsey talked for thirty minutes. I remember how puzzled and surprised Shevardnadze was by Woolsey—by what he said and what he didn't say. All the way back to Tbilisi the chairman kept repeating the same phrase: 'The American never mentioned the murder.' Woolsey had talked about all the things our countries were going to do together, but he never mentioned Fred Woodruff."

To the Georgians, the meaning of the oversight was obvious: The United States had decided that Freddie Woodruff was expendable. Woolsey later denied the omission, but the damage had already been done. The Georgians believed they'd been encouraged to resolve the matter of Freddie's death in any manner they deemed appropriate. And the sooner it was over, the better for all concerned.

"But why?" I asked.

Irakli didn't answer immediately. It seemed as though he was trying to decide how much he could trust me. Finally he spoke.

"Aldrich Ames," he said. "He met with Chairman Shevard-nadze when the CIA delegation was here in Tbilisi. Afterward we received a communication from Boris Yeltsin that caused us to become suspicious of Ames. Shevardnadze contacted friends in Washington and told them he was concerned that Ames was funneling information to Russia."

It was not an answer I had expected.

From the beginning, there had been whispers that Woodruff's murder was related to Ames's treachery. Now Irakli suggested that the Agency's decision to cover up that murder was also somehow related to the traitor.

Implicit in this suggestion was the inference that—at the time he met Shevardnadze to take possession of Woodruff's lifeless body—DCI Woolsey *already knew* about Ames's betrayal. If this was true, then the Agency had permitted a known traitor to travel to the former Soviet Union and drive (literally) to the Russian border. If Ames had continued just a few more kilometers north on the Old Military Road, he would have passed into Russia and beyond the reach of American justice.

What, I wondered, was important enough to justify such an audacious risk? And was Freddie Woodruff a casualty of that audacity?

As we drove through the unlit streets of Tbilisi, Lali was uncharacteristically silent. I think she was evaluating the risks of joining my idealistic crusade. When she finally spoke, I realized that she had transitioned from contractor to comrade.

"Why don't I call President Shevardnadze?" she said. "We can see him tomorrow."

I was surprised. It had never even occurred to me that I could talk to the Great Man himself. As it turned out, his private telephone number was on Lali's speed dial.

We arrived at his compound in the morning. There was an eight-foot wall, armed guards in business suits, an airport-style X-ray machine, and a metal detector. I wasn't sure whether it was a fortress or a prison.

I collected my thoroughly searched briefcase and turned to Lali. "Who pays for all this security around Shevardnadze?" I asked.

"You do," she said. "The first thing President Shevardnadze did after the Rose Revolution was call his friend Jim Baker. He asked him, 'Are the Americans going to continue my security or am I a dead man?' Your government agreed to provide this protection for the rest of his life."

One of the US-trained guards escorted us through the garden to the house. Along the way we passed the grave of Nanuli Shevardnadze. Lali said that she had been buried inside the compound so that her husband of fifty-three years could make his daily visits without leaving the sanctuary.

Shevardnadze met us at the door and embraced Lali with genuine affection. The former president was wearing a blue cardigan and seemed to welcome us as a distraction from the tedium of involuntary retirement. He led us into a spacious room that was in equal parts office, parlor, and library. He sat in an overstuffed leather chair, while we took the sofa opposite. I explained my client's concerns and enumerated the evidence supporting Sharmaidze's innocence.

"I remember Freddie Woodruff," he said. "He was helpful to me. He used to give me briefings on signals intelligence and Russian troop movements. But about Sharmaidze, I do not agree with you: He was adjudicated guilty by the court. He is guilty because the judge said he's guilty."

It was a shrewd answer. The former chief executive did not concern himself with truth; he focused entirely on process. Once the process was complete, it created its own kind of reality. And in the context of that reality, there was nothing more to be said about Sharmaidze's innocence.

I tried a different tack.

"I spoke with your former bodyguard, Eldar Gogoladze," I said. "He denied that he was fired after Woodruff's murder."

"Of course he was fired," Shevardnadze said. "He carried a foreign diplomat in his private car, he took him outside the city limits, he didn't have a chase car—he violated every security protocol. There was no reason not to fire him."

The answer had been quick and emphatic—but then the former president paused. His eyes twinkled and he smiled at some secret amusement.

"But there was something interesting," he said. "A few days after I fired Gogoladze someone reinstated him. I don't know who it was that did it—but it certainly wasn't me."

It was just as Irakli had told me: In 1993 the chairman of the Georgian State Council did not have the authority to hire or fire the head of his personal protection force. Governmental power lay somewhere outside the formal chain of command—and I had no idea where.

I needed to know a lot more about the recent history of Georgia.

The conversation drifted toward current events and the new government's campaign to arrest the old government's ministers.

"When I became president I knew there would be corruption," he said. "So I told each minister that I had two rules: 'First,' I told them, 'you are forbidden to steal *too much*. And second,' I said, 'you are forbidden to take the money out of the country.' "

Shevardnadze must have sensed my schoolboy contempt for this official tolerance of dishonesty. He seemed mildly dismayed by the unspoken judgment and leaned forward to explain.

"I was trying to build capitalism," he said. "Capitalism requires the formation of capital. And capital is blind: The money doesn't know how it was acquired—whether it was inherited or earned or stolen. But so long as it stays in the country, so long as it doesn't go to New York or London or Switzerland, the money is going to be put to work locally building businesses and creating jobs. And that's what I wanted to do."

This was an astonishingly pragmatic answer. This lifelong Communist intuitively understood how to harness the energy of greed for the common good. He was giving a master class in the art of Realpolitik.

Shevardnadze stood up, indicating the end of the interview. Lali and I retraced our steps and exited the compound. As we walked to the car, I noticed a man across the street with a long-lens camera. Clearly, someone had a continuing interest in knowing who visited the former president. As I looked at him, he snapped my picture.

I was now officially on the Georgian government's radar.

When we arrived home, I made a cup of tea and tried to figure out what impact the government's awareness might have on my efforts. I had thus far enjoyed easy access to people who had information about the murder and the investigation. But if the government chose to do so, it could hamper future access or—with regard to at least one important witness—block it completely. And that could be a real problem.

"Lali," I said, "I need to talk to Anzor Sharmaidze as soon as possible."

I'd never really thought of Anzor as a witness. After all, my belief that he had not committed the murder was the raison d'être for my involvement. Nevertheless, he did have unique knowledge about two things: the fact of his innocence and the brutal things the police had done in order to get him to deny it.

We organized the visit through attorney Tamaz Inashvili and a Western-funded ombudsman for prisoner rights. The four of us agreed to meet in the morning and ride together in Lali's car. The twenty-mile trip to the prison took just over an hour.

The aptly named Rustavi Isolator squatted at the end of a rutted dirt road. It was a bleak place. Twenty-foot-high whitewashed walls; shards of glass and razor wire; an apron of concrete and dead grass.

I felt queasy as we stepped through the iron door. I was walking into a cage and trusting that the guards would (eventually) allow me to leave. My freedom depended entirely on their willingness to comply with established rules and procedures—and if my investigation had taught me anything, it was that Georgians had a little trouble with rules and procedures.

The guards checked our credentials, searched our bags, and led us to the warden's office. Along the way we passed a group of inmates. As we approached, they turned to face the wall, clasped their hands behind their backs, and bowed their heads.

It was a synchronized choreography of the damned.

The warden jumped up as we entered. He was a short, thick man with an expansive forehead and a stubble of gray hair. He wore a Russian military parka and smoked nervously. His pale eyes betrayed apprehension: There was nothing good that could come from a meeting with an American lawyer.

We stood by the window as we waited for Anzor to respond to the warden's summons. The second-floor office overlooked the inner courtyard of the prison. There were rows of dilapidated barracks and, in the far corner, a garden.

"The convicts are permitted to grow vegetables," said the warden. "It is a privilege for good behavior."

After a few minutes I heard the sound of someone climbing the stairs. The footfalls were slow and unsteady, the breathing rapid and labored. A man finally appeared on the landing but did not enter the room. He was skinny, with ferret-like features. He was wearing a shabby leather jacket, a black crew-neck sweater, and dark wool pants. He had a close-cropped beard and unkempt brown hair. His eyes were rheumy, and he was cradling his left arm tenderly with his right. He swayed a little as he tried to stand still.

This was Anzor Sharmaidze.

The warden called him in and told him to sit at the conference table. He shuffled to a chair, sat down, and looked at us with passive indifference. He seemed decades older than his thirty-one years.

"Mr. Sharmaidze," I said, "I represent Georgia Woodruff Alexander, a sister of the man you are accused of killing. She believes that you are innocent and has hired me to get you out of prison."

It took a moment for him to understand my absurd assignment, but when he did the response was electric. He became agitated, glanced at the warden, and began to babble. Words gushed out of him like blood from a wound.

"I didn't do it," he said. "I wasn't there. The police beat me—they made me say I did it but I didn't do it. The worst was my feet; they beat the soles of my feet until I couldn't walk. They cuffed my hands behind me and hung me up by my wrists and beat me with iron pipes . . . but I didn't do it."

Then, as suddenly as it had appeared, the vitality was gone. All that remained was a broken little man with tears on his face. Lali touched his arm gently—a gesture of compassion and comfort—and he screamed in agony.

We pushed back the loose sleeve covering his left forearm and discovered an abscess the size of a grapefruit. There were red streaks tracing out from the center and the fetid odor of rotten meat.

Lali began to cry and I heard someone groan. It was me.

The warden called for the prison nurse—a grandmother in an old greatcoat. She examined the patient and announced that he had a temperature of 106.5 degrees.

"I expect that this boil will burst today," she said. "And when it does, he will die of blood poisoning."

The warden looked terrified. Having an inmate die was of no great consequence, but having an inmate die in front of an American lawyer was a disaster. He unlocked a cabinet behind his desk and gave Anzor two tablets from a small bottle.

"What else do you want me to do?" the warden asked.

"I want you to send him to a hospital," I said. The simplicity of my answer seemed to increase his anxiety.

"We send the van to the Tbilisi hospital on Saturday—but today is only Wednesday. We can't afford to make a special trip."

"How much would it cost?" I asked.

Whenever I travel in the Third World, I carry hard currency. US dollars have an amazing power to create opportunities out of thin air. I lay my hand on the money pouch tucked beneath my shirt and wondered if $5,000 would be enough to buy Anzor's life from this man.

He began to calculate.

"We would need a driver, two guards, the nurse, gasoline for the trip there and back," he said. "Perhaps . . . twenty dollars?"

They were loading Anzor into a van as we left. The next day Lali visited the hospital and paid the doctors $100 to keep him there for a month.

In many ways, the bullet that killed Freddie Woodruff in 1993 had ricocheted and hit Anzor Sharmaidze. It would have killed him in February 2004 if I hadn't gone to visit him in prison and paid to put him in the hospital. Native Americans say that if you save a man's life you become responsible for him. I had no idea what I'd just done.

CHAPTER 9

A VISIT TO THE PROSECUTOR GENERAL

One of the principal functions of a lawyer is to evaluate whether a client's goal is worth the effort and expense necessary to achieve that goal. This kind of cost-benefit analysis assures that the courts will not be overwhelmed with trivial matters and that any legal fee charged will be reasonable relative to the recovery. However, the analysis breaks down when the goal is to save a human life. In this circumstance, the burden of deciding normally shifts to the person paying the expenses: How much justice can that person afford?

And in this case, I was that person.

My client didn't have money to pay me. I was donating my time and paying all the expenses. It was a dubious business model that inspired me to look for creative efficiencies.

The Republic of Georgia was rife with corruption. Anyone who had authority was willing to exercise that authority in exchange for money. And the price wasn't always that high. I had, after all, gotten Anzor admitted to the hospital for only $20.

This experience raised an interesting question: Could I pay just a little more and buy Anzor's freedom entirely? And assuming that I could, should I?

There are (of course) practical problems with any bribery scheme. I would be required to trust a dishonest person. Would the payee keep our venal bargain or would he sell me out to an indignant prosecutor general?

Then there was the issue of who to pay and how much to pay them. Unlike people who had grown up in this culture, I had no understanding of the protocols of graft.

As far as I could tell, the most probable outcome of subornation was that I would pay the wrong person the wrong amount and end up sharing a cell next to Anzor. And in the process I would betray my basic nature.

None of that seemed like a very good idea. So I decided that—in all my dealings with the Georgian judicial system—I would abide by the ethical standards applicable to American lawyers. My adoption of those guidelines immediately imposed two imperatives: first, that I reject out of hand all possibility of bribery; and second, that I become licensed to practice law in Georgia.

Almost all courts permit out-of-state lawyers to appear before them on a case-by-case basis—and Georgia was no exception. I could represent my client in the Georgian courts provided that I filed the necessary paperwork. Obtaining a certificate of good standing from the State Bar of Texas was easy. Upon request (and payment of a small fee) an officer of the association certified that I was a duly licensed attorney.

However, this was only the beginning of the paper chase. It was also necessary to obtain proof that the association officer who signed my certificate was authorized to make that certification on behalf of the bar. This came in the form of a notarized affidavit from another bar employee. I was then required to submit evidence that the notary who attested to the affidavit had the requisite legal authority to administer an oath. This was satisfied by a certificate from the chief of the state agency that administers local notaries—that is, the Texas secretary of state. Proof that the Texas secretary had the power to certify notaries was in turn provided by the US secretary of state. And finally the US secretary's authority to certify state secretaries was confirmed by the Georgian ambassador to the United States.

I filed this sheaf of self-authenticating documents with the Georgian Ministry of Justice. The receiving clerk—who did not read or speak English—dutifully examined each official seal and then issued me a local law license. My first task as a newly minted Georgian lawyer was to locate and reinterview the remaining eyewitnesses who had testified at trial—the two women in the car and the two men with Anzor. Their testimony was the last link in the prosecutor's chain of evidence.

Elena Darchiashvili (the woman riding in the front seat of Gogoladze's Niva) lived with her mother in a house on Kekelidze Street. Lali called her to arrange a meeting, but as soon as Elena heard the subject of our interest she hung up. I sent a mutual acquaintance with assurances of goodwill and confidentiality but Elena became hysterical and slammed the door. Thereafter, every time I came to Tbilisi, Elena left the city and went into hiding.

These encounters were short on details but long on information. At the trial Elena had testified that because of her poor eyesight she could not tell the judge anything about the murder. Nevertheless, the prospect of talking to me was terrifying to her. This reaction suggested two things: first, she did *in fact* know what had happened to Freddie Woodruff; and second, someone had promised to hurt her if she ever revealed that knowledge. This threat of violence was encouraging confirmation of Anzor's innocence.

The other woman in the car—the barmaid who sat in the back seat with Freddie—was more problematic. No one seemed to know where Marina Kapanadze was or what she was doing. I located her mother, but she denied knowing even what country Marina was in. "She calls me sometimes, but I never know from where."

Freddie had thought Marina was a member of the local mafia, and a US embassy staffer had reported that she had confessed to being a spy. It was impossible to know the truth of these suspicions. However, Marina had accomplished the magician's trick of disappearing completely. By all indications, she was not an amateur.

I hoped to have more luck talking to the two men who had been arrested with Anzor on the night of the murder. I didn't think it would be difficult to locate them. After all, I was an experienced investigator and they were seemingly unsophisticated peasants. But finding Genadi Berbitchashvili and Gela Bedoidze proved to be a humbling exercise in frustration. Like Elena, they seemed to vanish every time I appeared—and I appeared in Georgia a half-dozen times trying to find them.

Anzor's court-appointed lawyer, Tamaz Inashvili, was helping me. He suggested that we go to Genadi's village at night. It didn't seem like much of a plan, but—since nothing else was working—I agreed and later that day folded myself into his Lada for the hour-long trip.

It was dark when we arrived. The village of Minarheki was a half-dozen hovels at the end of a bumpy dirt road. Each house had a dog and each dog had an attitude. With the exception of these aggressive mongrels, there didn't seem to be any life at all. I felt a vague "I told you so" sense of superiority. Before we set out, I had specifically asked Tamaz how he hoped to overcome the locals' well-known distrust of outsiders. I was sure that the villagers would hide in their houses and wait for us to leave. Instead of answering, he'd just looked at me and smiled.

Now—instead of apologizing and driving us home—Tamaz got out of the car, walked to the back, and opened the trunk. I could hear him rustling around and went to investigate. Then I saw the reason for his smile. He had brought two five-gallon jugs of red wine and about twenty pounds of barbecued beef. He tore off a piece of meat, took a bite, and threw the rest to the closest yelping mutt. The dog stopped barking and I saw a curtain move inside the house he guarded.

In a few minutes, an old man came out the front door. Tamaz told him that we were there to meet a man from that village named Genadi but that he had not yet shown up. "We have a little wine and meat," said Tamaz. "Would you like some?"

Soon every house was empty and every villager was standing around the car eating and drinking and talking. After he'd opened the second jug, Tamaz turned the conversation to the subject of our visit.

"Where is Genadi?" he said to no one in particular. "He's going to miss all the wine."

"He was here until a couple of days ago," said one man. "But the police came and told him to leave. They've sent him off two or three times and—after a week or two—they let him come home."

And there it was. For the price of a picnic dinner we had confirmed that the Georgian government was monitoring my travel and working to prevent me from speaking to the eyewitnesses. I was vaguely encouraged that they thought I was worth the effort, but at the same time their attentions made me nervous. I was no longer protected by anonymity and relative insignificance. I now needed the modest security provided by acting in a licensed capacity.

It was time to formally request reconsideration of Anzor's conviction. And that process started with the prosecutor general.

The procurator's office building was an intimidating place—a marble chicken coop with a barbed wire fence and armed soldiers patrolling the perimeter. Lali and I waited thirty minutes in an outbuilding while an adolescent corporal checked our credentials and confirmed our appointment. When we were finally passed through to the main building, the lobby was empty: no receptionist, no security guard, no building directory. Neither of us had ever been there before, and I wasn't sure where to go.

Lali smiled at my naiveté. "You Americans put your president's office on the ground floor of a white house," she said. "But every Georgian knows that the most important man has his office on the top floor."

The elevator doors opened directly into a secretarial anteroom. The young man behind the desk was watching television. He waved us toward a door that opened to reveal a second door. Lali noticed my confusion. "It's for eavesdropping," she said. "To frustrate people who try to listen at the door."

She knocked and we entered.

Irakli Okruashvili crossed the room quickly to greet us. The prosecutor general was surprisingly young and unexpectedly cordial. I was just beginning to wonder whether professional inexperience explained his unseemly exuberance when Lali turned to introduce us.

"Irakli is my private student," she said. "I've been teaching him English."

The prosecutor general looked me directly in the eyes and extended his hand. It was the practiced maneuver of a retail politician. We bonded over our mutual admiration of Lali. Notwithstanding his relative youth, this man was one of the most powerful people in the Georgian government. His position identified him as a member of Saakashvili's inner circle and a wunderkind of political judo. I felt confident that whatever I said to him would be communicated directly to the president.

"This is about the Woodruff murder?" he asked.

"Yes, sir," I answered.

There was another man in the room. Irakli introduced him as Zaza Sanshiashvili, chief investigator for the office. He was older and less urbane, but projected an air of maturity and calm intelligence. If Irakli was a big-picture strategist, then Zaza was his detail-oriented foot soldier.

"We've read the file," said Irakli. "What do you want?"

"I represent the dead man's sister," I said. "We have new evidence proving that Anzor Sharmaidze is innocent of murdering Freddie Woodruff."

Irakli looked at me blankly. I had the uncomfortable feeling that as far as he was concerned I hadn't said anything especially important or responsive.

"Yes," he said, "but what does the Woodruff family want?"

It took me a minute to understand the implications of this question: In the prosecutor general's world, the fact a man was innocent was no guarantee that the victim's family would not want to see him punished anyway.

"We want you to review the new evidence," I said, "to reopen the criminal case, reverse the conviction, and let Anzor out of prison."

Irakli looked perplexed. And suspicious.

"But why?" he asked. "Are you from the US government?"

"No," I said, "my government is not involved in this effort. I represent Freddie Woodruff's sister."

"But . . . why do you care?" he asked. "Does the family get money if Woodruff was killed by someone other than Anzor?"

It had never occurred to me that I would be called upon to justify my client's kindness. I had never thought to characterize her motivations or quantify her stake in the outcome. She and I shared a common heritage in which the justification was obvious—sometimes you do a thing simply because it is the right thing to do.

"No," I said, "there is no profit for the Woodruff family."

The prosecutor general remained incredulous. His silence was pregnant with skepticism. He wanted more.

"The Woodruffs are religious people," I said. "They believe it is a sin for them to allow an innocent man to languish in prison if they have the power to set him free."

Irakli began to fidget impatiently. Obviously, my client's true motivation was not in his mind a sufficient basis for her extraordinary request. I needed to think like a Georgian.

"Freddie had children," I said, "and the truth of his death matters to them. It is one thing if their father was killed by a drunk on the side of the road. It is another thing altogether if he died in combat with the enemy. So long as Anzor's conviction stands, they cannot claim their father was a hero."

Both the prosecutor general and his chief investigator nodded their heads in approval. This was an explanation they could understand: family pride in the courage of their honored dead.

"Good," said Irakli, "very good. Now tell me—what is your new evidence?"

I told him about the AFIP autopsy and the microscopic reconstruction of Freddie's skull fragments. "According to the American pathologists," I said, "this reconstruction proved with a hundred percent certainty that Freddie was shot in *the back of the head*.

This means that the prosecution's theory of *what* happened—that Anzor killed Freddie by shooting him in the forehead—is demonstrably false."

I told him about the US embassy official who'd observed that Freddie's body was in an advanced state of rigor when it was delivered to the hospital. "But rigor mortis does not begin until *at least* two hours after death," I said. "This means that the prosecution's time line—their theory of *when* the murder occurred—is wrong. And that means that Anzor has an alibi for the actual time of the murder."

I told him about the Batiashvili affidavit and the FBI memo regarding the Bureau's first inspection of Eldar's Niva. "The former head of Georgia's intelligence service swears that the police planted a shell casing from Anzor's rifle so they could tie him to the scene," I said. "And an FBI special agent reported that when he examined the car on the day after the murder there was no bullet hole in either the glass or the metal skin. This suggests that at the time of the shooting the car was stopped and the rear hatch was open—and that contradicts the prosecution's theory of *how* the murder occurred."

And I told him about the US Naval Observatory and the exact time of sunset in Natakhtari on August 8, 1993. "The eyewitnesses all testified that it was very dark when Freddie was shot. And the prosecution claimed that one of the reasons that Anzor fired his rifle was because Eldar had failed to dim his high-beams. But it is an objective fact that—even if the murder occurred as late as nine p.m.—it was not dark. This fact impeaches the witnesses and discredits the prosecution's theory of *why* the murder occurred."

The prosecutor general was taking notes. He asked a few more polite questions, told me to deliver copies of the relevant documents to the chief investigator, and promised to respond promptly. It was businesslike and mildly anticlimactic.

As he ushered us out of his office, I had the distinct impression that none of my so-called *new* evidence was particularly *new* to the prosecutor general. And if that was true, then simply telling him things that he already knew wasn't going to have much effect. I needed to re-engineer the process: to present my request in a way that made the government believe it was in their best interest to release Anzor.

In a complicated lawsuit it is often necessary for a lawyer to gain a deep understanding of the other party's interests: what they want and what they fear. With such detailed knowledge it is *sometimes* possible to formulate a settlement agreement that allows the parties—both plaintiff and defendant—to benefit from a resolution of their dispute. This is what I hoped to accomplish in my negotiation with the Georgian government.

But I had absolutely no idea where to start. I had a tourist's knowledge of Georgia, and I was never going to develop the kind of deep understanding that would allow me to efficiently empathize with the Georgian people. But I'd seen enough of the world to know that every society maintains a repository of its core cultural values and uses that chronicle to indoctrinate new arrivals. It occurred to me that if I could access that record I could learn (in broad concepts) the nuances of the Georgian psyche.

"Lali," I asked, "what's your favorite Georgian fairy tale?"

As it turned out, the answer was easy: *The Knight in the Panther's Skin*. It was every Georgian's favorite fairy tale. I spent the next week studying Shota Rustaveli's nine-hundred-year-old epic and extending my departure date. It gave me something to do as I waited for a reply from the prosecutor general. The FBI documents had forewarned me about the Georgian tendency to regretfully offer a critical meeting or interview for a day *after* the agents were scheduled to leave. It was a deft exploitation of our Western devotion to timetables. The Georgians could appear to be cooperative without actually having to cooperate. But I had read Rudyard Kipling and knew that only a fool tries to hustle the East. So I resolved to be patient and to always buy a ticket that could be changed without additional fees.

I marked the eleventh anniversary of Freddie's murder standing on the side of the Old Military Road three hundred meters north of the turnoff to the Natakhtari Drain. This respectful observance proved to be a useful experience: At 10 p.m. on August 8—an hour *after* the time when Woodruff was allegedly shot—there was still sufficient sunlight that I could read a book without difficulty. Clearly, the witnesses who swore to the presence of total darkness were being less than candid.

After a few days I called my client to report my general lack of progress. I was beginning to worry that the prosecutor general might be ignoring my request. But Georgia Woodruff Alexander dispelled that concern completely.

"Damn, Michael. What have you done?" she said.

She'd gotten an unannounced visit from Freddie's widow. Meredith's superiors at the CIA had questioned her about my activities in Tbilisi. Had she hired a lawyer? Was she trying to reinvestigate the murder? Did she ask for the case to be reopened?

"She was upset, Michael," said Georgia. "She told them she didn't have anything to do with it. And then she got on a plane and flew down here to Arkansas to talk to me."

According to Meredith, the prosecutor general had contacted the Americans to find out if I was acting on behalf of the CIA. The Agency had denied any association with me and said that they were completely satisfied with the outcome of the Georgian legal process.

"She said you were wasting your time, Michael—that there are a lot of prisoners in American jails that deserve your help more than Anzor does."

It was a sobering conversation. A covert agency that normally refuses to "confirm or deny" the identity of alleged associates had explicitly disavowed me. What little protection I had derived from ambiguity was now gone. In addition, the American government had expressed an opinion regarding an American citizen's application to reopen Anzor's prosecution: They were satisfied with the status quo.

This was a heavy and disappointing thumb on the scales of Georgian justice. My country had effectively vetoed the Woodruff family's request to free an innocent man.

I felt moderately queasy and immoderately disgusted. I needed a counterweight—something to offset this bureaucratic amorality. I needed a pugnacious ally who took pleasure in exposing duplicity and corruption. I needed narcissistic egoists with access to every home and office in Tbilisi. I needed the press.

Lali arranged the interviews. She had once again found the necessary names and telephone numbers in her oversized purse. But for her these weren't journalists; they were just current and former students to whom she had taught English.

I had meetings with several newspaper reporters over the following days—sitting in Lali's parlor wearing a suit and trying to explain the details of the FBI investigation. The journalists were young, earnest, and overwhelmingly female. They had studied the story and struggled to understand its broader implications. But their first question was always about me. Why was I doing this? After a while, the inquiry began to embarrass me. These young journalists simply didn't accept that curiosity and idealism were sufficient explanations for my quest. I worked hard to stay on message, to allow the evidence to speak for itself, to avoid speculation and criticism. I wanted to inform the public without inflaming their political masters.

"Michael Pullara is a soft-spoken man in lawyer shirt-and-tie and small specs," said one article. "He speaks slowly, answering questions unhurriedly and often via much back-ground. I should think this is how he gets answers—by quiet tenacity, rather than the bulldog approach. In Georgia he employs 'humility' to investigate rather than harsh noise. And he says he's 'insatiably curious' enough to listen to anyone who'll talk to him."

But the reporters were persistent in trying to assign both responsibility and blame. Who did this to Anzor? And should they be punished?

It was a dangerous line of inquiry with potentially lethal consequences. I answered very carefully. "The closest Pullara will go to apportioning blame is to make the Time culpable. 'It was a very fragile state. The consequences . . . could have resulted in the collapse of the state of Georgia or the US-Georgian relations or of Shevardnadze.' He thinks Anzor Sharmaidze may have been the necessary scapegoat of that Time; the sacrificial lamb of that lawless, chaotic, post–civil war period, which demanded 'hard decisions to save Georgia in 1993.'"

But the reporters were unsatisfied. To them, it was naive to suggest that law enforcement officials had arrested a possibly innocent man on the basis of some higher national ideals.

"Usually," said one reporter, "it's about saving their own skin."

And in this case the law enforcement official who had arrested a possibly innocent man was Eldar Gogoladze.

What did I think of him? Had he acted on the basis of a higher national ideal or to save his own skin?

The answer to this question was my Rubicon. If I publicly identified the former KGB colonel as a perpetrator, then he would become my blood enemy. And Eldar Gogoladze was a very dangerous man. I had known this day was coming since I interviewed him in his opulent office atop the Cartu building. I had examined the evidence from every perspective and come away with a single inescapable conclusion: Eldar was an unreliable witness.

And it was time that I said so.

"Gogoladze saw how it happened," I answered. "The level of his error suggests that he knows he is mistaken."

As I had hoped, this sent the reporters scurrying off to interview the man.

And in the meantime, I was going to be on TV.

After the collapse of the Soviet Union, there was a frenetic explosion of independent television stations in the newly emerging democracies. Western technological innovation had put the cost of creating a rudimentary TV channel within the easy reach of many people.

These stations became a rallying point for opposition political parties. They gleefully and effectively revealed official caprice, cupidity, and crime. The government would eventually take steps to corral these experiments in unrestricted free speech. But for the moment, the independent broadcasters could talk about anything they wanted to—and they wanted to talk about Anzor Sharmaidze.

ZTV operated out of a repurposed office building in the central business district. I arrived an hour early for the late-night news program and was ushered into the makeup suite (a cramped windowless room with lighted mirrors and three barber chairs).

There was a thirty-something man sitting in the third chair and having foundation rubbed on his face. Lali introduced him as Giga Bokeria—the son of her best friend and (incidentally) a close advisor to President Saakashvili.

Giga was a big man with a big head. He had penetrating dark eyes and restless energy. He looked at me with an open mouth and grunted as he got out of the chair.

"I know about this case," he said. "You should skip the lawsuit and apply to the president for a pardon."

And with that he was gone—off to an interview regarding some new European Union initiative in Georgia.

I was intrigued that someone in the president's inner circle knew enough about my project to offer a suggested solution. But there was a big problem with Giga's proposal: In order to be considered for a pardon, Anzor had to confess to a crime he didn't commit.

And that wasn't something he was eager to do.

The makeup artist rubbed foundation on my face. When she finished, I went outside to escape the heat and the acrid smell of perspiration. I walked slowly down the concrete stairs toward the cobblestone plaza. At the foot of the steps there was a gaggle of Georgian men having an animated conversation. I sidled up to this group and was immediately spotted by the man in the center. He barked something in Georgian and I apologized in English.

"You're American," he said, switching to my language. "Why are you here?"

I said something about Anzor and the man turned to face me.

"I remember the case," he said. "I was mayor of Tbilisi when Woodruff was murdered. I went to the jail to see the prisoner Sharmaidze."

He paused as if remembering. His eyes seemed to change focus as he looked more at his memory than at me. Then he whispered something, almost a sigh.

"Oh, how they beat that boy," he said.

The night was warm, but I felt a sudden chill. Just then Lali came to the front door of the building. It was time for the interview.

The manager at ZTV was one of Lali's former colleagues from Shevardnadze's office. He had handled public relations for the president and met her as an old friend. Once again, her stature gave me status.

He guided me into the studio—an oversized office made small by too much furniture and equipment. Tamaz Inashvili was sitting on a dais at the far end of the room. I took a seat next to him as someone gave me a microphone and earbud. I could hear Lali's voice through the earpiece. She had taken a place in the control room and was prepared to simultaneously translate everything that was said during the program.

The host and main interrogator was a skinny kid who could not have been more than five years out of university. He wore an electric-blue suit and rainbow suspenders. Seeing him reminded me of a fundamental fact about the Rose Revolution: It was as much intergenerational as it was political. The young had thrown out the old and taken their place at the table.

The man in rainbow suspenders was supported by a cast of four equally youthful correspondents. Each sat at a small desk with a large computer. I think the staging was intended to give the impression that the news team was using the Internet to fact-check every statement. But—as is often the case with manipulated impressions—this one was false. The computers weren't even turned on.

There was a prerecorded background video about the murder and the trial—images of Anzor standing in a courtroom cage wearing a heavy winter coat. Lali translated every word into my right ear. It was hard to concentrate on what I was seeing and at the same time on what she was saying. It only got worse when I talked and she translated my words into Georgian.

The moderator started slowly—who was my client?

I identified Freddie's sister, Georgia Woodruff Alexander. I wasn't worried that the audience would confuse her name with the name of their country. To a Georgian, I wasn't in Georgia; I was in Sak'art'velo.

I talked a little about my new evidence and the status of my application to the prosecutor general.

The host listened to the translation, smiled, and spat out a question. Even before I heard the translation, I knew it was aggressive: Wasn't this just an attempt to prove that Freddie died "in the line of duty" so that the family could get more money?

I took a breath. The question felt like bait—as though the host was trying to provoke a defensive reaction.

"No," I said softly. "There is no way for my client to profit from this. And Freddie's widow and children have already received all the benefits they can from the US government."

"Then why is she doing it?" he asked. "And why do we need an American lawyer to come to Georgia?"

"I've come because my client asked me to come," I said. "And my client asked me to come because she's discovered evidence that Anzor Sharmaidze is innocent. The Woodruffs are pious people, Christian believers. And they believe it is their obligation to help free the innocent."

"So you're some sort of hero?" he asked.

"Oh, no," I said. "The only hero here is Tamaz Inashvili. He has stood by his client at great personal risk. He has continued to fight for Anzor's freedom against almost impossible odds. He has demonstrated himself to be everything that a lawyer should be."

"So it's all for Anzor?" he asked. "You want him to get money?"

"Anzor was a soldier," I said. "And the murder of Freddie Woodruff was a dagger pointed at the heart of the new republic. The country called on Anzor to make a sacrifice for the people—

and he answered the call. He gave Georgia the very best years of his life. But the need for sacrifice has passed; the war is over. And when a war is over, the prisoners get to go home. It is time for Anzor to go home."

"But do you think he should get money?" asked one of the junior journalists.

"This is not a question for me," I said. "This is a question for Georgia and her people: Do you think he should get money? My only observation is that you or I would probably want a lot of money if we were wrongly forced to spend a dozen years in prison for a crime we did not commit. And—as the poet Rustaveli said a long time ago—the justice you give is the justice you will get."

A woman sitting at the second row of tables had stopped the pretense of computer use and was just listening. She and the host started asking a question at the same time, but she talked over him.

"Who did it?" she asked. "Who murdered Freddie Woodruff and framed Anzor Sharmaidze? And what do you think should happen to them?"

It was the most dangerous part of the interview. I checked my attitude and doubled down on humility.

"My client does not care who killed Freddie," I said. "Punishing the guilty will not make Freddie any less dead. We are only concerned about the wrongful incarceration of an innocent man. We're not asking the government to prosecute the real murderer or the people who framed Anzor. But if something happens to Anzor in prison, we will know that the people who framed him still have power in government. His continued safety will be evidence of the current government's innocence."

The producer gave a signal, the camera zoomed in on the host as he described the next night's program, and it was over. I was exhausted. I had no idea how long it had lasted.

Tamaz wanted to ask me a question, but we had to wait until Lali arrived to translate. Finally she did.

"How did you know?" he asked. "How did you know about the call?"

"What call?" I said.

According to Tamaz, the recent spate of activity had frightened someone involved in either the murder or the cover-up. They had found out that Anzor had a contraband cellphone, gotten the telephone number, and called him. They had told him that if he didn't drop the application to reopen his case, they would kill him in prison.

"I didn't know," I said. "I really didn't know. I was only trying to encourage the government to keep him safe."

The reality of the situation kept me awake most of the night. People were willing to kill to keep these secrets. And they'd already killed one American. What was one more?

A few days later Lali took me to a reception at the Sheraton Metechi Palace—EU diplomats celebrating EU diplomats for publishing a Georgian model commercial code. Several of the ambassadors recognized me from my recent appearance on television. One of them—an angular Italian in a gorgeous suit and red glasses—was particularly enthusiastic. He congratulated me with a gusto that suggested I had actually accomplished something.

The accolades seemed odd to me: I had been on TV, but Anzor was still in prison.

Just then I saw a man across the room with a long-lens camera. It appeared that I was a principal focus of his photographic interest. I moved several times in order to test this impression. I positioned obstacles between us, and (each time) he moved to clear the view. *Click-click-click-click-click*. I could hear the camera. And his voice as he excused himself through the crowd. He was American.

Apparently, the embassy had noticed me and wanted to build a file.

The call from the prosecutor general came first thing the next morning. We were invited to visit his office to discuss the Woodruff family request.

Lali and I arrived as scheduled and were processed through the front gate quickly. This time, we had an armed escort to the prosecutor general's office. The three of us and a rifle all rode together to the top floor. No one spoke.

The elevator opened to reveal a grim-looking secretary sitting stiffly at his desk. The television was off and the room was silent. The secretary walked across the room and opened the inner office doors—all without taking his eyes off me.

The prosecutor general did not rise to greet us. There were no handshakes or kisses on the cheek. He did not offer coffee and cognac or introduce the two other men sitting against the wall.

This was all business. And there was no room for effusive Georgian hospitality.

"We've considered your request relating to the prisoner Anzor Sharmaidze," he said. "You have not provided sufficient new evidence to justify reopening the case. The request is denied."

We'd just sat down and the meeting was already over. The look on the prosecutor general's face was clear—the matter was not open for discussion; we were expected to leave. Our escort was waiting for us in the anteroom. We rode the elevator in silence, but my mind was noisy. The difference between this and our first visit was unsettling. The charming Irakli Okruashvili had become the terrifying prosecutor general. And I had become the enemy.

"Why was he so angry?" I wondered to myself.

We drove across town for a prearranged meeting with Lali's best friend. She had invited us to visit her at the Tbilisi Chess Club. It was an unimpressive facility: a chalkboard, a few shelves of well-worn books, a dozen small tables with facing chairs, framed photographs, certificates. The clubhouse projected a plainness that belied its reputation as an epicenter of excellence.

There was a woman standing at one table arranging plastic chess pieces. She greeted Lali with a warm smile and surveyed me with dark dispassionate eyes.

Nana Alexandria was a genteel beauty with a ferocious intellect. A woman grandmaster, she had on two separate occasions competed for woman's world chess champion. As a youth she had represented the Soviet Union in chess tournaments throughout the world and, according to Lali, kept her close friends well supplied in Western fashions.

Lali made brief introductions and confided about our meeting with the prosecutor general. Nana sensed my disappointment and offered to distract me.

"Would you like to play a game of chess?" she asked.

I demurred. I'd already had more than enough crushing defeat for one day. Nevertheless, she persisted in trying to cheer me up as only a grandmaster can.

"The government controls all the formal levers of power," she said. "And as we all know the government doesn't play fair."

She was stating the obvious. But it was an unexpected admission coming from the mother of Giga Bokeria. Her son—the man I'd met in the makeup suite at ZTV—was one of Misha Saakashvili's key lieutenants and a central pillar of the government that she had just criticized.

I could feel her brain working, processing, formulating. After a moment of silence her eyes softened and she smiled.

"You need to expand the chessboard," she said. "You need to find an informal lever that will move the government."

It was cryptic advice from a world-class tactician—and as inscrutable as a fortune cookie. I sat in Lali's parlor all evening thinking about it. And then the electricity failed.

"Perfect," I thought. As I stewed in the darkness, I could hear Lali bustling in the other room. She carried a chair out on the front stoop, climbed up, fumbled with a few switches, and turned on the lights. She came into the parlor, beaming more brightly than the lamps.

"I had the house wired into two different electricity grids," she said. "It's how we do things in Georgia. If one way fails, we find another way."

I was too self-absorbed to take the hint.

It would take several months before I began to understand. In the meantime, I was going to have to file a lawsuit that I didn't want to file.

CHAPTER 10

"NO ONE INTERVIEWS MARINA"

Twenty-five years of law practice had taught me a simple truth: To a hammer, everything is a nail; and to some lawyers, everything is a lawsuit. Courtrooms are full of disputes that could have (and should have) been resolved by means other than litigation. Blinkered professionals use the blunt instrument of formal process even when a scalpel-like informal process would be more effective and efficient.

Now—because I could see no alternative but to lodge a formal appeal of the prosecutor general's ruling—I was about to join the ranks of these ineffectual advocates.

I would appear before a regional judge, be showered with accolades for my humanity, receive a respectful and deferential hearing, and lose. It would be an exercise in frustration leading inexorably to failure. The futility made my stomach hurt.

I wasn't used to being impotent. I was after all a lawyer—a priest of America's one true religion. I had studied the divine mysteries of the Constitution and been invested with the sacrament of due process. I could invoke the arcana of Law and perform the miracle of Justice.

But my religion wasn't practiced in Georgia. The authorities in Tbilisi didn't believe in an independent judiciary, the presumption of innocence, or reasonable doubt. As far as I could tell, they worshipped the arbitrary gods of Expedience and Self-Interest.

All this made it very hard to generate enthusiasm.

I sat in my office in Houston writing the petition. I sent each successive draft to Lali for translation and delivery to Tamaz Inashvili. He had agreed (on behalf of Anzor) to make a joint submission with the Woodruff family. Notwithstanding all our obvious deficiencies, we were, as far as Tamaz could see, the prisoner's only hope.

The more I worked on the petition, the more I realized that my evidence was inadequate to achieve my goal. I could prove that Anzor was innocent, but I could not prove who was *actually* guilty. I needed a stick to go with my carrot—a credible threat to expose the perpetrators. Without it, the government would never let Anzor out of prison.

A quest to identify the perpetrators was a huge expansion of both my portfolio and risk. My weapons were motions and subpoenas; I was ill-equipped to confront men with guns.

These thoughts were still in the formative stage when I called Lali to discuss other sources of information about the murder.

"Have you talked to Thomas Goltz?" she asked. "He was an American journalist in Georgia around the time Freddie Woodruff died."

I had never heard of Thomas Goltz. Ten minutes later I was talking to him.

"Freddie Woodruff was my friend," he said. "I used to bounce his daughter, Michal, on my knee. I published the first article about his murder, you know. It was in the *Washington Post*. I never thought that kid Anzor did it. What are you doing in Georgia? And who do you represent?"

It was a lot to absorb. But the man had asked a question and I needed to answer. I proffered my now-familiar explanation: I represented Freddie's oldest sister; we had new evidence of Anzor's innocence; we were trying to compel the prosecutor general to reopen his case and set him free.

The voice on the phone had no patience with these vagaries. What was the evidence? Where did it come from? And why did the Woodruff family care? He ticked through the important issues of my case with ruthless professional efficiency.

This was Thomas Goltz: intelligent, informed, audacious, opinionated. He was alternately gruff and charming, prickly and self-effacing. An intrepid adventurer with a knack for storytelling, he was widely connected and widely respected.

Each time I made a disclosure, he asked another incisive question. Thomas was forcing me to express for the first time my real view of the murder, the prosecution, and the various interests implicated by my client's application. He was forcing me to articulate the significance of my case in a wider geopolitical context.

"Freddie's murder created an existential crisis for Georgia," I said. "If they didn't fully investigate the murder, they might offend the Americans and lose crucial US support. But if they did fully investigate—and the evidence led back to Moscow—they might offend the Russians and lose their independence. The murder put the Georgians in such an elegant predicament that it's hard to believe it happened by accident."

Thomas shifted his inquiry from geopolitics to criminal culpability. If Anzor was innocent, then a lot of very powerful people were guilty of framing him. Did the Woodruff family want to see them punished?

I began to feel uncomfortable. "We're not interested in punishing anyone," I said. "Sharmaidze's conviction was an expedient and perhaps necessary political decision to protect the integrity of the republic in 1993. But the crisis has passed. Perhaps the time is ripe for Georgia to deal with these questions in a more direct fashion."

I was prattling on about the commitment to justice made during the Rose Revolution when a terrifying thought intruded: Thomas Goltz was a reporter and this was an interview. It was one thing to deal with neophyte Georgian journalists; it was quite another to share my unfiltered thoughts with an American reporter. I hadn't analyzed the implications of such a move. My mind frantically turned to my most secret fear—that the Georgian government would dispose of the inconvenience of international exposure by killing Anzor.

I began trying to control how Thomas would use the information I'd given to him. I talked about how dangerous this process was, how I needed to act with discretion, how publicity might anger the government and lead to unforeseen consequences.

Thomas responded to my clumsy manipulations with suspicion and professional pique. What was I playing at? This was an important story and he intended to tell it.

And that was the end of our call.

I have always been afraid of the US press corps. I grew up in the Age of Assassination and even as a child perceived a connection between notoriety and violence. And now I had inadvertently entrusted my case and Anzor's life to the American media machine. What I did not know was that I had also unwittingly touched Nana's "informal lever" that would ultimately move the Georgian government.

By the time I returned to Georgia, Thomas Goltz had published his article on an NGO website, and the Georgian news media had taken notice. One journalist—an intrepid young woman named Eliso Chapidze—had gone so far as to interrogate the prosecutor general regarding his reasons for rejecting the Woodruff application. She printed a transcript of the interview in a local news magazine and I read Lali's translation as I hopscotched from Houston to Paris to Prague to Tbilisi.

Eliso asked simple questions and the prosecutor general provided direct answers. He gave her, and in the process gave me, a point-by-point explanation of his decision and a turn-by-turn road map of his analysis. According to the article, the prosecutor general justified rejection of the Woodruff application on the basis of alleged procedural defects. The proffered list of objections was to me both unimpressive and unpersuasive.

But the poverty of his response was good news: The government's objections were more political than substantive. If the winds of politics blew a different direction, then Anzor might be set free. I lay awake on the plane trying to figure out how to make Eliso my ally. Clearly, she could obtain access and information that I could not. My mind and stomach churned as I struggled to invent a good argument that would persuade her to help me.

But it was all a waste of time. She was waiting for me at Lali's when I arrived.

Eliso Chapidze was not at all what I had expected. By the look of things, she was more schoolgirl than superhero. Brown hair, tan skirt, sensible shoes: She could easily fade into the background of any room. Except for her eyes—her eyes were alive with intelligence, vitality, curiosity, and zeal. They seemed to suck up every detail of my face and to draw words out of me.

Her greeting was warm but skeptical—the hopeful incredulity of a long-suffering disciple.

"Eliso is one of my students," said Lali. "She investigates political corruption—and she's very good at it. Last year they murdered her colleague and put Eliso in the hospital."

A wave of embarrassment washed over me. I felt like a trespasser, a tourist in someone else's war zone.

Eliso must have seen me blush, because she smiled. Then in broken English she said, "I will help you."

It was a simple promise but it made me feel a twinge of shame: No matter what I said, my words would never cost near so much as hers.

She told me about herself over tiny cups of sweet black tea. A graduate of Tbilisi State University, Eliso was an editor of *Resonance Daily*. She was thirty years old, unmarried, and childless. She spent her days and nights trying to expose other people's secrets: their bribery, extortion, torture, and murder. Armed with nothing more than native intelligence and a tape recorder, she investigated how rich and powerful Georgians were betraying the ideals of the Rose Revolution.

It was dangerous work. And to the elite of post-Soviet Georgia it sounded a whole lot like spying. In the West, a reporter represents the public's right to know. But in Georgia, the societal benefits of journalistic scrutiny are totally irrelevant. The scrutiny itself is a threat. And in the macho culture of the Caucasus if you threaten a man, he will respond with violence.

Later that evening, after Eliso had left, Lali continued to talk about this extraordinary young woman. She had interviewed Eldar Gogoladze for one of her stories. When she published an unflattering report about the former chief bodyguard, he called the magazine and threatened to kill her. In response, Eliso published a second equally unsympathetic article.

I made a silly joke that perhaps I shouldn't stand too close to Eliso—but Lali didn't laugh. She got up from the sofa and headed toward the kitchen.

"It looks to me that you're doing the same sort of thing that Eliso does," she said over her shoulder. "Perhaps it is I who shouldn't stand too close to you."

I had returned to Georgia to file the formal petition to reopen Anzor's criminal case. As grounds for this extraordinary remedy I relied on my so-called newly discovered evidence. I claimed that the FBI documents and the Batiashvili affidavit proved that the murder of Freddie Woodruff did not happen in the manner alleged by the prosecutor general. The government's case was, I said, predicated on expert and eyewitness testimony that was demonstrably false. As a result, Anzor could not have committed the crime for which he was in prison.

In addition, I submitted a personal letter from my client, the sister of the man Anzor was accused of killing. "I believe there are two tragedies here," she said. "Freddie's murder and the imprisonment of an innocent man. . . . Freddie loved Georgia. He would not want an innocent Georgian man punished for a crime he did not commit. Freddie would not want his death to result in an unjust punishment. Instead, he would want Georgia to use his sacrifice in a way that would improve the lives of all Georgians and increase the world's respect for Georgia."

She concluded her letter by explicitly declaring that—if the court reopened the case and released Anzor—the Woodruff family would not insist on a new investigation to find the real killer. "Please be assured that if Georgia acts with justice and mercy, we will be satisfied with whatever the government chooses to do."

Offering absolution to the perpetrators was in equal parts both gracious and calculated. It accurately reflected the character of Georgia Woodruff Alexander and at the same time assured the guilty parties that we had no intention of pursuing their punishment. I hoped in this way to diminish opposition to Anzor's release by those who would quite naturally be afraid if he were declared innocent.

Lali translated the petition and we filed it with the Supreme Court. I was as of that moment officially adverse to the Georgian government—a thought that made me feel small and vulnerable.

A few days after we filed, we collected Tamaz Inashvili from his office and headed for the Old Military Road. Anzor's lawyer had been searching for an alleged eyewitness who, according to rumor, had been present at the Natakhtari Drain when Freddie was shot. My Georgian colleague was excited when he called and this made his normally incomprehensible stutter even worse. There were lots of words, but all Lali could make out was "This could be the man."

The three of us drove past the turnoff to the Natakhtari Drain and into the village itself. Lali stopped the car in front of what had been a roadside restaurant—a now-defunct purveyor of authentic Georgian barbecue. There were still a half-dozen shaded picnic stalls scattered across the lawn in front of the kitchen. We slid into one to escape the noontime sunshine.

After a few minutes, a tall man in his early thirties came walking toward us. Anzor's lawyer hailed the dark-haired man, and we unfolded ourselves from the tiny booth to exchange the obligatory greetings.

Tamaz Tserekashvili was dressed in dark blue cotton slacks and a light blue cotton shirt, the official uniform of the guards at the Natakhtari Drain. He had seen Eliso's article and knew about our interest in the murder. The only thing he found surprising was that Anzor was still alive.

The circumstances made it hard to conduct the interview. Lali was forced to translate for everyone: English into Georgian; Georgian into English; stutters into fluency. Caught in the middle of this muddle was the witness: a man of modest education and more than a little apprehension. No one had talked to him about the murder for more than ten years. And as far as he could see, no good could come of talking about it now.

He'd been on duty in the guardhouse at the Natakhtari Drain that day and heard a woman screaming about a man having been killed. He walked the forty or so meters to the highway and saw a white Niva. It had pulled onto the gravel apron by the gate and was parked facing toward Tbilisi.

Close by—parked under the tree that had a tire nailed to it—was another white car: a late-model foreign sedan with the steering wheel on the right and damage to the driver's side door. This car, perhaps a Toyota, had been parked facing the Old Military Road all day long.

It had been driven by three or four young men dressed in guardian uniforms. Tserekashvili assumed they'd had a flat: He remembered how one of the soldiers sat on a tire in the middle of the road, stopping cars and asking for a spare inner tube.

The driver of the Niva had flooded the engine so Tserekashvili helped push start the car. Through the rear hatch he saw a man sprawled in the back seat: shot, bleeding, dying. One of the guardians—paramilitary soldiers from the Ministry of Internal Affairs—who was helping to push the car said he was glad that he and his friends didn't have any weapons with them; otherwise, they might have been accused of the murder.

As soon as the Niva had departed, the soldiers climbed in their car and drove off toward Tbilisi. Tserekashvili wasn't sure when or how they'd fixed the problem that had kept them marooned most of the day.

Anzor's lawyer handwrote the witness statement and Tserekashvili signed it. But he wondered why we needed it: Didn't we have copies of the statements taken by the police at the time of the murder?

I was still innocent enough to be surprised.

"You mean you were interviewed by the police?" I asked.

"Sure," he said. "By both the police and the security services. They talked to everybody who was there."

I felt a flash of anger followed closely by a surge of fear. No one had mentioned these witnesses at Anzor's trial. No one had contrasted their version of events with the sanitized descriptions offered by Gogoladze and the barmaid Marina Kapanadze. No one had talked about the mysterious guardians or the miraculously timed repair of their car. No one had presented any of the alternative theories of the crime supported by this evidence, because the defense had never been informed about Tserekashvili and the other eyewitnesses he'd just identified.

This also meant that someone powerful enough to manipulate the outcome of a murder trial was heavily invested in making sure that a nosy American lawyer didn't expose their conspiracy to frame an innocent man. Every insight into the tragedy of Anzor's predicament seemed to bring with it a corollary insight into the danger of my involvement. The process was maddening.

I asked Tserekashvili about the other witnesses and their testimony, but he was spooked. If we didn't have copies of the official statements, then we didn't have the government's blessing for our investigation, and that meant he didn't have the government's permission to talk to us.

The conversation was over. Tamaz Tserekashvili wasn't going to help us find any of the other witnesses. But we had his signed statement—and hopefully that would be enough.

Local journalists kept the story in the public consciousness over the next several days. I was interviewed a number of times for newspaper articles, twice for the evening news, and once for a dramatized reenactment of the murder. And so—on my third day back—when Lali told me we had an afternoon appointment, I assumed it was another reporter.

"No," she said. "It's Avtandil Ioseliani."

I recognized the name immediately. Prior to his seven years

as director of the intelligence and information service, Ioseliani had been the deputy director and Eldar Gogoladze's immediate superior. He was tall, dapper, and courtly. Short-cropped gray hair, tweed jacket, solid tie, beige slacks: He looked more like a professor than a spymaster. He had retired from the intelligence service in February 2004, the same month that Misha Saakashvili became president. And he had come to Lali's house to have coffee with me.

We sat in straight-back chairs with our knees a few inches apart. He kept his hands in his lap and spoke softly. Lali positioned herself just to my right and centered between us. Her translation was so fluid that I hardly noticed Avtandil and I were speaking different languages.

"I remember the events surrounding the Woodruff murder very clearly," he said. "I was just about to leave the ministry offices when Eldar's radio call came in. It was a few minutes past ten p.m."

The retired director had compassionate eyes. They gave the impression that he was seeing without judgment or expectation, but I was pretty sure that impression was wrong.

"I dispatched members of the presidential protection unit to find them on the road and went immediately to the Kamo Street Hospital. By the time I got there, Eldar had already arrived, dropped off the body, and gone home to take a nap—at least, that's what he told the unit members who arrived before me."

Eldar's deception was silly but not that surprising coming from someone who was both arrogant and incompetent. What was surprising was the fact that Avtandil had told me about it. Clearly there was no love lost between him and his former lieutenant.

"I sent unit members to Eldar's house with orders to bring him back immediately. They returned with him about twenty minutes later. He had showered and changed his clothes. I never knew what happened to the clothes he was wearing. We never tested them—or the small purse gun he always carried."

Avtandil paused to see whether I understood the significance of what he had just said. Satisfied, he continued.

"I told him to take his men, go back to the scene of the murder, and see what he could find. I told him he needed to do something to salvage his career."

I remembered that Gogoladze had subsequently been fired (albeit briefly) for failing to follow security protocols: He had carried a foreign diplomat in his car without prior approval and he drove the diplomat outside the city without a fully staffed chase car. I raised the issue with the former director.

"When I first came to Georgia, we met in his office at Cartu," I said. "Eldar told me that he hadn't used a chase car for two reasons: first, because it was Sunday and he didn't want to interfere in his unit member's family time; and second, because there was a gas crisis and he couldn't justify a second vehicle."

Avtandil threw his head back and laughed heartily. "Eldar cared nothing for his men or their family time," he said. "He hated them and they hated him. And as for gasoline—we were the security services. We had gas to go across town for coffee if we wanted."

I was amazed and slightly unnerved by Avtandil's willingness to implicate Gogoladze as a perpetrator. He had never said any of these things publicly before—so why was he telling me now? And what more would he tell me if I pressed a little?

"Eldar told me that the fatal bullet penetrated the car through the rubber gasket at the top of the hatchback window," I said.

It wasn't really a question. I was trying to avoid the confrontation of interrogation. But my caution was unnecessary. Avtandil had decided what he would and would not tell me before he ever arrived at Lali's house. And this was something he wanted me to know.

"I examined the car very carefully that night," he said. "Both inside and out. There was no bullet hole. Not in the gasket and not anywhere else."

The former director of the information and intelligence service had just provided me with independent confirmation that the bullet hole found several days later by forensic investigator

Zaza Altunashvili was not present on the night of the murder. He had unambiguously confirmed the observations made by FBI special agent George Shukin less than eighteen hours after the shooting: There was "no indication of glass or other part of the vehicle having been damaged by gunfire."

And in the same moment, he had revealed himself to be a knowing participant in the conspiracy to frame Anzor Sharmaidze for the murder of Freddie Woodruff.

His statement about the absence of a bullet hole was consistent with what I believed (and what I wanted to believe). But this evidence came from a man who had just (implicitly) confessed that he would embrace a lie in order to send an innocent man to prison. How was I supposed to figure out which statements to believe and which statements to disbelieve? It was an issue that had first revealed itself in my conversation with Gogoladze. And it was now imperative that I find a way to answer it.

Then—as if to emphasize the point—Avtandil hinted at involvement in the creation of the counterfeit bullet-hole evidence. "I took possession of Anzor's weapon that night," he said. "I locked the AK-74 in my safe and kept it there until we delivered it to the Americans." As a result, if Anzor's rifle was later used to make an after-the-fact hole in the Niva hatchback, Avtandil would presumably have been involved in removing the weapon from his safe.

"What about the woman who was with Freddie?" I asked. "Did you interview Marina?"

"No one interviews Marina," he said.

The former director paused for a moment. I got the sense that this was a topic he hadn't anticipated in advance. When he finally spoke, his tone was different: He was respectful, almost deferential.

"Marina Kapanadze is a person of very bad character," he said. "She was already well known to us. My office had a thick file on her . . . but it all disappeared during the revolution."

It was a surprising statement about a simple barmaid from the Sheraton Metechi Palace. I assumed it would take real power to purge a file at the intelligence and information service. If that was true, then Marina had friends in very high places and was in her own right very dangerous.

Avtandil stood up. "This has been very interesting," he said.

We shook hands and moved toward the door. He said something to Lali that she didn't translate, bowed slightly, and left.

"There is something I'm not supposed to tell you," she said a few moments later. "Something that Avtandil said as he was leaving."

I am by nature far too curious to encourage such discretion. I did my best to look plaintive and hoped that silence would goad her into telling me what he'd said. It worked.

"He told me that he'd come here to find out whether you were with the CIA or not," she said. "He's now sure that you are."

I didn't know whether to feel flattered or afraid. I hadn't done anything to create this erroneous impression. I was exactly what I appeared to be: a lawyer. But perhaps to a citizen of the former Soviet Union, an American lawyer's pursuit of truth is very like a spy's pursuit of secrets.

A few days later the Georgian Supreme Court sent word that they were remanding the Woodruff petition to the local regional court for a hearing on the new evidence. I was instructed to confer with the Prosecutor General's Office about procedural matters and so the next day I found myself sitting across the table from the junior lawyer who'd been assigned to handle the case.

The selection of counsel was calculated: The prosecutor general was saying that he did not believe the case was worthy of first-string talent. It was a none-too-subtle way of telling me and the press that he would defeat the application with little or no effort.

The young prosecutor was meticulous in a way that smacked of inexperience. He'd written out an agenda to assure that he didn't overlook any of the obvious issues: the Woodruff family's standing to bring the application; the authenticity of the alleged new evidence; the identity of new witnesses; and the fact that none of the old witnesses had changed their testimony. We touched on all the same points I'd discussed with the prosecutor general.

Halfway through an unnecessary discussion of scheduling, the door popped open. A gray man in a brown suit looked in, surveyed the room, and quickly slammed the door. Lali looked perplexed.

"It was the prosecutor Chanturia," she said.

I shook my head. The name didn't mean anything to me.

"Chanturia," she said again. "He was the prosecutor from Anzor's trial."

The prosecutor general had made an effort to create an appearance of casual indifference to the entire proceeding. However, Chanturia's conduct suggested something else entirely—concern. But that didn't make any sense to me. Why would anyone in the Prosecutor General's Office be concerned about a doomed application to reopen a twelve-year-old case? Perhaps there was something they feared more than losing.

The regional judge scheduled and rescheduled the hearing several times—once when I was halfway across the Atlantic on my way to Tbilisi. I began to get the impression she was testing my stubbornness, stamina, and credit limit. But there was a silver lining to all this delay. Eliso Chapidze persuaded Eldar Gogoladze to respond to the accusations that I was making against him. This on-the-record interview was his first public statement since Anzor's trial, and the former chief bodyguard gave a bravura performance. He said that Freddie had been his closest friend and therefore it was illogical to believe he could have been involved in the murder.

This was a specious argument: As Brutus eloquently proved to Julius Caesar, friendship is no guarantee of personal safety. But far more important than Gogoladze's self-serving non sequitur were the factual admissions that he made. He said that—at the time of the murder and for several days thereafter—he believed that a sniper had shot Woodruff through the open passenger's side front window. In addition, he said that immediately after delivering Woodruff's body to the Kamo Street Hospital he carefully examined the Niva 1600 and found no evidence of a bullet hole in the car.

It was a public reiteration of two statements he'd made to me in our private meeting. And it made me feel a savage pleasure. Gogoladze had inadvertently presented me with a golden opportunity to practice my skills as a trial lawyer. I quickly wrote and Lali quickly translated an Op-Ed piece for Eliso's newspaper, *Resonance*. The open letter applauded Gogoladze's willingness to come forward and challenged him to debate me. Lali contacted the program director at ZTV and persuaded him to invite Gogoladze, Irakli Batiashvili, and me to appear live on the station's evening news program.

My challenge was a gamble—but Gogoladze had already publicly acknowledged the fact of my allegations. As a result, he could not now pretend that he hadn't noticed the insult. Facing me had become a matter of honor. I began preparing immediately. I walked across the city in search of a model car and a toy soldier. There weren't many toys available in Tbilisi, but I found a small cache in a shop that sold school supplies. They had a serviceable SUV hatchback and a tiny Ghostbuster wearing a green jumpsuit.

I carried my treasures to Lali's house and thought about the impending confrontation. By the time I walked into the parlor, I had persuaded myself of one essential truth: What I was planning to do was very dangerous. And I was going to need some help.

"Lali," I said, "Do you know anyone with a gun?"

It was dark when we arrived at the ZTV studio. I felt uncomfortably exposed as I walked across the plaza to the front steps. The surrounding buildings blocked the wind and offered excellent sight lines. It was, I thought, an easy place for a sniper to kill an annoying American.

I waited in the lobby while Lali went to fetch the station manager. He came out and guided me through makeup and into a small office. It was separated from the main studio by a short hallway. There was a nondescript little man wearing an oversized sky-blue sport coat standing in the passage. He looked at me briefly with impassive eyes and then turned back to watch the people in the other room.

Lali saw me looking at him and smiled. "That's your bodyguard," she said. "When he's not busy protecting you from Gogoladze, he's a very capable handyman in my neighborhood."

The office was cluttered with unused cables and amplifiers. The only window was covered with a blanket. A small desk and chair stood arranged in front of a blank wall. And directly opposite, in the center of the room were lights, camera, and a video monitor.

Per my request the production staff had made me a separate studio.

I took off my suit coat and sat behind the desk. I laid out my toys on the tabletop while the station manager fitted me with microphone and earbud. I counted to five in order to test the sound levels and Lali responded into my right ear. She was again providing simultaneous translation for me and everyone who was watching.

The video monitor displayed the feed from both my camera and from the camera in the other room. I could see Irakli Batiashvili, the former chief of Georgia's intelligence and information service, settling into one of two chairs on the platform. Black turtleneck, black slacks, black leather jacket—he exuded sophistication and privilege.

Another man stepped up onto the stage. Shorter, older, balder, Gogoladze had chosen a button-down white shirt, black bomber jacket, and designer jeans.

"He looks comfortable," I thought. "And confident."

The station manager counted down to the beginning of the show then exited the room. I was alone. The host was the same skinny adolescent who'd interviewed me during my last appearance. He bubbled with enthusiasm as he reminded the audience about the murder of Freddie Woodruff. After providing a little background, he introduced his three guests and quickly segued to a prerecorded interview with Gogoladze.

"He was my best friend," said the former chief bodyguard. "I would never kill my best friend."

As evidence of his heartfelt sincerity, Gogoladze cited the financial inconvenience that Freddie's murder had caused him. "I was so upset about his dying in my Niva that I sold that car—at a loss!"

The recorded segment ended with a close-up of a single tear coursing down Gogoladze's cheek. It was unclear whether the tear was provoked by the death or the monetary loss. Either way, it was riveting drama.

I knew from experience that in Georgia interviews of this type were conducted with a single camera and a solitary cameraman. The interview portion of the video had been filmed at a different distance and from a different angle than the teardrop portion. Thus, the only way that the cameraman could have gotten the teardrop shot was if he repositioned the camera and lights for that specific purpose. And that probably meant that Gogoladze had managed to cry on cue. He was apparently fully committed to his role as the heartbroken hero.

The video monitor shifted from the prerecorded Gogoladze to the live one. He seemed to enjoy watching himself on television.

"How do you respond to the American lawyer?" the host asked him.

Gogoladze was ready for the question. His facial expression and posture changed from Grieving Comrade to Aggrieved Civil Servant. He was suspicious, pugnacious, and armed with a lifetime of experience in the intelligence service.

"What do we know about Michael Pullara?" he asked. Even in Georgian, his tone dripped with the suggestion of secret information. "Do we know whether he actually has a client? Or an office? Do we know whether he is really a lawyer?"

There is a saying among trial lawyers: If the facts of your case are bad, argue the law; if the law of your case is bad, argue the facts; and if the facts and the law are both bad, then argue the other lawyer.

Gogoladze was arguing the other lawyer. He wanted me to rise to the bait, to disregard the substance of my case and join him in an argument of my bona fides. He wanted me to fight his fire with my fire.

But sometimes it is best to fight fire with water. So I took a deep breath—and smiled. "Mr. Gogoladze is suggesting that I am not the best lawyer in the world," I said softly. "And he's right: I'm not. But I am the lawyer who is here. And if a great lawyer ever comes to take over this case, I will support him. But until then, I will do the best I can to represent my client's interests."

Gogoladze's shoulders slumped slightly. It was not the response he had expected. But he was ready with another line of attack.

"Even if you are a lawyer," he said, "this is not an area in which lawyers work. Lawyers do not investigate espionage operations. You are CIA—or worse you are a blind tool in the hands of a professional intelligence officer."

This was a dangerous attack: a frontal assault on my credibility as the victim's advocate. It was the kind of accusation that the typical Georgian would reflexively believe—that the truth behind every event was a struggle between powerful governmental forces. "Mr. Gogoladze is suggesting," I replied, "that I must be acting on behalf of an intelligence service because in his mind it would be crazy to confront the government unless you were supported by a powerful security agency. But I am not an intelligence professional. I am a man who disagrees with what the government has done and wants to make it right." I leaned forward toward the black lens of the camera. "This is what free people do," I said.

Gogoladze was utterly deflated. He had expected confrontation, and I had given him a bear hug of goodwill. It was time to take control of the conversation.

"I have a question for Mr. Gogoladze," I said. "In your recent interview you acknowledged that—on the night of the murder—you thought the bullet that killed Freddie had entered the car through the front passenger's side window. Is that correct?"

"Yes," he said. "I inspected the car at the hospital and didn't find a bullet hole anywhere: not in the metal, not in the glass, nowhere. So it had to be the open window."

"And two hours later, you walked into a roadside police station, pointed at Anzor Sharmaidze and his two companions, and said, 'Arrest them! They killed the American!' "

He smiled. He liked this part better. "Exactly right," he said.

"Then—four months later at the trial—you testified that Anzor and his companions were fifteen to twenty meters behind your Niva when you heard the shot."

"That's correct," he said. "I had just passed them on the road a second or two before."

"So my question is this," I said. "Why did you arrest the only three people on the planet that you absolutely knew could not have committed the murder that you thought had occurred?"

Gogoladze looked stunned. He had never before encountered American-style cross-examination and so was not prepared for its stinging consequences. He tried to say something but nothing worth translating came out.

I held up the toy SUV where it could be seen by the camera.

"In order for a bullet to enter the front passenger's side window of your car and strike Freddie Woodruff as he sat in the back seat *on the right*, it would have to have been fired from a very severe angle *in front and slightly to the right of the vehicle*." I inserted a red straw into the front passenger's side window of the toy car to show the path of the bullet. The straw pointed almost directly in front of the toy.

"And on the night of the murder that's where you thought the bullet had come from," I said. Holding the car and straw in one hand, I picked up the Ghostbuster with the other and positioned him forward of the SUV in line with the straw. "Here," I said. "The killer would have to have been here in order to shoot Freddie through the front passenger's side window."

Then I moved my little plastic soldier behind the car. "But you testified under oath that Anzor Sharmaidze was here—*behind the car*—when you heard the shot," I said. "So tell me, sir—why did you arrest Anzor?"

By now Gogoladze had recovered some of his balance. But he still didn't answer the question. Instead, he responded with anger and arrogance. "No one has ever questioned my professionalism!" he roared.

"I apologize, Mr. Gogoladze," I said softly. "This is the lack of legal skill I was talking about earlier. The truth is, I'm working as hard as I can to question your professionalism. I know housewives who are more professional than you. If you were really a professional you would have shot back at the killers or ordered the local police to close the road or at the very least been able to identify the location of the shooting. But you didn't do any of those things, did you? All you did was break down weeping for your friend who was shot. And any of the women here could have done that just as well as you did."

Gogoladze was speechless. It was unclear whether the cause was rage or humiliation. But one thing was certain: No one had ever talked to him this way. And if it weren't for the cameras, I would be paying the price for such insolence.

"So tell us, Mr. Gogoladze," I said. "Why did you arrest Anzor Sharmaidze? Did you think he fired a bullet through the open window and then ran to the back of the car before you heard the shot? Or did you think he had a special gun that could shoot around corners? Why did you arrest the one person in the world that you absolutely knew could not have committed the crime you thought had occurred?"

Gogoladze did not reply. He could not think of an answer, he could not run away, and the camera simply refused to stop looking at him. He was trapped.

And then I heard the soothing voice of Irakli Batiashvili.

An American boyhood: Freddie Woodruff, pictured here twice with his sister Georgia, grew up in the small town of Stillwater, Oklahoma, in the 1950s and '60s. At age eighteen, he moved to Searcy, Arkansas, a town that boasted all the elements of mid-century American prosperity—a drugstore, a department store, a Sears Roebuck catalogue store, a pool hall, a baseball field, and a one-screen movie theater. (*Photos courtesy of Georgia Woodruff Alexander*)

The makings of a spy: After college, where he displayed a gift for languages, Woodruff served in the US Army in West Berlin as a Russian interpreter. Recruited by the CIA in Germany, he went on to become fluent in German, Turkish, and Greek. A muscular, physically imposing man of the world, Woodruff is seen here fishing, standing in an outdoor market in Turkey, and aboard a ferry in a foreign shipping port, probably Saint Petersburg. (*Photos courtesy of Georgia Woodruff Alexander*)

Operative in a dangerous land: Following the breakup of the Soviet Union in 1991, the former Soviet foreign minister, Eduard Shevardnadze (above, center), known as "the Silver Fox," became the leader of the new country of Georgia. The capital, Tbilisi, was a dangerous place populated by many Soviet intelligence officers and sympathizers. Woodruff was sent to Georgia to train Shevardnadze's security force—the first such operation in the territory of the former USSR. In time the Silver Fox was pushed from power by the much younger, formidable Mikheil Saakashvili (below, right), whom the author confronted publicly, much to his own discomfort. (*Top: Viktor Drachev/AFP/Getty Images; Bottom left: Courtesy of Georgia Woodruff Alexander; Bottom right: Vano Shlamov/AFP/Getty Images*)

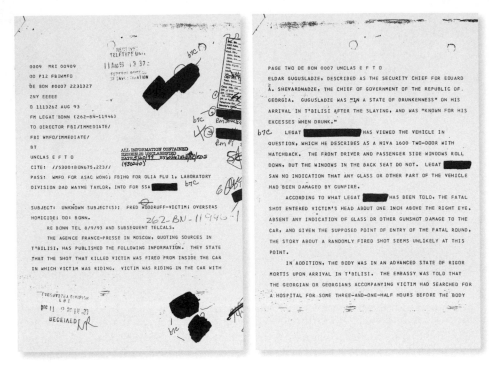

0009 MRI 00909

OO P12 FBIWMFO
DE BON #0007 2231327
ZNY EEEEE
O 111326Z AUG 93
FM LEGAT BONN (262-BN-11946)
TO DIRECTOR FBI/IMMEDIATE/
FBI WMFO/IMMEDIATE/
BT
UNCLAS E F T O
CITE: //5300:BON675.223//
PASS: WMFO FOR ASAC WONG; FBIHQ FOR OLIA FLU 1, LABORATORY
DIVISION DAD WAYNE TAYLOR, INTO FOR SSA ___

SUBJECT: UNKNOWN SUBJECT(S); FRED WOODRUFF-VICTIM; OVERSEAS
HOMICIDE; OO: BONN.

RE BONN TEL 8/9/93 AND SUBSEQUENT TELCALS.

THE AGENCE FRANCE-PRESSE IN MOSCOW, QUOTING SOURCES IN
T'BILISI, HAS PUBLISHED THE FOLLOWING INFORMATION. THEY STATE
THAT THE SHOT THAT KILLED VICTIM WAS FIRED FROM INSIDE THE CAR
IN WHICH VICTIM WAS RIDING. VICTIM WAS RIDING IN THE CAR WITH

PAGE TWO DE BON 0007 UNCLAS E F T O
ELDAR GUGUSLADZE, DESCRIBED AS THE SECURITY CHIEF FOR EDUARD
A. SHEVARDNADZE, THE CHIEF OF GOVERNMENT OF THE REPUBLIC OF
GEORGIA. GUGUSLADZE WAS "IN A STATE OF DRUNKENNESS" ON HIS
ARRIVAL IN T'BILISI AFTER THE SLAYING, AND WAS "KNOWN FOR HIS
EXCESSES WHEN DRUNK."

LEGAT ___ HAS VIEWED THE VEHICLE IN
QUESTION, WHICH HE DESCRIBES AS A NIVA 1600 TWO-DOOR WITH
HATCHBACK. THE FRONT DRIVER AND PASSENGER SIDE WINDOWS ROLL
DOWN, BUT THE WINDOWS IN THE BACK SEAT DO NOT. LEGAT ___
SAW NO INDICATION THAT ANY GLASS OR OTHER PART OF THE VEHICLE
HAD BEEN DAMAGED BY GUNFIRE.

ACCORDING TO WHAT LEGAT ___ HAS BEEN TOLD, THE FATAL
SHOT ENTERED VICTIM'S HEAD ABOUT ONE INCH ABOVE THE RIGHT EYE.
ABSENT ANY INDICATION OF GLASS OR OTHER GUNSHOT DAMAGE TO THE
CAR, AND GIVEN THE SUPPOSED POINT OF ENTRY OF THE FATAL ROUND,
THE STORY ABOUT A RANDOMLY FIRED SHOT SEEMS UNLIKELY AT THIS
POINT.

IN ADDITION, THE BODY WAS IN AN ADVANCED STATE OF RIGOR
MORTIS UPON ARRIVAL IN T'BILISI. THE EMBASSY WAS TOLD THAT
THE GEORGIAN OR GEORGIANS ACCOMPANYING VICTIM HAD SEARCHED FOR
A HOSPITAL FOR SOME THREE-AND-ONE-HALF HOURS BEFORE THE BODY

Death of a CIA agent: Woodruff was shot to death on August 8, 1993, while sitting in the back seat of a white Niva 1600 sedan driven by the head of Shevardnadze's personal protection force, twenty miles northwest of Tbilisi in a mountainous border region. He was forty-five years old. The redacted teletype report authored eighteen hours after the murder by FBI legal attaché George Shukin expressed skepticism about initial reports that Woodruff was killed by a "randomly fired shot." Below, a hospital photo of Woodruff's body. (*Top: FBI document; Bottom: Georgian police*)

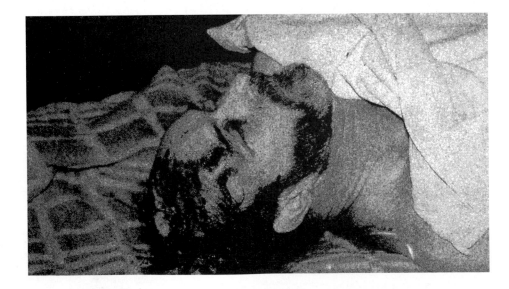

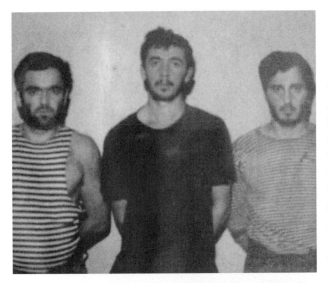

Entry hole of bullet

к 0930 ГГ

Large tree

Approx. location of Vehicle at time of bullet impact

Shooter Position

Cover-up of a murder: Anzor Sharmaidze, pictured on the night of his arrest standing between Gela Bedoidze and Genadi Berbitchashvili, was said by Georgian authorities to have confessed to the murder of Woodruff. But he later said he had been tortured and forced to make a false confession. Center and bottom: Labeled FBI photographs of the white Niva 1600 showing the location of the bullet hole and of the alleged locations of both the car and Sharmaidze on the Old Military Road. The Georgian report of finding a bullet entry hole in the car conflicted with the description of the car given by an FBI special agent on the day after the murder and suggested that Georgian authorities had tampered with the evidence in order to bolster their account of Woodruff's death. (*Lineup photo: Georgian police; Location photos: FBI*)

The long investigation: The author (large photo, center) made more than a dozen trips to Georgia in his quest to free Anzor Sharmaidze and discover how Freddie Woodruff was murdered. His inquiry was covered by local Georgian newspapers and television. Below, Georgian medical examiner Levan Chachuria, shown with his own car, a Niva 1600 similar to the one in which Woodruff died. He testified that the CIA agent was shot in the forehead, a conclusion diametrically opposed to the one reached by the US Armed Forces Institute of Pathology. (*Photo courtesy of the author*)

Framed for murder: Above, Anzor Sharmaidze, at the author's first meeting with him in prison, a bleak, isolated facility with walls topped with razor wire and broken glass. "I didn't do it," he said. His eyes were rheumy and he was cradling his left arm tenderly. He seemed decades older than his thirty-one years. His arm, it was discovered, had an enormous infected abscess and he was in danger of dying. The author paid for him to be taken to a hospital. Below, a photo taken of Sharmaidze three years later, during an interview with *Wall Street Journal* reporter Andrew Higgins. After an article appeared in that paper, Sharmaidze was released, but his day-to-day existence would remain very difficult. (*Photos courtesy of the author*)

Hall of Mirrors: Above, the February 21, 1994, arrest of Aldrich Ames, by FBI agent Dell Spry. Ames pled guilty to espionage and was sentenced to life in prison. The author corresponded with Ames and made many attempts to visit him at the federal penitentiary in Allenwood, Pennsylvania. Some letters were lost or never arrived. Others made it through. The CIA reviews and censors all of Ames's incoming and outgoing mail, and strictly controls his visitors. The Agency refused all of the author's requests for a face-to-face visit. Nonetheless, Ames professed to know nothing about how or why Woodruff was killed. "Aldrich Hazen Ames," said G. L. Lamborn, a twenty-six-year veteran of the CIA, "is the reason why Freddie Woodruff was murdered." (*Photo: FBI; Letter: Courtesy of the author*)

May 21, 2018

Mr. Aldrich Hazen Ames
Register No. 40087-083
Allenwood USP
U.S. Penitentiary
P.O. Box 3000
White Deer, PA 17887

Re: Freddie Woodruff

Dear Mr. Ames,

I am writing to request that you put me on your visitors list so that I can come and talk to you. I have written twice before but have no way of knowing whether you have received my other letters.

I represent two of Freddie's family members – a sister (Georgia) ▮▮▮▮▮ ▮▮▮▮▮▮▮ Although I did not know Freddie personally, I grew up with his three sisters, took classes from his father and went to church with the whole family.

My work on this case started out as a personal attempt to give the family a sense of closure. However, over the years it has become something more than that. FBI Special Agents and CIA officers have told me that I know more about this case than anyone else.

If you agree to meet with me, I will tell you everything I know about Freddie's murder and my investigation. I promise to answer all your questions as thoroughly and forthrightly as I can.

As far as my questions for you are concerned, if you want to talk to me, you will; if you don't want to talk to me, you won't. I recognize that you're a skilled professional and that I cannot manipulate or cajole you into talking about anything you don't want to talk about.

Mr. Aldrich Hazen Ames
May 21, 2018
Page 2 of 2

I've been told that you have a keen interest in history. If there is any particular book I can bring or send to you, please let me know.

In order to put me on your Approved Visitor List you will need to fill out and send to me a Visitor Information Form (BP-A0629). I will fill it out and return it to the Bureau of Prisons.

Thank you for your kind consideration of this request.

Very truly yours,

Michael A. Pullara

"Eldar," he said. "You know that the murder did not happen this way. The killing of Freddie Woodruff was the work of a great regional power."

Great regional power was code language understood by every Georgian: It meant Russia.

Gogoladze was quiet for a second or two. Then, without looking up, he responded to the former minister. "Yes," he said. "That is true."

Eldar Gogoladze—the principal eyewitness—had just confessed that Anzor Sharmaidze did not kill Freddie Woodruff. He had just acknowledged that the Russians had killed the American CIA officer. I felt exhilaration, exhaustion, and awe. And all I wanted was to get back to Lali's house as quickly as possible.

The next day Gogoladze was fired from his job as vice president at Cartu Group. That afternoon I sat on the bed in Lali's guest room and tried to puzzle out the connection: Why would acknowledging Russia's role in Woodruff's murder get Gogoladze fired by Georgia's biggest oligarch?

Lali tapped on the door and walked in without waiting for an answer. In her hand she had a copy of a videotape of the previous night's program. "I saw my neighbor as I was coming in," she said. "He's a lawyer too, you know. He graduated Moscow State University with a red diploma—highest honors! He came out as I was parking my car. 'I saw your American on television last night,' he said. 'It was impressive. The West does not usually send us A-level professionals.'"

To be adjudged A-level by a superbly educated Georgian was a big compliment—the first and best I would receive. I was savoring the words when I heard a loud knock at the front. I followed Lali to the entry hall and was standing there as she unbolted the four locks and swung open the reinforced metal door. It was my bodyguard, the little man in the oversized sky-blue sport coat I'd seen standing in the hallway between the two studios at ZTV.

He'd come for his $20.

"Thank you very much," I said, with Lali translating. "Knowing that you were there gave me a lot of confidence."

The little man bowed and turned to leave, but I stopped him.

"May I see it?" I asked.

He smiled in a way that made him look taller as he unbuttoned his sport coat. There, in a small holster on his hip, was an antique revolver. Not much of a gun, really. But big enough to give me courage.

CHAPTER 11

A GEORGIAN EDUCATION

The day of our courtroom proceeding finally came. A TV news crew was waiting for Lali and me outside the courthouse. Waiting for me in the lobby was a stumpy peasant woman dressed all in black. Gray hair peeked out from under her headscarf. I judged her to be about sixty, but her eyes looked older. Her hands were worn and calloused. They shook as she reached toward me. She touched the hem of my coat and rubbed it gently between thumb and forefinger.

Lali gasped. "It's Anzor's mother," she said.

Complex commercial litigation is a bloodless practice. It is more often than not millionaires suing billionaires over money that neither one needs for his next meal. I never meet my clients' parents and no one ever anoints me as his or her last best hope. As a result, I wasn't prepared for this mother's tidal wave of adoration. I began to panic as it washed over me: a salty ocean of expectation. I hoped she would like me as much when we left.

Tamaz Inashvili was already in the courtroom. He had agreed to sit second-chair and advise me on the nuances of Georgian law and procedure. I expected the presentation to be fact-intensive and so didn't anticipate any discussion of substantive law; nevertheless, I wanted to be prepared.

The accommodations were spare: two tables, a metal desk, a few wooden chairs. But the layout told me a lot about litigation in Georgia; there was no spectators' gallery, no jury box, no court reporter's desk. Georgian process occurred in relative secrecy, with no permanent record other than the final order. If a particular piece of evidence was problematic, the government-appointed judge could ignore it with impunity.

In addition, there was a noticeable dearth of symbols in the room, a complete absence of the mythic and patriotic images that define a community's understanding of Good and Evil. There were no reminders of the struggle for human dignity, the inalienable rights of Man, or the sanctity of Law. In the absence of these tokens, the room felt less like a Temple of Justice and more like a Bus Station of Pragmatism.

All in all, the setting did not inspire confidence.

The young prosecutor—the same one with whom I'd previously met—had already arrived and was seated at the table directly in front of the judge's metal desk. Tamaz, Lali, and I were relegated to the second table: one that was perpendicular to and to the side of the other participants.

"That's where the prosecutor general always sits," said Tamaz, "in the center."

The regional judge entered the courtroom from a door behind her desk. She was young but wore her black robes comfortably and with confidence. Lali spoke first, saying that she was prepared to translate the proceedings simultaneously (Georgian to English for me and English to Georgian for everyone else). There were a few introductions and then the judge asked for opening statements.

Tamaz and I had discussed the possibility of his making a brief statement regarding the legal standard governing my client's request to reopen the murder case. I hadn't vetted his remarks but assumed they would be limited to a few sentences about the relevant sections of the criminal code. I was wrong.

He stood up and began talking. And talking. And talking. He reviewed the history of the case, the details of the investigation, the principal issues of the trial. He described the allegations of torture and the suspicious provenance of Anzor's confession. He urged all the same arguments he had made twelve years before.

And he ate up my time.

Over the years, I have paid a lot of legal consultants a lot of money for advice on how best to influence judges and juries. One of the pearls of rhetorical wisdom that I acquired from these pundits is called the Rule of Primacy: People remember best that which they hear first. And the first thing my judge was hearing was a chaotic torrent of almost indecipherable stutters. Tamaz seemed agitated, almost defensive—as though someone had insulted his professionalism. He listed one after another the heroic efforts that he made on behalf of Anzor Sharmaidze until he and everyone else in the room were tired. And then he sat down.

I was mad and confused. I had no idea why Tamaz had hijacked my hearing. I had evidence to present and arguments to make. But this was the first time I'd tried to do it with someone literally talking over me. Lali listened to me and spoke to the judge at the same time: a kind of human megaphone that heard soft-spoken English and spoke amplified Georgian. I had to disregard Lali's voice while at the same time searching for the judge's time-delayed reactions. Normally, I watch my audience for nonverbal cues: facial expressions, postural changes, eye movements—all these things give me hints about how the person is reacting to what I've just said. But with simultaneous translation, I had to guess first which statement the judge was reacting to and second what her reaction meant in the context of Georgian culture.

I processed through the Batiashvili affidavit, the Tserekashvili witness statement, and the FBI reports without any objections from the young prosecutor. This was by itself remarkable. In American trial practice, testimony and documents are carefully scrutinized before the finder of fact is allowed to consider them as evidence. Lawyers argue the minutiae of intricate rules regarding what is reliable and authentic. These procedural skirmishes often decide the outcome of a case.

But in a Georgian court, evidence was not required to meet a minimum standard of trustworthiness prior to it being presented to the judge. This absence of procedural safeguards made me feel unmoored. I finished my presentation and sat down. The young prosecutor shuffled through some papers, stood up, and—instead of addressing the court—began talking to me.

"Are you trained as an investigator?" he said.

This direct communication from opposing counsel was an unexpected turn of events. In American courts, the rules require that lawyers argue *to* the judge (and not *with* each other). This simple protocol tends to increase civility and decrease fisticuffs.

Nevertheless, I'd been asked a question and the judge was quite obviously waiting for an answer.

"I'm not exactly sure what my colleague is asking," I said, addressing the judge, "but I am trained in a variety of techniques that are useful for investigating complex cases."

"Ah, so you are a lawyer and an investigator," said the young prosecutor. "Are you also a pathologist?"

This struck me as a particularly bizarre question. My first thought was that it related to the AFIP expert opinion that the fatal bullet entered Woodruff's skull not above the right eye but above and behind the right ear. The young prosecutor was trying to discredit the message by discrediting the messenger. It was a clumsy tactic.

"No," I said. "I'm not a pathologist; I'm a lawyer. And as a lawyer, I routinely rely on expert reports—especially if I'm dealing with a subject about which I don't have specialized education, training, or experience."

The young prosecutor smiled. "Do you have an expert report regarding the onset of rigor mortis?" he asked. "Or is this an area in which you have specialized education, training, or experience?"

The young prosecutor had set a neat little trap and I had blundered into it. He had correctly identified a hole in my evidence: Even if the judge accepted my evidence of rigor, there was no expert evidence proving how long it would take for that rigor to occur.

I muttered something about having consulted generally accepted medical textbooks and promised myself to be less arrogant.

"The former minister Irakli Batiashvili," said the prosecutor. "Did he personally see the police plant the shell casing?"

"No," I said. "It was his deputy—Shota Kviraya. He saw the police plant this evidence and reported the fact to Minister Batiashvili."

"So you do not have an eyewitness?" he asked.

The question provoked an insight: Cross-examination of counsel was how Georgian lawyers made objections to their opponent's evidence. That meant I was in the middle of a legal argument about the admissibility of my evidence and I didn't even know it.

I looked at the prosecutor again. He didn't seem to be nearly as young as I'd previously thought.

"I don't have an eyewitness," I said. "But I do have Shota Kviraya's superior officer. And Kviraya's report regarding the planted evidence is precisely the kind of oral communication that Minister Batiashvili relied upon in the ordinary course of his duties. As a result, the statements in the Batiashvili affidavit are admissible as evidence."

The judge nodded. She seemed pleased that I had finally figured out what was going on. Meanwhile, the prosecutor held up a black-and-white photograph mounted on foam board.

"This picture was taken by the American FBI," he said. "As you see—it clearly shows the bullet casing at the scene of the murder. Do you believe that the FBI was part of a conspiracy to frame Anzor Sharmaidze?"

"The photograph accurately depicts what the special agents saw," I said, "but they saw it nine days after the murder. The photograph doesn't prove that the bullet casing was there continuously for nine days. As far as the FBI and the photograph are concerned, the casing could have been placed there just a few minutes before the special agents arrived."

"What about this photograph by your FBI?" he asked, as he held up another black-and-white image. "It shows a bullet hole near the rubber gasket at the top of the hatchback window. If, as you claim, this hole was made after the fact, how did the bullet get inside the passenger compartment of the Niva?"

It was the question I'd been wrestling with for years: How do you kill a man inside a car without breaking the glass or puncturing the metal? As it turned out, the answer was fairly simple. "The car was stopped and the rear hatch was open," I said.

The young prosecutor seemed surprised and slightly off balance. It was not the answer he was expecting. "But that would mean all the witnesses are lying," he said.

I didn't respond immediately, hoping the silence would emphasize the elegance of his observation. "Yes," I said. "That's exactly what it would mean."

The prosecutor's brow furrowed. He wasn't having nearly as much fun now that I was fighting back. "It is an interesting theory," he said. "But does any of your new evidence involve *even* one of the eyewitnesses from the trial changing their sworn testimony?"

I'm not absolutely sure, but I think I saw the prosecutor smirk.

He knew that Anzor's companions had been spirited away each time I came to town. He knew that Elena Darchiashvili went into hysterics every time I tried to approach her. And he knew that Marina Kapanadze had disappeared to another country.

"No," I said. "None of the eyewitnesses have changed their sworn testimony."

The judge asked if I had any additional evidence, complimented my altruism, and adjourned the hearing. She was out the door before I had time to stand up. I had expected a ruling on my application and so was bewildered by her rapid departure.

"What happens next?" I said to no one in particular.

"Telephone justice," said Lali. "She goes to her chambers and awaits a call from someone in the president's office. They will tell her how to rule."

The unfairness of the process made me want to yell at somebody. I chose Tamaz.

"What the hell were you doing in the hearing?" I said. "You

wasted my best chance listing all the things you've done for Anzor. What was that about?"

He looked at me blankly for a moment then pointed at Anzor's mother.

"I wanted her to hear what I'd done," he said. "She promised to give me a cow if I saved him from execution—and she lied. She never gave me the cow. You can't trust her."

Telephone justice and legal fees paid in cows. I really was a very long way from home.

Finding out that the Woodruff application would be decided by the president had the unavoidable effect of dampening my enthusiasm for the Georgian judiciary. As I waited for the regional judge's order, I thought about the implications of "telephone justice" and concluded that I had fundamentally misjudged the process in which I was involved. I had seen a familiar form, a regional court, and assumed that it was invested with a familiar substance, judicial independence.

It was an amateur's mistake. Nevertheless, realization of this colossal error led to an important insight: I was pleading my case to the wrong person. I needed to persuade Misha Saakashvili, the president of Georgia. And that meant I needed to know a whole lot more about him and the culture that had produced him.

Georgia is what used to be called an honor-and-shame society; that is, a society in which the primary mechanism for gaining control over children and maintaining social order is the inculcation of shame and the complementary threat of ostracism. By contrast, America is a guilt-and-innocence society—one in which control is maintained by creating and continually reinforcing the feeling of guilt (and the expectation of punishment now or in the afterlife) for certain condemned behaviors.

Soviet society did a very poor job of allocating opportunities and rewards among the people on the basis of talent and initiative. As a result, individuals tended to rely heavily on social networks and kinship in order to obtain economic advantages. Nowhere was this more true than in the already clannish environment of Georgia. And—as Soviet society disintegrated and chaos ensued—the clan became even more important. It was the principal mediator of an individual's success (or failure) and the primary arbiter of an individual's honor (or shame).

It was into this cultural landscape that the future president had been born on December 21, 1967. His father was a physician; his mother a university professor. They divorced when he was three, and Misha was raised by his mother's family. And the putative head of the clan was her brother, Temur Alasania.

On one level, Misha's uncle Temur was a successful Soviet diplomat who'd spent twenty-four years at the United Nations working on disarmament issues. On the other hand, he was, according to many sources, a KGB general and illegal arms dealer. Whether by dint of armament or disarmament, he had become powerful, wealthy, and well placed to help his young nephew.

As a child Misha studied at the First Experimental School and then at the 51st Secondary School—elitist academies that educated the children of high-ranking officials and the occasional plebeian genius. According to one of Misha's classmates, "Mere mortals did not attend our schools. At the beginning and end of each day, there were so many black cars crowded around that you could easily mistake it for a meeting of the Communist Party Congress."

Misha was remembered not for his academic excellence but for his stylish Western clothes. "Saakashvili did not study very well," said the classmate. "All the children knew that he'd gotten into the First School because of his uncle, Temur Alasania. At a time when it was difficult to buy quality clothing, his uncle Temur would send him jeans from America. It was very noticeable: a classic gray mouse in good jeans."

He attended university in the neighboring Soviet republic of Ukraine, and while there, he performed abbreviated military service as a border guard at the Kiev International Airport. By the time he graduated, the USSR had collapsed; Georgia had declared independence; Zviad Gamsakhurdia had been deposed; and the bloodiest part of the Abkhaz war had ended.

Misha spent a few months in Tbilisi as a translator for Western human rights organizations and then departed for Columbia University Law School and Uncle Temur's Brooklyn apartment. The US Department of State had awarded him a fellowship reserved for emerging leaders from Eurasia. He interned at the United Nations, married a Dutch law student, and upon graduation took a job at a prestigious New York law firm.

As I studied this biography of privilege, I began to perceive the presence of intelligent design. Whenever they were confronted with the possibility of danger to their favorite son, the Alasania clan chose the certainty of safety over the possibility of heroism. Thus, unlike so many other young men in Georgia, Misha had not joined the army or mafia in search of glory and political advancement. Instead, he had been steered out of harm's way and into convenient and advantageous safe havens.

The recognition of this pattern was an important realization: Any appeal for Misha to take a selfless and heroic stand on behalf of Anzor Sharmaidze would be wasted effort. His history suggested that whenever confronted with a difficult choice, he would choose the option that promised the least probability of personal risk and greatest possibility of personal benefit.

For Saakashvili, survival was a fundamental family value.

In 1995 Misha was approached by Zurab Zhvania, an old friend from Georgia who was working on behalf of then president Shevardnadze to recruit talented young Georgians into government service. He accepted the call and returned to Tbilisi after almost a decade of living abroad. He was elected to parliament, appointed minister of justice, and given the task of cleaning up the country's criminal justice and prison system. The following year he resigned in an angry (and politically popular) protest of intractable official corruption.

During this period Misha caught the eye of the American embassy. The US ambassador, Richard Miles, was a veteran of regime change in the Balkans. He had arrived in 2002 with a stern warning for Shevardnadze. "We would like to see stronger leadership," he said. It was an unusually blunt and public criticism of a long-standing US ally.

Miles began actively grooming Saakashvili to lead the succession. Misha was routinely filmed in front of his US diplomas and awards. George Soros—the Hungarian-American investor, philanthropist, and political activist—flew him and his followers to a Soros-sponsored seminar in Belgrade on how to stage your own "Velvet Revolution." It didn't matter that Eduard Shevardnadze was godfather to his oldest son (the eponymous Eduard Saakashvili). Misha was the anointed leader of a US-sponsored campaign to replace the existing government, and personal loyalty wasn't going to stand in the way.

In November 2003 Saakashvili surged to the front of widespread protests over corrupt parliamentary elections. For twenty days he and a huge crowd occupied the center of Tbilisi. Protesters waved flags, shouted slogans, and carried long-stem red roses. These flowers became the irresistible symbol of their insurrection. Western broadcasters descended on Tbilisi and breathlessly described the democratic dreams of an impoverished Georgian people. But no one bothered to report on the odd detail that was (for me) the most provocative question: Where did all those poor people get red roses in the middle of winter?

A possible explanation emerged later. In early 2004 a former member of the Georgian parliament said that Soros "spent $42 million ramping up to overthrow Shevardnadze." The billionaire philanthropist allegedly rented a fleet of buses for the protesters, imported a forest of roses, and generally bankrolled the coup d'état.

In revolution, as in everything, amateurs focus on theory and professionals focus on logistics—and in matters of revolution Soros was definitely a professional. As it turned out, even the transition of power was a stage-managed affair. Misha stormed the parliament on live national television while Shevardnadze escaped out the back door. Saakashvili marched to the lectern, looked directly into the camera, and drank the deposed leader's still-warm glass of tea.

The new president promised that Georgia would be ready for European Union membership within three years, would have reconstituted borders within five years, and would operate under the rule of law almost immediately. Nevertheless, he used his party's supermajority to push through constitutional amendments that increased executive authority and curtailed judicial independence. This was the legal infrastructure that made telephone justice a practical reality.

In addition, Saakashvili appointed several of his family members to lucrative posts in the government. He made Uncle Temur a member of the national security council. And, though his position was officially "unofficial," it was rumored that none of the security chiefs could make a single decision without him. Not surprisingly, the Alasania clan became the dominant business group in Georgia.

As I studied Saakashvili's meteoric rise, I began to wonder what impact the process itself had on his thinking: What did the Rose Revolution teach Misha? My best guess was two things: First, the process demonstrated that his power derived from and depended entirely on the Americans. His status as a popular messiah flowed from the people's belief that he was supported by the US and therefore could deliver US aid. Second, the process showed that pedestrian notions of friendship and loyalty were utterly irrelevant. The Americans had unceremoniously unseated Eduard Shevardnadze, the man who negotiated the end of the Cold War and the collapse of the Soviet Union. They would not hesitate to do the same and worse to Saakashvili.

"He needs the Americans," I thought, "and he needs the Americans to need him."

It made for a complicated, complex, and convoluted relationship—exactly the kind of Byzantine intrigue at which Georgians had excelled for fifteen centuries. In order to actualize this uneven partnership, Saakashvili installed several well-connected Americans at the highest levels of his administration. One of these,

Daniel Kunin, was the thirty-three-year-old son of former Vermont governor Madeleine Kunin. In 2003 Misha appointed him senior advisor to the Georgian government. I had hoped that this young expatriate might embrace the Woodruff petition as a small step in the process of creating the rule of law in Georgia. But I was mistaken. Kunin stayed far away from me and my work.

More than a week had passed since the hearing and I was no closer to communicating directly with the president. There was no deadline for the regional judge to act, but prudence dictated that I assume her ruling was imminent. Sensing my frustration, Lali offered me a distraction: dinner at the home of Carolyn Clark Campbell, the CEELI liaison who had referred me to Lali, and her husband, Lance Fletcher. When we arrived, they apologized for their apartment, saying their permanent residence was being reconstructed. Nevertheless, their temporary digs were utterly agreeable to me: It smelled like home.

While Carolyn bustled in the kitchen, Lance played host. He was officially the president of Junior Achievement of Georgia and the deputy rector of the country's oldest private university. In these capacities he promoted both entrepreneurship and liberal arts education. However, it was his unofficial activities that captured my imagination: He was a confidential advisor to Misha Saakashvili and a member of the young president's kitchen cabinet.

Lance had a vague familiarity with my case—but my questions about whether the Woodruff petition had been discussed with Saakashvili were met with circumspect silence. Nevertheless, I pressed what I thought was the most practical argument supporting intervention by the president: If he released Anzor, Misha could demonstrate his bona fides to the American public as a US-style civil libertarian while creating an unsolved crime to lay at the feet of his enemies.

The stubbornly blank look on Lance's face made me feel exposed as a novice. He was in the most polite way possible stating the obvious: I had no business giving political advice to a modern-day Machiavelli. Fortunately, I was rescued from further embarrassment by the delivery of lasagna. Carolyn carried her kitchen conversation to the dinner table. She was in the middle of describing for Lali the speech she intended to give the next day at Tbilisi State University. She and Lance had been asked to participate in a forum celebrating the first anniversary of the Rose Revolution.

And Misha was expected to attend. Then, unbidden, Carolyn offered me a golden opportunity: If I arrived at the invitation-only event with her and Lance, I wouldn't need any credentials to get in. I could sit with them and perhaps visit with one of the president's advisors after it was over. Lance was silent. It was pretty clear he didn't think my showing up was a good idea. Nevertheless, I accepted.

And that's how I came to be standing in front of President Mikheil Saakashvili asking that he grant the Woodruff petition and release Anzor from prison. It had seemed like a pretty good idea when I first raised my hand. After all, the fact of telephone justice appeared to be widely acknowledged among the public. But it is one thing for the public to suspect improper influence by the executive; it is another thing altogether for the president to admit it.

Implicit in my request was the assumption that the president and not the local judge would decide Anzor's fate. It was an explosive allegation. It presumed that there was no judicial independence and that all authority lay in the hands of the president. The fact that this was *true* was irrelevant. It was politically impossible for the president to publicly engage the substance of any plea to circumvent the judiciary. So he evaded my request by characterizing it as an insult to Georgian sovereignty.

His response was sly, clever, and terrifying. He shouted, the crowd cheered, and I tried to appear inoffensive and unthreatening. Suddenly the tirade was over: The audience leapt to their feet and began applauding madly for the young president. He barely acknowledged the ovation. His attention was fixed on reprimanding the functionary who'd handed me the microphone. After that, he was gone.

Altogether his remarks had taken more than two hours. As a consequence, none of the other speakers made their presentations. If my brain had been functioning, I would have found it mildly ironic that Misha's disingenuous rant had prevented Carolyn from talking about her success in establishing an independent judiciary in Georgia. But as it was, my mind was a jumble of self-criticism. The three-mile walk back to Lali's house was a blur. I played and replayed the interaction in my mind. I muttered my analysis and excuses and generally worked myself into a frenzy. Try as I might, I could not escape the conclusion that Saakashvili's wrath would fall not on me but on the helpless Anzor Sharmaidze. I had made a mistake. And I didn't know how to fix it.

Three days later, the regional judge issued her ruling. Apparently, Misha didn't want to reopen Anzor's case. The decision ran to seven single-spaced pages. It summarized the arguments made by the prosecutor general and adopted each of them in turn: The Batiashvili affidavit was inadmissible because it didn't identify which of Batiashvili's two deputies saw the police plant a shell casing from Anzor's confiscated rifle; the FBI documents were inadmissible because they did not identify the specific individuals who supplied the information to the special agents; the FBI memorandum stating that (in the hours immediately after the murder) there was no bullet hole in the car was erroneous because FBI photos (taken several days later) clearly showed the presence of a bullet hole in the rear hatch; the US pathologists' opinion that Woodruff had been shot in the back of the head was disproved simply by looking at the obvious entry and exit wounds depicted in the autopsy photos.

On page five the judge turned her attention to the handwritten witness statement of Tamaz Tserekashvili. In his affidavit, the guard from the Natakhtari Drain had averred that he heard a woman scream about murder, saw a mortally wounded man in the back of a white Niva, and observed three guardians sitting on the side of the Old Military Road trying to fix their car.

"Regarding the Tserekashvili affidavit," the judge wrote, "the prosecutor stated that the petitioners have presented—not a witness statement by *Giorgi* Tserekashvili—but a witness statement by someone called *Tamaz* Tserekashvili. Even if the petitioners could manage to pass off *Tamaz* Tserekashvili as *Giorgi* Tserekashvili, the Tserekashvili affidavit would have to be rejected because *Giorgi* Tserekashvili gave a statement to the investigators the day after the murder. In that statement, *Giorgi* Tserekashvili said that he remembered in detail the time of the crime: it occurred shortly after he began watching a film ("Lazare") that started that night at 22:00. *Giorgi* Tserekashvili's sworn statement (in which he mentions that it was dark when the crime occurred) is supported by the testimony of El. Vardiashvili and other witnesses who happened to be near the water pump station at that time."

The regional judge's finding was illogical: The fact that one witness (named *Giorgi* Tserekashvili) testified one way did not prevent another witness (named *Tamaz* Tserekashvili) from testifying a different way. There was nothing in logic or law that required that *Giorgi* and *Tamaz* be the same person. After all, the Woodruff petition was all about finding *new* evidence—and *Tamaz* was certainly new.

But as far as I could tell so were Giorgi Tserekashvili and El. Vardiashvili. I had never heard of either one of them. Vice Consul Lynn Whitlock had not mentioned them in her daily summary of the Sharmaidze trial. Attorney Tamaz Inashvili had not mentioned them in his defense of Sharmaidze or in his conversations with me about the facts. None of the investigative reporters mentioned them in their stories about the murder. And the young prosecutor had not mentioned them in either his written filings or his oral argument regarding the Woodruff petition.

Nevertheless, the judge had mentioned them. Apparently,

there were two more eyewitnesses to the events surrounding the Woodruff murder. The fact that these witnesses had not been disclosed to the defense or called to testify by the state suggested that their evidence was problematic to the prosecutor general. And that made them more than a little interesting to me.

However, the judge's decision made clear that evidence known to the police but not disclosed to the defense was not "new evidence" for purposes of reopening the Sharmaidze case. That meant that even if I could find Giorgi Tserekashvili and El. Vardiashvili they wouldn't help me win my case in court.

But my Georgian education had taught me I was never going to win my case there anyway. I would win my case if and when the president decided it was in his best interest to give me what I wanted. In the meantime, I needed to keep my case alive in the courts so that when the time came Misha would have a vehicle to reopen the Sharmaidze investigation. However, all my attempts at persuasion and pressure would be aimed not at the judiciary but at the executive.

I drafted an appeal to the Supreme Court requesting review and reversal of the regional judge's decision. This filing assured that the case remained pending and that I as counsel remained pertinent to the process. But that filing only solved my procedural problem. I needed a new strategy: a carrot-and-stick approach that promised to reward the president if he did the right thing and to punish him if he did not.

Clearly, I did not possess such powers on my own. But Saakashvili's near-total dependence on the United States made him susceptible to pressure from the West. I just needed to figure out how to generate that pressure.

In the meantime, my urgent concern was protecting Anzor. I had challenged the president because I assumed that as an American I was untouchable. But I had forgotten that I was not the only person at risk: There was an innocent prisoner whose life I pretended to care about. And my foolish arrogance could easily get him killed.

CHAPTER 12

"YOU NEED TO GET THAT FILE"

Thomas Goltz had already heard about my face-off with Saakashvili. A Georgian acquaintance had written him to say that I was now radioactive. "Since that Q&A with our president, whenever people hear about the Woodruff case, they don't have any desire even to meet with Mr. Pullara," he reported. "Everyone loved the president's answer to him—that Georgia is a sovereign nation just like the US or any other country. The simple fact is, there are so many other important issues in Georgia today, no one really cares about a guy who was killed back in 1993 or another guy who's been in prison for more than 10 years."

I had called Thomas for comfort and guidance. The more I thought about it, the more I regretted my encounter with the president. I was genuinely afraid for Anzor's safety, and Goltz was the only American I knew who understood the Georgian mind.

I was especially interested in his thoughts about Misha's dependence on the US. "It's his Achilles' heel," Goltz said. "Saakashvili can pound his chest about Georgia's sovereignty, but—when *Bush* comes to shove—he's going to do exactly what the US tells him."

"But that doesn't really solve the problem," I said. "How do I get the US to exert pressure on a country that most people have never heard of?"

Thomas was silent for a moment and then chuckled. "We need CBS *60 Minutes* to do a story about this," he said.

That's how I came to be in New York City in January 2005. Thomas contacted *60 Minutes* producer Peter Klein and generated enough interest in the story to justify a meeting—provided that I pay my travel expenses to Manhattan. I didn't mind: People take you more seriously if you're willing to put your own money into something.

Peter and I met for lunch and talked for two hours. I barely touched my soup and salad: I was busy telling my story. It was by now much rehearsed and had a very particular rhythm, but Peter kept pulling me off-script with well-timed and well-conceived questions. I finally finished my narrative and steeled myself for a lecture about the practical difficulties of getting a Third World story on an American broadcast.

But Peter took the conversation in a completely different direction.

"Let's do it," he said. "We'll go to Arkansas; we'll go to Tbilisi; we'll go to Washington, DC. Bob Simon can be the correspondent. He likes to do stories about the intelligence agencies—and he's gonna like to do this story."

It took a moment for me to respond. I'd been struck dumb by the ease with which Peter could make a decision to change my life. I had expected it to be much harder.

As we were parting, I asked Peter whether I needed to keep his decision a secret from the Georgians. "You can tell them *60 Minutes* is coming," he said. "It may encourage them to keep Anzor safe."

I looked at my watch and did a quick calculation. It was 3 p.m. in New York and 11 p.m. in Tbilisi. If I hurried, I could still reach Lance Fletcher by telephone.

He answered on the fourth ring but gave no hint whether I had awakened him. He listened without interruption while I gushed. The numbness had given way to excitement.

"We need to tell the Georgian government," I said. "We need to warn them that the American news media is interested in Anzor. We need to give them a reason not to hurt him."

I paused to breathe and give Lance an opportunity to congratulate me.

"Let me think about it," he said. His tone was flat, noncommittal, final. It was not at all the fulsome response I had expected. But none of that mattered. Because he did think. And he did tell. And he did warn. And sixteen days later President Saakashvili announced his intention to reexamine the conviction of Anzor Sharmaidze on the basis of new evidence.

"The Prosecutor's Office intends to reopen the murder case of the American diplomat," he told his national security council. "I have discussed the issue with the prosecutor general. We want to carry out an open and transparent investigation of this case." He concluded his public remarks by directing his government "to cooperate with the American lawyer." A few days later the Supreme Court dutifully reversed the regional judge's order and reopened the case of Anzor Sharmaidze.

I had won the first round. The prosecutor and I were going to reinvestigate the Woodruff murder and reexamine the evidence of Anzor's guilt.

But success left me with more questions than answers. In my experience, the only thing more perplexing than a loss I can't explain is a victory I can't explain.

I contacted Peter Klein to inform him about Saakashvili's announcement. "Congratulations," he said. "But there's a problem: CBS isn't going to renew *60 Minutes Wednesday* for next season—and that means I'm not going to be able to do the story."

He said a few nice words—that we should keep in touch, that he admired what I was doing—but the final message was unequivocal: I should try to get the story produced somewhere else because it wasn't going to be produced on CBS.

From start to finish my relationship with *60 Minutes* had lasted eighteen days.

I sat in my office for the better part of an afternoon trying to understand all that had happened. I had solicited the American press—not as a part of some master plan but as a last-ditch effort to save Anzor from the consequences of my incompetence. When Saakashvili learned that *60 Minutes* was going to publicize in America his injustice in Georgia, he did justice in Georgia.

I appreciated the extraordinary response, but it seemed out of proportion to my phone call. There had to be more to the story, I thought. And there was. A few weeks later Saakashvili made another announcement: George W. Bush was coming to Tbilisi.

I heard it on the evening news and laughed out loud. In an instant, all the metaphors became real: By involving American news organizations, I had inadvertently expanded the Georgian chessboard. By proposing to tell Anzor's story to the American public, I had unwittingly threatened Saakashvili's Achilles' heel. And by doing it all just before George W. Bush's visit, I had accidentally maximized my leverage.

Mikheil Saakashvili had shown me the one way I could move him: American news coverage about Saakashvili at a time when Saakashvili needed a positive image in the US. And presumably, the more desperate his need, the more he could be moved. But at almost the same moment that I learned the lesson I lost the lever. CBS was not going to do a story. This meant I had two big tasks in front of me: first, to work with the prosecutor general to reinvestigate the murder of Freddie Woodruff, and second, to find a Western journalist who could publicize the plight of Anzor Sharmaidze at a moment when Saakashvili needed positive press in America.

I found help with both tasks from my client, Georgia Woodruff Alexander. I had called her to report on the loss of CBS.

"Gosh, Michael," she said. "If you need a reporter, why don't you call that Jamie fella—the one that did the movie about Freddie."

It had never occurred to me that someone had done a movie about the murder of Freddie Woodruff.

"Oh, yeah," she said. "He made a video of the barmaid, Marina Kapanadze, and talked about how she might have been involved in Freddie's murder." I got a copy of the movie: a documentary with the titillating title *Sexpionage: The Honey Trap*. It was the story of KGB "swallows"—nubile young women recruited to tempt and entrap diplomats, businessmen, and soldiers. The Cold War narrative featured (for the most part) giggly Russian blondes who were a decade past their prime; sinister intelligence officers who sold human flesh to buy secrets; and hapless Westerners who'd been caught between them. But one part of the film was distinctly different: grainy footage of a buxom waitress standing behind an ornate wooden bar. The production values suggested that the video had been obtained surreptitiously and without the woman's knowledge. But I immediately recognized the woman. It was Marina Kapanadze.

I contacted Jamie Doran at his home in England. We made plans to meet in Washington, and I spent the intervening two weeks trying to learn about him. An Irishman from Glasgow, he began making television documentaries in 1994. In addition to *Sexpionage*, he had produced a three-part series on the USSR's first nuclear bomb and a biography of Yuri Gagarin. The content of these three films suggested that Doran had a measure of access to Soviet intelligence. It was, I thought, a relationship that could come in handy.

We met in the lobby of his hotel. I identified him from a picture I'd found online: brown curly hair, ruddy complexion, a slight paunch. He wore loose-fitting slacks, a wrinkled shirt, and a corduroy sport coat. His smell arrived before he did—a miasma of stale beer and cigarettes. I came to recognize it as his unconscious calling card.

"Let's find a pub," he said, "someplace I can have a beer and a fag."

There was a Guinness-style pub within easy walking distance. We settled into a booth and Doran began to drink, smoke, and talk. He had just returned from Afghanistan, where he had purchased an interview with the Uzbek warlord Abdul Rashid Dostum. He told me how he sat knee-to-knee with the notorious general and (by dint of Gaelic charm and intellect) gained the psychopath's grudging respect. He told me how he had been recruited by MI6 and invited to try out for the Manchester United Football Club. And he told me how he had secretly recorded

Marina Kapanadze in the Piano Bar—and her reaction when she learned about it.

"She didn't seem upset," he said. "She laughed, flirted with me, told me to stay until closing. She said she'd give me the best sex of my life."

His eyes sparkled. It was obvious that he enjoyed telling this story.

"But as she was locking up, four men came in. They grabbed me, frog-marched me down to the lobby. My bodyguard—a guy from the local mafia that I'd hired to protect me—was down there. He confronted them, told them that if they killed me it would be a matter of honor: He'd have to kill them and their whole families."

He paused. He seemed to be gauging my interest, my acceptance. Whatever he saw, it made him smile.

"The next day was my birthday," he said. "When I woke up and realized that Marina hadn't killed me, I felt born again."

It was an odd interview. Doran spent a lot less time on my story than on his own—almost as though he was trying to convince me of *his* status and stature. Nevertheless, it was entertaining. Just then my cell phone rang. I stepped outside to take the call. It was my client, Georgia Woodruff Alexander.

"Michael," she said, "I just talked to somebody that Freddie used to work with, somebody from the CIA. I told him about what you were doing and he said you should call him. He's driving to California now, but he said he'd meet with you if you want."

"What's his name?" I asked.

"Bob," she said. "Bob Baer."

In my office, within arm's reach of my desk, was a bookcase. On the second shelf wedged between dozens of other books were two paperbacks that I'd read not more than six months before. They were first-person accounts of the life of a former CIA operations officer, Bob Baer. The nonfiction books had been optioned by Hollywood and were on their way to becoming a major motion picture staring George Clooney.

He answered on the second ring. He already knew about me

and the reopening of Anzor's criminal conviction. "We believe that he's innocent," I said.

"Of course he's innocent," growled Baer. "Freddie was murdered by GRU."

Over the course of my investigation, I'd encountered several witnesses who suspected that Woodruff had been murdered by agents from Soviet military intelligence. But this was the first time anyone in the US government had asserted it as a fact.

"Yeah," he said, "the Russians killed Freddie. But I don't want to talk about it on the phone. I'll be in California tomorrow. Come and see me."

I stumbled back into the bar and sat down. Doran was the one who was drinking, but I was the one who felt drunk. I told him about my extraordinary conversation and Baer's invitation to meet him in Newport Beach.

"Let's go to California," he said. "We can leave in the morning."

I was a little surprised at how quickly *my* invitation had become *our* trip to California. But so long as Baer did not object, I could see no harm in cultivating a relationship with an Irish documentarian.

We arrived at LAX just after noon, rented a car, and drove down the coast. Our meeting with Baer was scheduled for the morning. We took rooms at the Holiday Inn Express and the next day met the retired CIA officer at a trendy open-air shopping mall. He was waiting for us outside a coffee shop. Blue jeans, T-shirt, work boots—he looked more ironworker than superspy. His arms and chest were thick. He was a man who had once spent a lot of time in the gym.

Introductions were quick and perfunctory. Even so, I stumbled a little. I was nervous and tongue-tied—overexcited to meet a real live CIA man. Fortunately, Doran had offered to take the lead. "Leave it to me," he'd said. "I know how to deal with these intelligence types."

We sat equidistant around a circular metal patio table. Doran started his conversation with Baer the same place I'd started mine. "We think that Anzor is innocent," he said. Then almost imperceptibly he leaned back. He was waiting, creating an opening for Baer to fill.

But Baer was stubborn. So we sat in silence. After a moment Baer leaned forward and offered his own open-ended declaration. "This has already been fully investigated," he said.

I wasn't sure, but when he leaned back it looked a little theatrical—as though he was making fun of Doran. If so, Doran didn't seem to notice.

I nodded, waiting for more, waiting for anything. But this was not serve-and-volley conversation. It was two men, expert in the arts of manipulation, attempting to use silence as a weapon. Neither would relent and relinquish the illusion of control.

And so we sat for thirty minutes in intermittently punctuated silence, shook hands, and went our separate ways.

"I think that went well," said Doran. But I said nothing. It was my turn to be silent.

As I reconsidered the day, I realized that I had chosen to make a mistake. I had embraced Doran's self-professed expertise with intelligence officers because I was nervous about talking to Baer. As a result, I had condemned myself to watch style get in the way of substance.

It was an expensive lesson but not necessarily beyond redemption. Having tried and failed to manipulate Baer, I saw no real downside to humility and transparency. If all else fails, tell the truth. And so I called him again.

"Bob, I'm not as smart as you," I said. "I don't have your training or your experience. And I won't ever be able to manipulate you into telling me anything that you don't want to tell me. On the other hand, if you ask me a question, I'm going to tell you everything I know on the subject. I'm not going to keep any secrets. I would appreciate it if you'd talk to me. But if you can't, I understand."

Baer could have made me wait, made me squirm a little bit— but he didn't. He just started talking. The barrel-chested immovable object I'd seen sitting on the opposite side of the patio table became almost chatty.

The metamorphosis was remarkable. But I couldn't help feeling that Baer modulated his personality the way a spider fine-tunes his web: a process that is endlessly fascinating to observe—unless you're the prey.

"Freddie's murder wasn't up to GRU's typical standard of professionalism," he said. "It was clumsy and ham-handed—too many witnesses, too many variables, too many things that could go wrong."

"What about motive?" I asked. "Was the motive related to his work—perhaps something the Russians viewed as threatening?"

"The Agency never identified a credible motive," he said. "But you have to understand—Freddie wasn't working *against* the Russians. In fact, he did a lot of work *with* the Russians. So it didn't make any sense for the Russians to kill him. There just wasn't any profit in it."

"But if the operation wasn't up to GRU standards and the Russians didn't have a motive, perhaps they didn't do it."

"No, the Russians killed him," he said. "We identified the shooter. He was former Soviet Special Forces. And the Bureau interviewed him."

I had by now spent a great deal of time believing in the mystery, believing that Freddie Woodruff was murdered by "person or persons unknown." And I had spent a lifetime believing that if the good guy catches the bad guy, then the bad guy gets punished. But if Baer was telling the truth—if the US government really had identified the shooter and still allowed Anzor to languish in prison—then my reality was a naive fantasy. And that was a truth I wasn't eager to learn.

Baer seemed to sense my ambivalence. He was quiet as I tried to put the puzzle pieces together. An assassination that was hastily conceived and sloppily executed. A killing that could not be rationally related to the victim's work. No obvious motive and no clear beneficiary. Little effort to hide the who and how, but maximum effort to obscure the why.

Then it hit me: The fact that it was so difficult to identify the beneficiary of the murder suggested that the motive for the murder was (as least in part) to protect that beneficiary from being identified. And I knew there was at least one person in Freddie's orbit whose true identity the Russians were desperate to protect.

"What about Aldrich Ames?" I asked.

Baer answered with a growl of approval. "Good question," he said. "You need to talk to Special Agent Dell Spry."

I'd heard the name before. He was part of the FBI task force that investigated the CIA mole. According to the caption on a photo beamed around the world, Spry was the agent who put the cuffs on Ames the day he was arrested.

Baer gave me his number and I called that same afternoon. Spry didn't pick up, so I left a message. He later told me that he wouldn't have called back at all if I hadn't mentioned Bob Baer by name. Both then and later, the fact that Baer had talked to me was the passport that gave me entrée to the tight-knit fraternity of intelligence operators.

We met in Atlanta. Spry was starched, creased, and buttoned-down. He wore a crew cut, a conservative striped tie, and a smile. He was polite, respectful, and poised. He exuded honesty and integrity. He was very clearly a methodical man whose attention to detail made him dangerous. His speech was slow and his Southern accent thick, but his mind was sharp and fast. He was a tier one counterintelligence operator whose activities were authorized at the highest level of the US government. And he had a reputation among America's secret keepers as a man who could connect the dots and find people who didn't want to be found.

I'd brought my entire file. Baer had encouraged me not to ask questions, so I started at the beginning and told Spry everything I knew and everything I thought I knew. When I was finished, he reached into my stack of documents and pulled out the heavily redacted letterhead memorandum. "I wrote this," he said, "all twenty-five pages. You've done a good job of filling in the blanks."

He paused for a moment. He appeared to be deciding something.

"I remember this case," he said. "It left a hole in me."

And then he started at the beginning and walked me step-by-step through his investigation. He was as candid and direct with me as I had tried to be with him.

"You're right about the film," he said. "Freddie borrowed a camera and checked out five canisters of thirty-five mm film from the embassy stores. The Georgians only returned four canisters—and those had all been overexposed. Elena told us that just after the shooting she saw Marina pulling film out of canisters and exposing it to light. That caused us to view the film as a critical piece of evidence."

He turned to the next page in the memorandum and stared at the blacked-out paragraphs. "On the way back from Mount Kazbek they stopped at a pub: a kind of beer-and-barbecue place. It was Sunday afternoon and the little restaurant was supposed to be closed, but there were several cars there, supposedly people that Marina knew. Eldar told Elena to wait in the car while he, Freddie, and Marina went inside. They stayed about thirty minutes, and when they came out, Marina said she was cold and asked Freddie for his coat."

I was entirely focused on his words. It was only when he paused for a drink of water that I realized my heart was pounding.

"It's standard procedure to identify the target of an assassination for the shooter. You really don't want him to make a mistake and kill the wrong person. It can be done several different ways—light a cigarette when they walk up, put out a cigarette when they walk away, give them something, take something from them. We think that the shooter was there at the pub and—by taking Freddie's coat—Marina was identifying him as the target."

The facts were coming too fast to memorize. I asked if I could take notes.

Spry nodded. "We know that Freddie was investigating smuggling operations in Georgia," he said, "drugs and weapons. We know that he had a camera with him. And we know that he was a consummate professional. All that together means he was probably taking pictures the whole time: inside the pub, outside the pub, on the highway. We believe that Freddie probably photographed the assassin and that Marina probably destroyed that photograph. We also suspect she may have taken Freddie's handgun. He always carried a weapon but we never received it from the Georgians."

My writing was becoming an illegible scrawl. My hands were shaking. And in my excitement I momentarily lost sight of Baer's good advice.

"Bob said the Bureau identified the shooter," I said. "That you actually talked to him."

Spry paused and looked at me without expression. "Have you ever gone to a Georgian wedding?" he asked.

It was a jarring turn in the conversation and I immediately regretted my question.

"No," I said. "I never did."

"Everyone is invited," he said. "It doesn't matter whether you know the family or not. In Georgia, it's bad manners to walk by a wedding and not go in to celebrate. But the noise! The singing, the shouting, the music, the laughter—you can hardly hear yourself think."

He paused for a moment—just long enough to notice the anxiety that his unexplained digression was causing me. "I made a friend in the Georgian security service. One day he called me and said, 'Let's go to a Georgian wedding.' And we went—because at a Georgian wedding no one can overhear your conversation."

Spry smiled and his eyes twinkled. "He told me that the day after the murder the police had stopped a man at the Tbilisi train station—a Russian born in Kazakhstan who was using the name Vladimir Rachman. When they searched him, they discovered that he was carrying a silencer and two canisters of tear gas. The police arrested the man for possession of military paraphernalia, and almost immediately, the Russian Ministry of Defense began pressing the Georgian government to release him. The man had been in Spetsnaz [Russian military intelligence special forces], had fought in Nagorno-Karabakh, and been wounded in the left hand. The Georgians let him go and the man went to Azerbaijan. And my friend thought the whole thing might be relevant to the Woodruff investigation."

I stopped taking notes and just listened. I'd never heard anything like this in my life.

"I took the five identifiers—name, country of origin, military organization, duty station, distinct physical injury—and asked Bob Baer to see if he could find the man. A few weeks later, on a Sunday morning, Bob called me. 'You'd better get in here,' he said. 'I found him.' And he had. A perfect match on all five identifiers. I now had the man's name, his aliases, his contacts, and his photograph."

It was a mind-boggling accomplishment. The CIA had found a single needle in a worldwide haystack.

"Then I went back to the Georgians. I told them that we'd identified this man; that we knew he'd been arrested right after the murder; and that—given the severity of his offense—we were sure he would still be in prison. I told them that we wanted to meet him as soon as possible. And then we sat back and watched while the Georgians reached out to the Russian Ministry of Defense and begged them to find this man and return him to Tbilisi."

The image made me laugh: the FBI secretly watching as Keystone Cops constructed one lie in order to protect another lie.

"After a few weeks they called and told us that he was available. So we went back to interview him—me and my partner on the case, Special Agent Dave Beisner. It was definitely our guy. And on the surface, he looked and smelled the part of an inmate in a Georgian prison. But his hands weren't calloused; he wasn't suffering from malnutrition, tuberculosis, or fleas; and his beard had recently been trimmed. He told us that he didn't know much about Freddie's murder except that the CIA man had been shot in the back of the head. He offered to help us with some other stuff and asked for political asylum in America. We talked about that for a while and then circled back to Freddie. I asked him how he knew that the bullet had hit Freddie in the *back* of the head and he said that he'd read it in a newspaper somewhere. But that was a lie. We'd collected and translated every newspaper article in the world that had ever mentioned the murder of Freddie Woodruff—and not a single one of them had ever said that the bullet struck him in the back of the head. The only people who knew that fact were the FBI, the pathologist who'd done the microscopic reconstruction of bone fragments, and the man that fired the bullet."

It wasn't a confession, but it did suggest that Rachman had been present at the murder or that he had talked to someone who had been present.

"We traced his movements in the weeks after the murder—where he went, what he did. When he left Georgia he went to Azerbaijan and met with the minister of internal affairs. So we went to Baku and had our own meeting with the minister. He didn't really want to cooperate at first. He was mostly concerned that the FBI knew about his meeting with a possible assassin. But I pressed him, 'Do you really want me to go back to Washington and tell my president that you would not help America with this important case?' And that did the trick. He gave us a one-page document that Rachman had given him—a CV for a company called Mongoose. In the document, the company took credit for killing the CIA man in Georgia and offered to do murder for the ministry at a cost of one thousand dollars per bullet."

"But who hired him to kill Freddie?" I didn't realize I'd asked the question out loud until I saw the look on Spry's face. But he wasn't offended. I think he knew the impulse was irresistible.

"When I took over this case, I ordered a second Bureau-wide search for documents related to the murder. I wanted to see every piece of paper from every government agency or public source that referred to the shooting of Freddie Woodruff. During the course of that search, I became aware of information concerning an event that supposedly occurred a couple of months *before* Freddie was killed. A high-ranking member of Russian organized crime allegedly attended a meeting in May or June of 1993 at the Hotel Rossiya in Moscow—a kind of board of directors meeting chaired by Russian Defense Minister Pavel Grachev and attended by the Ministry of Defense, GRU, and the Russian mafia. During the meeting, one of the people in attendance complained that they needed to 'do something about a troublesome CIA officer named Freddie Woodford and a Georgian named Eldar Gogoladze to whom he'd gotten too close.' At a subsequent meeting held after August 1993, someone asked, 'Whatever happened to the troublesome CIA officer in Georgia?' The person asking the question was told not to worry about it, that the problem had been taken care of."

The story knocked the breath out of me. The murder of an American intelligence officer sanctioned by the Russian minister of defense himself? It was hard to imagine that Freddie was involved in anything of sufficient importance to merit the compliment of Grachev's notice.

"Is it possible that the whole thing was made up?" I asked.

"It's possible," he said. "The memo was allegedly written before the murder, but it wasn't produced in response to the FBI shooting team's search request. The official explanation for this failure was that the memo referred to the targeted CIA officer as Wood*ford* and not Wood*ruff*. But flimsy excuses like that tend to diminish an investigator's confidence in the reliability of the evidence."

"What about Moscow?" I said. "Did you ever follow up there?"

Spry chuckled. "Yes and no," he said. "I made a plan to go there. And I applied for country clearance. And I briefed the FBI liaison at the State Department. But while I was on the plane bound for Russia someone revoked my country clearance. The FBI legal attaché in Moscow met me at the airport and told me I had to get on the first flight home—because without official country clearance, I had no authority to do anything in Russia."

"Who revoked your country clearance?" I asked.

"I don't know," he said. "You'll have to ask Ambassador Strobe Talbott."

It was a completely incredible story told by a completely credible man. But some of it was still awfully hard to believe. At a time of near total anarchy—when patrons at the local Sheraton Hotel were asked to check their guns at the door—the Georgian police had randomly stopped a Russian man at the train station and arrested him for carrying a silencer and tear gas. At a moment when the FBI investigation had identified a hired assassin but not yet identified his employer, the Bureau discovered a report in its files that provided the precise evidence necessary to steer the inquiry.

I couldn't help believing that the facts were true but the story was false. The puzzle pieces needed to be reassembled to make a different picture. And for that, I needed more evidence.

"Nothing about this case is simple," I said. "The regional judge hinted that there might be eyewitnesses. But if they exist, I have no idea how to find them."

Spry looked at me quizzically. "Do you have a copy of the Georgian investigation file?" he asked.

"No," I said. "The only investigation file I have is from the FBI. In light of what they did to Anzor, I didn't think the Georgian files would be of much use."

The special agent leaned forward, looked me in the eye, and touched my arm. "You need to get that file," he said.

CHAPTER 13

A LETTER FROM THE AMERICAN AMBASSADOR

I returned to Tbilisi in March 2005, sixty days before President George W. Bush's scheduled arrival. The Georgians were literally painting the town. They paved every inch of highway Bush would drive on, painted every facade he would see, and washed every window he might care to look through. They illuminated monuments that had always stood in the dark and turned on fountains that had been dry for more than twenty years. Old people walking on Rustaveli Avenue were warned not to loiter lest they be renovated against their will. And it was all completely artificial: creating the appearance of prosperity where none existed. If George Bush was Catherine the Great, then Misha Saakashvili was Grigory Potemkin and Tbilisi was his village.

I had come back in hopes of getting the Georgians to make good on the promise of reinvestigation. But time was short and opportunity was fleeting: When George Bush left town, my leverage would leave with him. Lali had gotten me an appointment with Zurab Adeishvili, the newly installed prosecutor general. He had formerly served as head of the Ministry of State Security. A diminutive man in a gray suit, he had a narrow face, penetrating black eyes, and a perpetual expression of mild incredulity.

He was in every sense unremarkable, until he opened his mouth. As soon as he began to talk, he revealed himself as the kind of man that one underestimates at one's peril. I had come prepared for intransigence. As a consequence, Adeishvili's first question left me speechless. "What do you want us to do?" he asked.

"That depends largely on both your capabilities and your commitment," I said. "What tools do you have, what manpower can you allocate, what support can you get?"

Sitting on the opposite side of the room was Zaza Sanshiashvili, the chief investigator for the Prosecutor General's Office. He had been in each of my prior meetings with the former prosecutor general, Irakli Okruashvili.

"Perhaps Mr. Zaza and I can meet briefly, discuss these issues, and present a plan of action for your review," I said.

After a murmur of approval, our newly formed committee adjourned to the chief investigator's tiny office. Mr. Zaza settled in behind his desk and gestured toward a suspicious-looking electric kettle.

"*Chai?*" he said.

It was an act of hospitality and respect. Not at all what I had anticipated from a chief investigator. I looked around the room for some hint that would allow me to resolve the dissonance between expectation and experience. The only personal artifacts in the office were two Georgian Orthodox icon prayer cards taped to the wall.

Mr. Zaza was a man in his late fifties or early sixties—and so had lived most of his life under the cloak of state-sponsored atheism. His high professional position suggested that he had at least publicly observed the official policy.

"Is he a recent convert?" I wondered. "Or perhaps a lifelong secret dissenter?" Either way, the prayer cards suggested that the chief investigator had an affection for epic myths of justice and mercy.

He passed Lali and me tea bags and mismatched cups. He stood up to pour the boiling water and sat down to wait for our first sips. Then he laid his hand on a sheaf of red rope folders stacked in the middle of his desk. "I've already reviewed the file from the first investigation and the evidence you submitted in support of your claim," he said. "Your evidence is not in a form that complies with our rules."

"Then we should begin there," I said. "Retrace my steps and collect the evidence in a form that can be used in your courts."

It was an uninspired suggestion, and he responded with a sigh of undisguised disappointment. "I've already talked to Irakli Batiashvili and Avtandil Ioseliani," he said. "They both confirm the statements given to you."

I could feel his patience slipping away. I needed to say something substantive or I was going to lose his confidence. I looked again at the prayer cards and decided to take a chance.

"The truth is, Mr. Zaza—I don't know how to reinvestigate this case. My goal is to get an innocent man out of prison. I want to do whatever is necessary in order to accomplish that goal."

I watched him closely as Lali translated my words. The lines around his eyes softened, his shoulders eased downward, his hands opened ever so slightly.

The chief investigator had relaxed. "What you need to do," he said, "is reinterview the eyewitnesses who testified at trial, the three people in the car with Woodruff, and the two boys on the side of the road with Sharmaidze. If they change their stories and testify that the defendant is innocent, then he'll be released. In order to prepare for those interviews, you need to obtain properly authenticated copies of the FBI documents. And you need to gain access to the special agents, scientists, and doctors who authored those documents. The authors have to testify that the documents are accurate before a Georgian court can accept them as real evidence."

"And how do we do that?" I asked.

"We write a letter to the US ambassador," he said. "We ask the Americans for help."

The committee had a plan. We trooped back upstairs, presented our proposal to the prosecutor general, and spent the next thirty minutes drafting a letter to Ambassador Richard Miles. In addition to a broad request for assistance, the letter asked the US government to confirm the observations by Special Agent George Shukin (that there were no bullet holes in the Niva) and the AFIP pathologist (that Freddie was shot in the back of the head). "I would like to affirm our interest to properly investigate the murder of Mr. Woodruff and to adequately address all the questions that have arisen in the past ten years," the prosecutor general wrote. "Let me assure you that your involvement will substantially facilitate the process of this investigation."

I was almost buoyant as we left the building. The US government would provide the prosecutor general with authenticated copies of the documents they had given me; FBI special agents would brief Georgian investigators regarding their observations and conclusions; and the fact of Anzor's innocence would be established.

This was good news that I needed to share. Lali and I headed across town to see Anzor's attorney, Tamaz Inashvili. The route to his office took us by several blocks of dilapidated Stalin-era apartments. Lali slowed down and pointed toward one of the indistinguishable mint-green buildings.

"That's where they found Zhvania's body," she said. "It was just last month."

The prime minister of Georgia had allegedly been playing backgammon in a squalid little apartment. After several hours without contact, his bodyguards broke down the door. Zurab Zhvania and a twenty-five-year-old male companion were dead. According to the official report, both men had died from carbon monoxide poisoning caused by a poorly ventilated gas heater.

But no one believed the official report. The circumstances of Zhvania's death, an apparent same-sex encounter with a younger man, made a public investigation problematic. Georgia is a macho culture and homosexuality is an embarrassment. As a result, the government had a ready-made excuse for its failure to perform a thorough and transparent inquiry.

Nevertheless, the staging of the scene was so clumsy that

most people saw the sexualized context as a contrived attempt to distract from the truth, that the popular prime minister had been murdered somewhere else and then moved to the apartment. And it was generally agreed that there was only one person in the country who had both the power and the resources to kill Zhvania and orchestrate a cover-up: the president, Mikheil Saakashvili.

"I need to be very careful," I thought. If reasonable Georgian people believed that Saakashvili was capable of killing his own prime minister, then I needed to believe he was capable of killing a tiresome Texas lawyer.

I was still thinking about it when we arrived at the Ministry of Energy Regulation.

Inashvili was working there in the Legal Department. At the same time, he continued to serve as Anzor's criminal attorney. It was a thankless job that made him adverse to the people who paid his salary. He listened politely as I described my meeting with the prosecutor general, but he didn't share my enthusiasm. He was, I learned, distracted by other developments.

"Anzor got married," he said. "His new wife is living with the Sharmaidze family. And I'm pretty sure she was put there by the government to spy on us."

The Woodruff family's petition had made Anzor a minor celebrity. He'd been interviewed on television, quoted in the newspaper, and discussed at dinner tables. As a result of this short-lived notoriety, he had for a time become the object of feminine interest and attention. And one of these pen-pal relationships had blossomed into romance.

"It's the only thing that makes sense," Inashvili said. "Why else would a healthy woman marry a prisoner?"

Lali, whose ex-husband had been imprisoned for involuntary manslaughter, smiled. "There is one advantage," she said. "Come nightfall, you always know where your man is."

I had worried about the effects that publicity might have on my case. But I had never imagined that one of those effects might be a prison wedding. Nevertheless, it was highly improbable that the Georgian government would waste any effort trying to seduce Anzor Sharmaidze. He didn't know anything about the murder and he didn't know anything about our case. But Inashvili's suspicion did tell me something about the cultural attitude toward personal and political relationships: Georgians wed and bed for convenience, opportunity, and advantage; not necessarily for love.

For example, President Saakashvili had offered to stand shoulder-to-shoulder with America in its post–9/11 wars. And he backed this offer with Georgian blood and treasure: He sent two thousand soldiers to Iraq and sixteen hundred soldiers to Afghanistan. This commitment of manpower was, on a per capita basis, second only to that of the US, and it made Georgia a major player in the coalition forces. But to the average Georgian, the country didn't have much reason to be fighting in these faraway conflicts.

The official justification for involvement was thin—that after two decades of constant need Georgia could finally demonstrate its ability to give something back and thereby hasten its entry into NATO. But the idea that Georgia could make a material contribution to the war effort or get NATO membership was (at best) theoretical.

The real motivations for Saakashvili's commitment were much more practical and much more self-serving. First, his active support for the American wars made his political survival a matter of US national interest. In the eyes of the US government, any threat to Saakashvili was a threat to Georgia's continued participation in Iraq and Afghanistan. Second, his commitment of Georgian troops meant that the country would be spending millions of dollars on matériel and munitions—and all of those transactions would be handled by Misha's uncle Temur. The Alasania clan would get rich and at the same time cultivate the support of Western defense contractors.

But American interest in Georgia went much deeper than an accommodating politician and deployment of a few thousand soldiers. Georgia was a strategic asset to America—an outpost of US influence that was literally inside the territory of the former Soviet Union. It was for the US what Cuba had been for the USSR. And the Russians were just as annoyed at American trespass within their sphere of influence as the Americans had been at Soviet trespass ninety miles off the coast of Florida.

Shortly after the White House announced that President Bush would expand his trip to Moscow with stops in the former Soviet Republics of Latvia and Georgia, the Russian foreign minister sent a letter of protest to the US secretary of state. A Kremlin spokesman called the side trips "a kind of slap in Russia's face"—comparable to Putin visiting Washington between stops in Havana and North Korea.

The American reply was neither diplomatic nor conciliatory: Bush would visit whatever countries he wished whenever he wished to visit them. In retrospect, the timing of the visits seemed unnecessarily provocative. They were scheduled to coincide with the sixtieth anniversary of the allied victory over Nazi Germany—a victory that had cost the USSR more than 20 million lives.

The ill-timed visits were the kind of symbolic insult that often provokes a symbolic response.

Air Force One arrived in Tbilisi from Moscow on the evening of May 9. While in Russia, the American president had reviewed a Victory Day Parade and laid a wreath at the Kremlin's Tomb of the Unknown Soldier. However, during his twenty-hour stay in Georgia there would be no mention of either the Second World War or Soviet sacrifice.

The US delegation traveled from the airport to Old Town Tbilisi via the recently repaved and renamed George W. Bush Highway. The guest of honor was greeted by the locals with a program of diatonic singing and frenetic dancing. He clapped in time to the raging tempos, and as he was leaving the stage wiggled his hips and did a very credible Texas two-step, seeming to genuinely enjoy the excesses of Georgian hospitality.

The next day, Bush spoke to 150,000 Georgians (and me) in Freedom Square. As he noted in the speech, the location had played a central role in the country's history. It was the place where Soviet shock troops had attacked peaceful Georgian protesters and where those same Georgians had declared independence from the Soviet Union. It was the epicenter of the Rose Revolution and the birthplace of Georgian self-government. It was hallowed ground—like Constitution Hall, Yorktown, and the Alamo all rolled into one.

The American president thanked the Georgians for their contributions to the War on Terror and praised them as an inspiration for color-coded revolutions around the world. He paid homage to Zurab Zhvania and extolled him as a leader in a global democratic tsunami. He encouraged Georgian efforts at reform and dangled the possibility of a closer relationship with NATO.

And then he tried to speak Georgian. The goal of his linguistic misadventure was "*Sakartvelos gaumarjos!*"—the traditional toast "Here's to Georgia!" But the syllables rebelled and refused to march in the right order. Nevertheless, the Georgians were happy for the effort and cheered all the way through the translation.

The choir sang the relevant national anthems, the politicians exchanged affection and awards, and Mr. Bush waved goodbye. And then it was over.

A few weeks later I received a report from Anzor's lawyer, Tamaz Inashvili, regarding the status of the prosecutor general's reinvestigation. Irakli Batiashvili—the former head of Georgia's information and intelligence service—had formally confirmed to the government everything he had informally revealed to me: that Woodruff had been murdered by the GRU; that Eldar Gogoladze had been involved; and that Anzor Sharmaidze had been framed. Likewise, Avtandil Ioseliani—one of Batiashvili's two deputies and Gogoladze's immediate superior—confirmed that on the night of the murder he did a thorough inspection of the Niva; that there was no bullet hole in the rear hatch; and that Gogoladze had disappeared from the Kamo Street Hospital for one hour immediately after dropping off Woodruff's body. According to the status report, Batiashvili and Ioseliani each provided substantial additional details to the chief investigator and independently gave statements that were entirely consistent one with the other.

The chief investigator had not yet interviewed the two women who'd been riding in the Niva, Marina Kapanadze and Elena Darchiashvili; the two men arrested with Anzor, Genadi Berbitchashvili and Gela Bedoidze; or the US embassy staffer who had observed the onset of rigor mortis. The investigator's attempts to interview Gogoladze had so far been frustrated by that witness's unexplained disappearance.

Tamaz and Lali were busy locating additional witnesses for the reinvestigation—the people in Kazbegi with whom Freddie had lunch on the day of the murder; the people in Natakhtari who saw Freddie's body on the night of the murder. They asked me to contact the FBI and expedite delivery of the materials requested in the prosecutor general's letter to the US ambassador. In response to my inquiry, the Bureau advised that they had no record of the Georgian request. The FOIA clerk told me that the prosecutor general's letter had not yet been conveyed to them, which suggested that the request was still being considered by the State Department.

Nevertheless, I was encouraged. Even though George Bush had left town, the Georgians continued to do a rigorous reinvestigation of the murder. As far as I could see, there was every reason to believe that as soon as the FBI delivered authenticated copies of its files, the prosecutor general would acknowledge Anzor's innocence, the court would set aside the conviction, and the government would release the prisoner.

But once again I was being naive.

The issue in this case had never been whether Anzor Sharmaidze was *in fact* guilty of murder. The Georgian government had known from the beginning that he did not kill Freddie Woodruff. Instead, the issue was and always had been whether it was in the Georgian government's immediate best interest to publicly acknowledge the fact of Anzor's innocence. And as I was about to find out, the Georgian government's perception of its immediate best interest was something that could be easily manipulated by certain external forces, one of which was the United States.

This particular part of my education started with an e-mail. The chief investigator had contacted Lali and Lali had contacted me: The prosecutor general wanted a meeting—in person, in Tbilisi, as soon as possible. It seemed an awfully long way to go for a conversation, but the prosecutor general was a serious man so I assumed it was a serious matter.

A week later Lali and I were standing in his office. There were no preliminaries. He came straight to the point. "I received a reply from the American ambassador," he said, and handed me a letter on US embassy letterhead.

The document was terse and categorical. The United States had no interest in reinvestigating the murder of Freddie Woodruff. America was satisfied with the original Georgian investigation and with the prosecution of the accused. The US government declined to produce the requested FBI documents and refused to make its investigators available for interview.

It was a devastating development. And it didn't make any sense. My country—the champion of liberty and justice for all—was deliberately obstructing due process for Anzor Sharmaidze. It was acting with conscious intent to deny freedom to the innocent and at the same time grant immunity to the guilty.

It was mind-boggling. I simply could not comprehend how such petty cruelty served US national interests. Nevertheless, the implications of US opposition were obvious and immediate. The Georgians could not resist the will of their US patron. If the Americans did not want to reinvestigate the murder of Freddie Woodruff, then the Georgians would not reinvestigate it. They would go through the remaining motions, but the conclusion was now preordained.

After a few minutes of postmortem conversation, the prosecutor general thanked me for coming and said goodbye. The chief investigator walked me to the elevator and shook my hand. Just as the door was closing he said something that made Lali laugh.

"What was that about?" I asked.

"Nothing," she said. "I was just surprised to hear him say he was sorry."

I was sorry too. And angry. And frustrated.

It was a significant setback and an inexplicable exercise of American power. Why was the United States so committed to keeping an uneducated Georgian man in prison for a crime he did not commit? It all seemed so wasteful and unnecessary. The part I couldn't get over was the seeming irrationality of US opposition. After all, reinvestigation of Freddie's murder appeared at least on the surface to serve American interests: It would allow Georgia to burnish its credentials as a modern democracy committed to the rule of law and at the same time provide the US an opportunity to identify and potentially to punish the real perpetrator of Freddie's murder.

But the US didn't want any of that. And I couldn't figure out why not. The question gnawed on me. Eventually, I realized something obvious: The fact that the case was a big deal to me didn't mean that it was big deal to the US government. America's opposition to reinvestigation of the Woodruff murder was not based on some baffling antipathy to Anzor Sharmaidze. Rather, that opposition was a very small, perhaps insignificant, part of a much larger US strategy to achieve a much more important US goal.

Anzor was merely collateral damage in a great game of political and diplomatic confrontation. It was a chilling insight. And I needed someone a whole lot smarter than me to help me understand its implications. So I called Bob Baer.

I told him about the status of my case and my view of advantages that the US could accrue from reinvestigation of the Woodruff murder. I was trying hard to be efficient.

"If the US can identify the real murderer," I said, "then they can avenge Freddie's death and deter future threats to agents in the field. I understand Realpolitik but—"

"You don't know shit about Realpolitik," he interrupted. "Nobody is ever going to avenge Freddie's death. If you're the US government, you don't start down that path unless you're willing to launch the Eighty-Second Airborne—because that's what it's ultimately gonna take. The question always is: Are you willing to go to war over one man's death? And every CIA officer who ever went into harm's way knows that the answer to that question is an emphatic 'Hell no!' "

The words stung. I felt unmasked as an amateur and a fool. But he was right: I didn't know anything about Realpolitik. That was the domain of specialists, foxes who know many small things. I was at best a generalist, a hedgehog who knew two or three big things.

And so after I'd recovered from the embarrassment of my telephone call I attempted to do an inventory of that knowledge. I sat in a dark room and searched the corners of my mind. The results were not encouraging.

First, I knew that the US government did not want a full, fair, and public investigation into the murder of Freddie Woodruff. They had suggested as much when they subverted the second FBI inquiry and confirmed it when they interfered in my reinvestigation.

Second, I knew that the possibility of Russian involvement in the murder was a patently obvious issue that the Americans and Georgians had scrupulously ignored. Notwithstanding all the Russian smoke, the investigators had gone out of their way to avoid seeing a Russian fire.

And third, I knew that the only leverage I would ever have involved well-timed use of the Western news media. I needed a well-researched story, a crisis in Georgia, and the biggest megaphone I could find.

Henceforth, I would stop depending on the courts and start

relying on the press; I would stop trying to use the Americans to pressure the Georgians and start trying to use the Russians to pressure the Americans; and I would stop trying to prove Anzor's innocence and start trying to prove someone else's guilt.

In other words, I would have to go find the real killer. And that meant I had to go to Moscow.

CHAPTER 14

THE SEARCH FOR THE REAL KILLER

In 1994 Jamie Doran made a documentary about Soviet nuclear weapons. During the course of production he became friends with several members of the Russian elite. One of those was Maria Semenova. Maria—who goes by the nickname "Mousia"—lived in a wooded compound outside Moscow's third ring road. Stalin had given the spacious country house to her maternal grandfather after he built and detonated the USSR's first atomic bomb. As a result, Mousia had grown up with neighbors named Rostropovich, Shostakovich, Brezhnev, Andropov, and Sakharov.

That's where Jamie and I stayed when we went to Moscow.

Mousia was shy, unpretentious, and wickedly clever—the product of very good genetics: One grandfather was chief designer of all Soviet nuclear weapons; the other grandfather was awarded the Nobel Prize for Chemistry. But her natural intelligence and ruthless honesty were a handicap in the Soviet Union. She saw through the fundamental deceit of Marxism-Leninism and became apostated from all "isms."

I'd come to Moscow with a pocketful of crisp new hundred-dollar bills. Jamie said it was a city where you could buy anything you wanted—but you had to pay cash.

I wanted information. And everyone knew that information was expensive. To get what I needed we turned to one of Jamie's contacts—the Colonel. A slender and elegant man with a fondness for all things Italian, he was a fixer for Western journalists and had a source inside the office of the SVR archivist. I briefed the

Colonel on the high points of the Woodruff murder and offered my conjectures on what documents might exist in the Russian files.

"No," he said. "We don't tell him what we want. We ask him to tell us what is available."

We got the answer four days later. The Colonel called and demanded that we meet him in his apartment. He was already angry and afraid when he answered the door.

His source had contacted him in a panic. "You've ruined me," the source said.

According to the Colonel, the source had made a routine request for documents relating to the killing of CIA officer Freddie Woodruff. But instead of getting files from the archivist, the source got a visit from SVR security officers.

"You cannot have these documents," they told the source. "And it's not worth your life to ask for them again."

The Colonel was furious. We had caused him to burn a valuable asset and he would get nothing for it. He demanded to know what we were playing at.

"Do you have any idea how dangerous this is?" he said. "Leave. And don't ever come back."

The archivist's refusal was an unexpected outcome. Prior to approaching the archivist I'd done extensive research on Russia's information black market. A vigorous backdoor business had always existed, but with the collapse of the organized economy the illicit information industry had exploded. Government secrets became a commodity that could be easily monetized for hard currency. Foreign spies submitted shopping lists, and opportunistic clerks trawled through confidential files to fill their orders.

One American intelligence officer told me that the United States had paid millions of dollars for a trash bag. It was the waterproof wrapping around a packet of secret documents that had been passed to the KGB by a mole *whose true identity was unknown to the Russians*. But there was a fingerprint on the trash bag. And the CIA was able to use this print to identify the traitorous mole as FBI senior special agent Robert Hanssen.

Why, I wondered, would the SVR allow such treasures to escape willy-nilly out the back door while responding with such vehemence to an archivist's request simply to examine a decade-old murder? Their reaction suggested not only that they were involved in the Woodruff killing but that his assassination was directly relevant to deeper and perhaps more contemporary secrets.

I didn't have the resources, expertise, or inclination to investigate this bigger mystery. Nevertheless, I needed to know the subject of Russian concern so that I could assess the risks and formulate a strategy. Once again, Jamie knew someone who might be able to help.

"Igor is connected," Jamie said. "He knows everybody. He can tell us what they're worried about."

And so, a few days later, the British documentarian and I were sitting in an apartment talking to a KGB officer. It was surreal. This sort of thing didn't happen in real life. But it was happening to me. Igor talked matter-of-factly about things I'd never heard of, never even imagined. I suspected it might all be a lie. But even so, it was a fascinating story.

According to Igor, a few days before the USSR dissolved (on December 26, 1991) the national and regional leaders of Soviet intelligence met at a dacha near Moscow. They were there to solve an unprecedented problem: How would their agencies continue to function in the absence of a central government that had for decades funded their operations?

The men in attendance were custodians of a highly professional security apparatus. But they knew with absolute certainty that if they did not immediately find an alternative source of funds their organizations would quickly disintegrate. It was a desperate time that called for desperate measures. And their solution was both pragmatic and amoral: They created a narcotics cartel.

They called their venture "Friends United" and chose a Chechen intelligence officer, Usman Umaev, as the first principal director. The Friends used SVR and GRU assets to smuggle opium paste out of Afghanistan to a processing lab in Shali, Chechnya. In the summer of 1993, they began using Chechen trucks guarded by Mkhedrioni (the mafia army led by Jaba Ioseliani) to drive tons of refined morphine through Georgia to the Black Sea ports of Poti and Batumi. From these ports the product typically continued to either Romania or Turkey, although one enterprising lieutenant arranged to export the heroin directly to the Caribbean on ships that had brought in Colombian cocaine.

I recognized the smuggling routes that Igor was describing. They were the same ones that Freddie Woodruff had identified to the CIA in his thirty-page memo on narcotics trafficking in the Caucasus. But I didn't say anything about it. And as it turned out, I didn't need to.

Igor already knew. "I can say with ninety-nine percent confidence that Woodruff was not killed because of Aldrich Ames," he said. "Rather, the American was killed because of what he knew about this drug smuggling operation."

According to Igor, prior to 1995 the Georgian arm of the cartel was owned fifty-fifty by Mkhedrioni and Shota Kviraya, the deputy chief of information and intelligence services who told Batiashvili that the police had planted a shell casing from Anzor's rifle for the FBI to recover. The Georgian joint venturers paid the Shevardnadze family 10 percent of their profits as consideration for not interfering in cartel business. After 1995, Kviraya owned the Georgian business by himself and began paying the Shevardnadze family 20 percent of the profits. Notwithstanding this expense, Kviraya's share was more than $4 billion.

It was a fantastical story. But on the surface it seemed conveniently consistent with what I knew or, at least, consistent with what I *thought* I knew. And that made me suspicious. Why would the SVR respond so ferociously to the archivist's request if the Woodruff murder and the content of the requested file related only to Russia's well-documented participation in narcotics trafficking? And why would the Russians provide me a former KGB officer to explain that relationship while at the same time preventing me from obtaining a file that ostensibly explained exactly the same thing?

It bothered me that I could not answer these questions. And so in the end Igor's insistence that the Woodruff murder was *not* related to Aldrich Ames had the paradoxical effect of redoubling my commitment to investigate the possible relationship. Fortunately, there was a vibrant cottage industry of former KGB officers willing for a fee to elucidate the unwritten history of the KGB. One of those was the affable and garrulous Stanislav Lekarev, a former member of the KGB First Chief Directorate (foreign intelligence) who had worked undercover in London as a Soviet film executive. He spoke English with a slight British accent and seemed to have adopted completely the manners and mannerisms of the West.

"Call me Stan," he said. "I'm happy to help you. I'll do anything I can to free an innocent boy from prison."

The motion picture arts were a natural cover for Lekarev. His father had been an actor on stage and in film, his mother a stage actress and acting instructor. He spoke knowledgeably about topics ranging from film production to acting techniques. He considered himself an expert on Hollywood accounting and the use of sex as a weapon.

"Do you remember Clayton Lonetree?" he asked. "He was one of mine."

Lonetree had been a Marine guard at the US embassy in Moscow in 1985. He was seduced by a Russian woman who worked as an embassy telephone operator. Under duress, Lonetree delivered embassy floor plans and top secret cables to the KGB. He was ultimately arrested, convicted of espionage, and sentenced to thirty years in prison.

"If I know your birthday," Lekarev said, "especially if I know where you were born and exactly what time, I can do your horoscope and tell you what kind of woman you like. This is what we did. Then we slowly introduce the woman to your subconscious— passing on a street, sitting on a bus—until finally you meet. After the relationship has developed, the woman invites you home to meet her uncle Vanya. The uncle—in truth a KGB officer—tells you that we will kill the woman unless you give us an embassy document. No matter what you provide, we praise you lavishly when it is delivered. After that, we own you."

I didn't know whether to laugh or cry. But I knew one thing for sure: He wasn't kidding.

"What about Aldrich Ames?" I said.

"Ah, Mr. Ames," said Lekarev. "Prior to 1991 Ames was a treasure. His identity was known to only three or four people in the Russian government. One of those people was Vladimir Kryuchkov—the head of foreign intelligence and later the chairman of KGB. He betrayed Ames by killing all the agents that Ames had identified. After that, it was only a matter of time before the CIA identified Ames as a mole."

I was busy scribbling notes as fast as I could. Lekarev anticipated my next question.

"By 1993 it was highly unlikely that the SVR would kill Woodruff to protect Ames," he said. "In fact, I suspect that the SVR sacrificed both Ames and Hanssen to protect an even more important agent."

It was a diabolical idea: that the Russians killed Woodruff not to save Ames from discovery but in order to draw attention to Ames and away from someone else.

"But what if they did?" I asked. "What if the Russians did kill Woodruff because of Ames? How would they do it?"

"You have to remember the conditions that existed in 1993," he said. "The central government wasn't functioning. There was no vertical *coordination*—the top couldn't tell the bottom what to do. However, there was still strong horizontal *cooperation*. Intelligence officers could contact their peers in other organizations and get them to do things."

Lekarev took a piece of paper and drew an XY axis graph.

"Coordination was down here in the negative numbers," he said. "But cooperation was over here in the positive numbers. That's how they did it."

I looked at the graph. It was a simple and terrifying indictment of post-Soviet Russia: a highly effective killing machine with no central command authority. Brawn without brain.

"In 1993 Georgia was essentially still a part of Russia," he said. "Shevardnadze didn't want to join Yeltsin's Commonwealth of Independent States; he wanted to align himself with the West in hopes of getting Western aid—but that didn't matter. Russia had its army, GRU, and SVR all over Georgia. There were Russian loyalists everywhere in the Georgian government. So anything that Russia wanted to do in Georgia, they could do quickly and without concern."

Lekarev was silent for a moment—remembering, calculating, or (perhaps) just acting. Then he leaned forward and lowered his voice.

"GRU was doing this kind of thing back in 1993," he said. "And I think there's a seventy-five percent chance that they killed Woodruff. Someone from SVR would have called them and asked for a favor. GRU wouldn't have even known why they were killing him. They would have just done it."

"Who?" I said. "Who would have called GRU?"

"It's hard to say," said Lekarev. "It would have been organized through Igor Giorgadze. He was Group Alpha and loyal to Moscow. As for who made the request, there weren't very many people who knew about Ames. My guess would be Ames's handler, Victor Cherkashin."

Lekarev was quiet. He seemed to be waiting for me to say something, but I couldn't figure out what it was. Finally, he spoke.

"Why don't you ask him?" he said. "He's in town promoting his book."

It was not an idea that had ever occurred to me: to make a cold call to a foreign espionage agent and ask him if he had instigated the murder an American CIA officer. But I'd done sillier things over the course of this adventure, so I decided to give it a try.

Mousia made the initial contact. She'd gotten Cherkashin's phone number from his literary agent. She told him a little bit about my project in Georgia. He agreed to meet us at the Moscow Art Theatre the next morning. It was an inspired choice of location: the place where Konstantin Stanislavski developed method acting—the subtle art of pretending to be sincere and emotionally authentic. It was mildly ironic that a master manipulator had chosen this particular venue as our meeting place.

We entered through the side door. A custodian was waiting to let us in. He pointed us to a staircase leading to the basement.

Cherkashin was waiting for us in the bar: a semicircular cave with banquette seating for a dozen. He was sitting on the near end by the privacy curtain—an unremarkable septuagenarian in a black suit, white shirt, and unfashionable tie. My first impression was of a grandfather. I thought he might have peppermints in his pockets.

Jamie took the lead. He launched into a game of "Small World"—naming KGB officers he knew or had interviewed. I couldn't tell whether he was trying to put Cherkashin at ease or to establish his own substance and credibility. But the retired KGB officer was already comfortable and he seemed to have taken Jamie's measure with a glance.

The Englishman was still talking, but Cherkashin was looking at me.

"I know the Woodruff story," he said. "I'm sorry that he's dead, but we did not kill him."

He spoke perfect English. The accent was faint, the timbre warm and genial, and the volume low enough to pull me forward in my seat. He had used words and sound for effect and had taken control of the room with a single sentence. It was a strangely familiar experience.

And then I saw it: Jamie and I had been managed this way once before, by CIA officer Bob Baer. In that instant I made a decision. I did not have the skill to play games with this grandmaster. I would therefore relate to Cherkashin in the same way that I related to Baer: I would be forthcoming, honest, and humble.

This was a formidable man. And I would treat him with respect.

"The FBI did two investigations of the murder," I said. "The second investigation focused on the possibility that Woodruff was killed in order to protect Aldrich Ames."

It wasn't really a question; more of an invitation. And Cherkashin studied me for a moment before he accepted.

"No," he said, "killing Woodruff would not protect Ames. Woodruff was a field officer—a nose that provides information to a brain. And in this case, the brain was at CIA headquarters in Virginia. If we wanted to protect Ames, then we would have had to kill Milt Bearden."

It was an illogical deflection. Bearden was chief of the Soviet/East European Division—a position two levels above Woodruff in the CIA organization chart. Killing him would not protect Ames because Woodruff would still know (and be able to report) any compromising statements that Ames had made.

"The FBI suspected that Ames may have inadvertently betrayed himself while out drinking with Woodruff," I said. "They hypothesized that Woodruff was assassinated before he could return to the US to prevent him from reporting that information."

"Impossible," he answered. "As I recall, Woodruff was scheduled to depart Georgia less than three weeks after Rick left the country. So there simply wasn't enough time to make a plan and execute it. We just couldn't move that fast."

This was a truly unexpected defense: Russian intelligence could not have murdered Woodruff because even with twenty-one days lead time they did not have the necessary efficiency or competence to do the act. This excuse was so inane that it made me wonder whether Cherkashin was working hard to make me think that Russia was not involved or working hard to make me think that it was.

"Ames's history of betrayal is pretty strong evidence that he would sacrifice Woodruff to save himself," I said. "It wouldn't be the first time that he caused someone's death."

"Rick is not a bad man," Cherkashin said. "When we first began working together, I told him that I wanted to keep him safe and that—in order to accomplish that objective—I needed to know the names of anyone with whom I should *not* share his information. He thought about it for a few minutes, took out a piece of paper, and wrote down a list of people for me to avoid. But he never intended to cause anyone's death. It was simply good tradecraft."

Cherkashin was leaning forward; his elbows were resting lightly on his knees; his hands were moving gently in the breeze of his words. It was a sincere and emotionally authentic performance. But the script was a lie.

Whatever else might be said about Aldrich Ames, he was not stupid. As an experienced intelligence officer, he knew that the people he identified to the Russians would be arrested, tortured, and executed. But for the perfidious Ames, the math was simple: They would die so that he could live (and make money).

Irrespective of his posture and prose, Cherkashin's message was clear: If Ames caused Woodruff's death in an effort to keep himself safe, it was simply good tradecraft.

"I think about Rick very often," he said. "I'm sorry that he ended up as he did. I wish there was something I could do."

Cherkashin sighed and sat back. He seemed truly discomforted at the thought of Ames's circumstances: life in federal prison without possibility of parole. His brow was slightly furrowed, his eyes sad and a little moist, his lips pursed and turned down at the ends. It was all too perfect. And I wondered how far he'd carry it.

"Have you tried to contact him?" I asked. "Have you written?"

He tilted his head, shrugged his shoulders, and smiled wistfully. "No," he said. "I do not have the necessary information."

Unbeknownst to Cherkashin, I'd been in communication with Ames. We'd exchanged a few letters about my project and his visit to Georgia. Not surprisingly, Ames claimed to know nothing that could shed any light on the murder.

"I can give you his address," I said. "You could write him."

It was as though I'd given the man an electric shock. His back stiffened, his eyes widened, his hands shot out in front of him defensively—palms forward, fingers spread, ready to push away an assault.

"No, no, no, no, no," he said. "Thank you, but no."

The mask had slipped aside—and in the process given me a lens through which to interpret the remainder of the matinee. He quickly recovered himself and began the leaving ceremony. "You're doing a very noble thing," he said. "I just wish there was more I could do to help."

"Perhaps there is," I answered.

He raised his eyebrows and turned his head slightly. He was inviting me to tell him more.

"I would like to interview Igor Giorgadze," I said.

His expression changed immediately. The grandfather was gone. In his place was a hard-as-nails KGB officer.

"What is that to me?" he asked. The tone was sharp. This was all business.

Giorgadze had been appointed director of Georgia's information and intelligence service following the country's defeat in the battle for control of Sukhumi. In 1995 he was implicated in the attempted assassination of Eduard Shevardnadze and fled the country. Since then he had been prominently featured as a fugitive on Interpol's Most Wanted List and as a commentator on Moscow's news programs.

"The Americans and the Georgians present themselves to the world as champions of justice," I said. "But I believe that they have knowingly and intentionally perpetrated a great injustice against Anzor Sharmaidze. I need to talk to Mr. Giorgadze in order to prove both Anzor's innocence and the fact of American and Georgian hypocrisy."

Cherkashin was sitting back, listening. His eyes were veiled, his face without expression. His hands were resting on his stomach. He drummed his fingers. Twice.

"This is interesting to the KGB," he said. "Go home. We'll call you."

"Here in Moscow we stay at—"

"We know where you stay," he interrupted. "Go home. We'll call you."

Over the next several days Jamie and I waited by the phone at Mousia's house in the woods outside of Moscow. When no call came, I flew home to Texas and Jamie flew home to England.

Shortly after my arrival in Houston, I reached out to Milt Bearden, the division chief that Cherkashin had identified as the brain at CIA headquarters in Virginia. He was nonplussed by my report.

"Why would Victor want to kill me?" he asked. "What did I ever do to him?"

The call came ten days later. It was from Cherkashin's daughter, or at least a woman who claimed to be his daughter.

"We've arranged a meeting with the person you asked about," she said. "You are to rendezvous with your contact at nine a.m. on Friday at Domodedovo Airport. And don't be late: You have a plane to catch."

The time allowed was too short for me to get there from Houston, but just enough for Jamie to fly in from London. He and Mousia arrived at Moscow's second busiest airport on time and were met by a man who identified himself only as an associate of Cherkashin.

"Give me your cell phones," the man said. He removed the battery from each device and returned the lifeless gadgets to their owners.

"You can have the batteries back after we return," he said. "Now follow me."

He led them around security and directly to a departure gate. A counter agent saw him coming and opened the boarding door just for them. No one asked to see their boarding cards, which was fortunate because they didn't have any.

Two-and-a-half-hours later they landed in the Black Sea city of Sochi.

There was a van waiting for them on the tarmac. They took

it north past a waterpark, a half-dozen grand spa hotels, and a sanatorium, then the driver turned left and they entered the seaport. He parked the van next to an oceangoing motor yacht and pointed his passengers toward the gangplank.

"There," he said. "Go there."

The trio clambered aboard, and thirty minutes later the ship was under way. Jamie, Mousia, and their mysterious companion headed due west.

It was dark when the captain asked Jamie to come to the bridge. He wanted the Western journalist to see the navigational instruments so he could verify the ship's location.

"We're in international waters," the captain said.

As if on cue the lookout announced the presence of a ship directly astern. It was another oceangoing motor yacht. The helmsman began gunning the engines and the crew scrambled to link the two vessels. After the ships had been lashed together, a catwalk was laid between them. A stocky man in a black suit, red tie, and orange life preserver walked across.

"I am Igor Giorgadze," he said. "I understand you want to talk to me."

They conducted the interview in the ship's salon. Jamie asked questions and Mousia translated. They filmed the whole thing and when it was over gave me a copy of the video.

Jamie's first query was the obvious one. "Why are we meeting in the middle of the Black Sea?"

Giorgadze glanced up and to the right. This was a question he had prepared for and he was remembering the answer. "There are people who wish to do me harm," he said. "They want to criticize and embarrass any country that gives me sanctuary—and I don't want to put any country in that position."

"Isn't it true that you're living in Russia under the protection of the SVR?" said Jamie.

"I have good relations with the SVR," Giorgadze said. "And I also have good relations with the special services in Turkey, the

US, and throughout South America. But no one is supporting or protecting me. If they were, I wouldn't have to wait eleven years to return to Georgia."

"Who is it that wants to harm you?"

Giorgadze's eyes narrowed. The muscles around his mouth tightened slightly.

"The president, Misha Saakashvili," he said. "He has offered five hundred thousand US dollars to anyone who gives information about my location. And he has a group of killers who are searching for me."

"Why would Saakashvili want to kill you?"

"I am a competitor," he said. "Shevardnadze believed that Georgia needed to ally itself with the US, and Saakashvili is fulfilling that policy. I have a different vision. I believe that Georgia should be the Switzerland of the Caucasus—good relations with all, alliances with none."

"The Georgian government claims you attempted to assassinate Eduard Shevardnadze," Jamie said. It wasn't really a question; more of a declarative statement intended to provoke a response. And it did.

Up to now, Giorgadze's hands had lain folded in front of him. His voice had been soft, his cadence measured, his sentences punctuated with thoughtful pauses. But this reply was different. The former KGB general looked down and to the right before speaking; words came out of him with strength and confidence, and he gestured by chopping at the air with a stiffened right hand.

"I am offended by this accusation," he said. "At that time, both the US and Russia agreed that Shevardnadze should be president of Georgia. So assassinating him would have been stupid. To which of the Great Powers would I turn for support after I killed their beloved Silver Fox? But the worst part, the most insulting part, is that the Georgians accuse me, Igor Giorgadze, of unprofessionalism."

I stopped the video and watched the diatribe over again. Giorgadze did not look like an outraged man nearly so much as he looked like a man pretending to be outraged. It was a tell, a change in a poker player's behavior that gives a clue to the hand he is holding.

This was, I suspected, how Giorgadze acted when he was lying.

"I can prove that I did not try to kill Shevardnadze," he continued. "I was trained in Department Thirteen of the First Chief Directorate of the KGB—executive actions, assassinations, wet works. I am an expert in these things. The Georgians say I tried to kill Shevardnadze. But Shevardnadze is not dead. As a result, the only reasonable inference is that I did not try to kill him. Because if I had tried, he would be dead."

"But why would Shevardnadze accuse you if you did not do it?" Jamie asked.

Giorgadze smiled. It was like someone had flipped a switch. In an instant his affect changed completely. He was once again composed, reflective, and spontaneous.

"Let me tell you a joke," he said. "Shevardnadze and his young grandson were on a balcony overlooking Tbilisi when the old man asked the boy what he wanted to be when he grew up. '*Babua*,' the boy said, 'when I grow up I want to be president of Georgia!' A few seconds later Shevardnadze called to his wife. 'Nanuli, come quick!' he said. 'Our poor grandson just fell off the balcony and died!'"

The big man chuckled. He liked his joke.

"This was democracy under Shevardnadze," he said. "If he identified you as an opponent, then you would be oppressed, arrested, murdered. I was an opponent—a serious candidate to replace him as president—and so he turned on me."

"What about Freddie Woodruff?" Jamie asked. "Were you behind his murder?"

The switch flipped again. It was his tell—not anger, but pure aggression.

"I did not know Freddie Woodruff and I was not involved in his murder," he said. "In August 1993 I was working in the Ministry of Defense—trying to identify Gamsakhurdia sympathizers that were still in the government."

"Then why did Shota Kviraya accuse you of arranging the murder on orders from Moscow?" Jamie asked.

"Because of Shevardnadze," he answered. "He did it to discredit me. But it is not a serious theory. There is no proof to support it."

"And what about Mkhedrioni?" said Jamie. "Were you involved with them?"

"Jaba Ioseliani was the number two man in the country," said Giorgadze. "I worked with him in the government but had no other association with him or his organization. Everybody knew that Mkhedrioni was half-criminal. But we were on the same side of the barricade—and that was all that mattered at the time."

"So if you did not kill Woodruff," said Jamie, "who did?"

"Woodruff's death was nothing more than an unfortunate accident," he answered. "That is the official verdict and the only one for which there is any evidence."

"Do you feel any shame that Anzor Sharmaidze is in prison for a crime he did not commit?" asked Jamie.

Giorgadze did not object to the assumption of innocence implicit in the question. The switch had flipped again. It was the sober, reflective professional who answered.

"There are many such people, in jail for crimes they did not commit," he said. "And I am sorry for that. But that is how Georgia was working at the time—and that is how Georgia is working today. Look at the death of our late prime minister, Zurab Zhvania. Everybody knows that he was murdered and everybody knows who did it. He was a rival to Saakashvili, so Saakashvili eliminated him. Nevertheless, the government insists on telling us that he died from bad air and bad sausage."

I watched the video several times and came away with two conclusions:

First, I was pretty sure I could tell when he was lying. The abrupt torrent of words and explosion of confidence seemed to emanate from an entirely separate part of his brain. But suspecting a lie was not the same thing as knowing a truth. If I was to have any hope of discovering the true nature of his involvement, I would need to find someone who was both close to Giorgadze and willing to be transparent with an American lawyer.

Second, from Giorgadze's perspective, everything that happened in Georgia was inextricably connected to everything else that happened in Georgia. No single event could be understood without an appreciation of its historical context and knowledge of the relationships among the people involved in the transaction.

So what was the true historical context of Freddie Woodruff's murder? And what were the relationships among the people who benefited from Anzor's continued incarceration? The answer to these questions lay buried in old investigation files that the Georgian government did not want me to see.

CHAPTER 15

"THEY BEAT ME"

Jamie committed to producing a documentary about the quest to liberate Anzor Sharmaidze. In preparation for filming in Georgia, we hired a local journalist to locate Gela Bedoidze and Genadi Berbitchashvili—the two men who'd been arrested with Anzor and who'd testified against him at trial. Not only did Magda Memanishvili find the witnesses, she got copies of sworn statements they'd given the prosecutor general during his reinvestigation of the criminal charges.

As counsel for Georgia Woodruff Alexander, I was entitled to receive copies of all such statements. However, Giga Bokeria—Lali's godson and Saakashvili's chief lieutenant—had personally vetoed my request for the affidavits on grounds that I was a foreigner and therefore could not be allowed to see such potentially embarrassing documents.

When I finally got to read them, I understood why he thought so. Both Gela and Genadi had repudiated their prior testimony. They now claimed that they'd been tortured and threatened and made to memorize and recite a fabricated story. They now swore that at the time of the murder, they were thirty kilometers away; that they never made it to the Old Military Road before being arrested; and that Anzor was *completely innocent*.

"We lied," said Genadi. "But we were in a horrible situation. I would have signed anything they put in front of me and sworn to anything they told me to say."

The witness statements were a parable about the caprice of fate.

Gela, Genadi, and Anzor spent most of August 8 going from place to place drinking. They found a black-market tanker truck and filled Gela's car with gasoline. Anzor complained that he hadn't seen his family in months and begged his companions to drive him home to Pansheti. Just outside of Mtskheta, eight kilometers before the turnoff to the Old Military Road, they stopped to help three girls whose Fiat was out of gas.

"I entertained myself with two of the girls while a third siphoned gasoline out of my tank," said Gela. "After they left, I turned the ignition and the low-fuel light came on. The girls had emptied the tank."

The boys no longer had enough gas to make it to Anzor's house. Genadi suggested that they go to a nearby police post; he had colleagues there who might help them get more gasoline. They'd only been at the Nerekvavi police post a few minutes when security officials arrived from Tbilisi and arrested them.

It was a meaningless string of random events stumbling drunkenly toward tragedy—and evidence of Anzor's innocence.

I was surprised to discover that the prosecutor general had actually reinvestigated the case. After months of silence, I'd begun to believe that the court order requiring reexamination was nothing more than a clever ploy to distract, delay, and ultimately disappoint. Nevertheless, the prosecutor general had been in possession of these witness statements for almost half a year and he'd done nothing to end Anzor's torment. The implications of this inaction were clear: Notwithstanding its promise to do justice and love mercy, the new government of Misha Saakashvili had joined the old conspiracy against Anzor Sharmaidze.

The only way I had to end this evil was to expose it.

Meanwhile, I had to just get on with business. This was the second time I'd come to Georgia with Jamie. During the first trip we drove up to Anzor's family home in Pansheti. It was a humble structure perched between a two-lane road and a slope that seemed to fall away forever. There was a cold drizzle when we arrived, and clouds had formed below the house. The mist parted for a moment, and I saw cows grazing on the mountainside and a river a mile below on the floor of the valley.

It was sublime. And seeing it made me sad.

"This is one of the things that Anzor lost," I thought.

A shirtless man in his early thirties was working on the engine of a rusted-out car. He came toward us with a wrench in his hand but stopped when Lali hailed him.

A strong family resemblance belied the need for any introductions: This was Anzor's younger brother. He led us into the house. The front door opened into a small room that served as kitchen, dining room, living room, and workroom. Anzor's mother was sitting near the fireplace, hand stitching a pair of torn pants.

She smiled when she saw us. This—and the bright colors of her clothes—were starkly different from our first meeting at the courthouse. She was gracious and hospitable. We were guests in her home and she was proud to have us there.

She served tea while Jamie set up his camera, and then she sat for an interview. The questions were uninspired but essential: How does it feel to have your son wrongly convicted of murder? What do you think about the Woodruff family's effort to get Anzor out of prison?

She dutifully exposed her pain and confessed her admiration for American generosity. Quite obviously, she would say or do anything to help her child.

We said our goodbyes and left as the sun was going down. On the drive back to Tbilisi I realized anew the harsh inflexibility of the Old Military Road. It was carved out of an ascending valley, and the mountains on either side formed a funnel. A traveler on the road had to either continue north into Russia or return south via the same route taken in. There was simply no other way out of the valley. And that made this road an ideal place for an ambush.

Once Freddie Woodruff turned north toward Kazbegi, a shooter could wait for him at the mouth of the funnel near Natakhtari with 100 percent certainty that the CIA officer would return to that point. But the combination of uncertain timing, gloaming darkness, and multiple occupants in a fast-moving vehicle made a single-shot kill highly improbable. To increase the odds of success, an assassin would need help—from outside the vehicle, inside the vehicle, or both.

Identifying those helpers would be key to solving the puzzle. In the meantime, we had a documentary to make. Both Georgia Woodruff Alexander and Dell Spry would join Jamie, Mousia, and me in Georgia—she as the woman whose concern had inspired reexamination of Anzor's conviction and he as the FBI special agent whose investigation had gotten closest to discovering the truth. Lali would provide our room, board, and transportation—giving over her entire house and housekeeper for two weeks and hiring her nephew and his van to squire us around the city.

Jamie's plan was to retrace my steps, reinterview the witnesses, and reenact the murder. And he started at the top with Eduard Shevardnadze. The former president still lived in a self-imposed internal exile. Nevertheless, he was bright, congenial, and a little impish.

Jamie made small talk in a transparent attempt to inflate his résumé. "You know, I've met Mr. Gorbachev before," he said.

The old politician smiled. "I have met him more," he replied.

Shevardnadze confirmed on camera everything he'd told me in our first meeting—his reliance on Freddie Woodruff; his distrust of Eldar Gogoladze; and his belief in Georgian judicial process. But he was coy about current events in Georgia and declined Jamie's invitation to cast suspicion on Igor Giorgadze or to criticize Misha Saakashvili.

"I am alone with my memories," he said. "Such things no longer concern me."

Over the next several days we quickly replowed ground it had taken me a long time to till. Jamie interviewed Avtandil Ioseliani, the former deputy minister who had been Eldar Gogoladze's direct superior in August 1993. The retired security officer confirmed that Eldar had gone home (to take a nap) immediately after he delivered Woodruff's body to the hospital and that when he returned, Eldar was freshly showered and wearing a new suit of clothes. More importantly, the deputy minister described how—on the night of the murder—he had carefully inspected Eldar's Niva and determined that there was no bullet hole in the vehicle.

This dovetailed nicely with Jamie's interview of the ballistics expert, Zaza Altunashvili. He confirmed that when he examined the Niva a few days after the murder there was a bullet hole in the rear hatch and that the size of that hole matched exactly the size of the bullets fired from Anzor's gun.

We had hoped to do an on-camera interview with Irakli Batiashvili—to get him to confirm that the police had planted a spent cartridge case from Anzor's rifle for the FBI to find. But there was a problem. The Georgian prosecutor general had arrested the former minister and current opposition politician.

The prosecutor accused Batiashvili of committing high treason by providing "intellectual support" to insurgents in the breakaway province of Abkhazia. The only proof of his crime was a fabricated recording that pieced together snippets from several unrelated telephone conversations. In the final product, Batiashvili allegedly encouraged the leader of a rebel group "to not give in"—but the forgery was of such poor quality that the prosecutor general didn't offer the tape as evidence at trial. Nevertheless, Batiashvili was found guilty and sentenced to seven years in prison.

It was apparently a very dangerous thing to be accused of a crime in Georgia—and even more dangerous to be perceived as a potential candidate to replace Saakashvili.

Magda scheduled an interview with a retired Georgian security officer—an interrogator with a specialty in torture.

I was antsy as the hour approached: eager to see the definitive face of evil, eager to feel the thrill of moral superiority. But the torturer turned out to be an unremarkable man, disappointingly average, a banal civil servant glad for the chance to discuss his expertise.

He sat on Lali's couch and calmly described the mechanics of breaking a person's mind and body. "It isn't difficult," he said.

Jamie quizzed him about the abuses that Anzor claimed to have endured.

"I would cuff their hands behind their backs and then suspend them in the air by their wrists," he said. "It didn't take long for both shoulders to dislocate—gravity does all the work. But I found that holding them down and beating the bottoms of their feet was more efficient. They knew immediately that if they didn't give me what I wanted, they would never walk again."

"What about the prisoner Sharmaidze?" Jamie asked. "Did you interrogate him?"

"I don't remember," said the torturer. "Too many people, too long ago—and I never really spent much time trying to get to know them."

The next day Tamaz Inashvili joined us for a trip to the prison. Anzor had been moved twice since I filed the Woodruff petition and was now at a facility on the edge of Tbilisi. We arrived in mid-afternoon, but the guards wouldn't let us in.

"No cameras," they said.

Someone informed the warden of a disturbance at the front and he came to investigate. He was a massive human being: six feet, eight inches of intimidation. And he wasn't happy to see me.

Lali began arguing for our entry and the warden began coloring with rage. I pulled her back from the combustible conversation for a warning.

"Be more careful," I said.

Lali frowned. She seemed insulted.

"One person's already been assassinated and another person's been framed for murder," I said. "Killing you or me would be nothing to them."

She blanched. And sputtered a little. I think until that moment she'd actually forgotten the dangers inherent in our quixotic little project. But when she remembered, it frightened her.

"Then I quit," she said. "I don't want to get killed. I quit. It's not that important."

I left her to calm down and returned to the jailer. Tamaz had turned the conversation toward procedure, and the two men were discussing whether ministry approval was necessary before cameras could be admitted.

"We already have approval from a higher authority," I said. "The president went on national television and directed his government to cooperate with the American lawyer. And I am that American lawyer."

The giant's eyes widened. He remembered the speech and the president's commitment.

"If you'd like to call President Saakashvili to discuss it," I said, "I have his cell phone number."

"No," said the warden. "We don't need to bother the president." He turned and barked a few orders. The guards opened the steel door and rushed to pick up our equipment bags.

I held out my hand to Lali. She took it and we walked inside. By the time we got set up, it was dark. The guards escorted Anzor from his cell and parked him by one of the buildings in the courtyard. He stood facing a wall with his hands clasped behind his back. It was the pose that prisoners were required to assume in the presence of guards, and like all the rules it was enforced with swift and terrible violence.

Anzor was wearing a black turtleneck sweater, a black leather jacket, and dark slacks, clothes he had received from home. In a Georgian prison, only the guards wore uniforms.

Jamie placed him on a concrete step in front of a whitewashed background. The setting was austere, a perfect complement to Anzor's aggressive indifference. After more than a decade in prison, tourists like us were not even mildly interesting to him.

The truth was that we were wasting his time. Anzor didn't know anything about the assassination of Freddie Woodruff. He could once again deny his involvement in the murder, but he couldn't tell us what really happened that night on the Old Military Road.

Nevertheless, Jamie asked and Anzor answered.

He spoke softly and without affect, as though he were describing trivial things that had happened to someone else. He replied to each inquiry with monotone and apathy. There was no resistance in him, until Jamie asked him to describe the torture.

"What's the point?" he said.

"It's for the Western viewers," Jamie said. "They need to understand why you confessed to a crime that you didn't commit."

Anzor seemed to wilt. He focused his eyes on a spot near his feet and sighed. I had the sense that he was watching his young self be brutalized and feeling pity for that lost boy. The look on his face reminded me of Mary in the *Pietà*, except that the broken body Anzor held was his own.

His soft voice became a whisper. "They beat me," he said. "They tied my hands behind my back and hung me from a pipe. And beat me. They held me down and beat the bottoms of my feet with a stick. They hit me with guns and threw me into walls. They punched me and kicked me and stomped me. I wanted to die but they wouldn't let me."

He paused and looked up at Jamie. "Is it enough for your Western viewers?" he asked.

I felt indicted by the question, unmasked as a parasite that feeds on the pain of others. My adventure was his nightmare. And it made me want to vomit.

Afterward, I pulled Anzor aside and mumbled a few words of encouragement. He looked at me with sad dead eyes and grunted. "I just want to go home," he said.

Two days later Tamaz showed up at Lali's house with Gela Bedoidze and Genadi Berbitchashvili. I think Tamaz had been waiting to see how we treated Anzor at the prison. His arrival with the two key witnesses suggested that he was more or less satisfied.

Life had not been kind to Gela and Genadi. The two boys who'd been arrested with Anzor were hardly recognizable in these middle-aged men. Alcohol and indolence had ravaged their bodies and stolen their vigor. But it was the arrest on August 8, 1993, that had ruined their lives.

With the camera rolling they both confirmed their written statements: They were tortured; they lied; Anzor was innocent. He was never on the Old Military Road; he never shot at the Niva; he didn't kill Freddie Woodruff. The trio was in the wrong place at the wrong time because Anzor wanted to see his mother in Pansheti.

Gela and Genadi had finally told the truth. But neither man seemed to get any relief from the act of public confession. They were still terrified, still sweating, still trembling, still jumping at every sound. It took me a moment to realize what I was seeing: Their lies had never been the cause of their fear. Instead, they were afraid of the powerful people whose secret crimes they had witnessed. They were afraid of what would happen if the people who tortured and framed Anzor began to view them as a threat.

They had been desperately afraid of those people for more than a dozen years. And that fear had crippled them. Nevertheless, from my perspective that fear of retaliation was compelling evidence that this time Anzor's companions were telling the truth. In my experience, if a witness says something that puts them at risk of prison or death, the only reason they do it is because the statement is true. And that was exactly what Gela and Genadi had done: They had confessed to perjury and they had accused some very dangerous people of some very serious crimes. They were either telling the truth or they were crazy.

Their recantation demolished the last shred of evidence supporting the prosecutor's case. I could now prove that Anzor did not kill Freddie. And proving that fact was an essential step in getting the US government to stop using the Sharmaidze conviction as an excuse not to reexamine the Woodruff murder. So long as Anzor was in jail for the murder, they had a facially plausible reason not to reinvestigate.

Once I eliminated Anzor as an excuse, I might be able to get them to help me identify who killed Freddie and why they killed him.

I was sitting in Lali's parlor trying to think of clever ways to engage the local embassy in that effort when Georgia Woodruff Alexander proposed a somewhat more direct approach.

"Why don't I go talk to the ambassador?" she said. We made a call and got her an appointment. The next day Lali's nephew drove her to the US embassy—a gated compound dominated by a new thirty-thousand-square-foot building. We had decided that she would go alone in order to demonstrate that her commitment to the reinvestigation of Freddie's murder existed independent of my influence.

She met with Ambassador John Tefft and a political officer from the embassy staff. In an interesting coincidence, the second man had the same job title as Freddie when he pretended to work for the Department of State. Both the ambassador and the officer were gracious, courteous, and apparently befuddled. They claimed to know nothing at all about the Woodruff murder or the family's attempt to liberate Anzor. This seemed odd since it was Ambassador Tefft who had signed the letter endorsing the Sharmaidze conviction and declining the prosecutor general's request for FBI assistance in a reinvestigation.

"They didn't answer any of my questions," she told me. "I asked them if they were going to name the new building after him or put up a plaque or something. But they hadn't thought about any of that stuff. They'd just left Freddie behind."

The next day I went to the embassy. I had called ahead. I wanted to meet the political officer who'd sat in on the prior day's meeting. I assumed he was the local station chief and my best opportunity to talk directly to the CIA. I showed up on time and the receptionist put me in a hallway lobby to wait. I'd been sitting there thirty-five minutes when the political officer finally showed up. He seemed indignant.

"You can't just come here and expect to see the ambassador," he barked. He had a short beard and wore a blue blazer. He looked more like a junior professor than a diplomat.

"That's all right," I said. "You're the one I wanted to see."

We had our meeting right there in the lobby—another petty discourtesy intended to distract me. But I had a goal in mind and I wasn't going to be flustered by ego manipulations. I knew that the political officer would write a report summarizing our conversation and that his report would be circulated to people at the Agency who were interested in the murder of Freddie Woodruff. I wanted those people to know what I had discovered and how I had discovered it. And I wanted them to know that they could trust me. So I told him everything.

He listened attentively, asked a few relevant questions, and then rushed me out of the building. I left the embassy grounds thinking that it had been an unsuccessful meeting. It would be a few weeks before I found out how wrong I was.

By the time I got back to Lali's house, Jamie had already gone out for an interview. He and Magda had been working for some time to get Eldar Gogoladze. The former bodyguard was reluctant to speak since the last time he did so publicly it had cost him his job. But he was a vain little man and could not pass up the opportunity for self-promotion. Jamie did the interview accompanied only by a local cameraman. Gogoladze was suspicious of the technician and made an effort to intimidate him. "Who are you?" he said. "I know where you live."

The interrogation produced no material revelations on the case. Gogoladze still claimed that the boys were twenty meters behind the car when he heard the shot; still claimed that on the night of the murder he thought the bullet had come in the front passenger window; and still claimed that he didn't find the entry hole because the hot bullet had melted the gasket around the rear window. The only new detail to come out of the interview was Gogoladze's request that Jamie ghostwrite his autobiography. "I've had a very exciting life," he said. "And I know a lot of secrets."

The two men had bonded over their mutual antipathy toward me. Jamie didn't like me because I was a provincial who had criticized his drinking. Gogoladze didn't like me because I was an interloper who had interfered in his comfortable life.

And he was angry about it.

"It would be so easy for me to kill him," Gogoladze told Jamie. "He doesn't have any security, he doesn't exercise any caution, and I have a long gun that would be the perfect tool for the job. I've already given the matter quite a bit of thought."

I caught up with Jamie and the crew later that night at a pub. They were there with Dell Spry.

There was a hint of glee in Jamie's voice as he recounted his conversation with Gogoladze. He seemed particularly amused by Gogoladze's threat and how he had smiled as he pretended to aim the rifle. But the retired FBI special agent took it very seriously. "You're leaving tomorrow," he told me. "Eldar has means and motive. We aren't going to give him opportunity." Spry walked me out of the bar and led me through the shadows back to Lali's house. "Get your hands out of your pockets," he said. "When somebody says they want to kill you, it's because they want to kill you. You need to be ready to fight."

I left the next day. Jamie and crew continued working in Tbilisi for another week. They followed Spry as he retraced the FBI's post–Aldrich Ames investigation; they organized a poignant meeting between Georgia Woodruff Alexander and Anzor's mother; and they filmed a dramatic reenactment of the murder using one of the local community's best actors.

But it was all for naught. There'd been difficulties between Jamie and me. And shortly after returning to England, he abandoned the project. It was a dispiriting blow, but I knew I would have to press on again, by myself. I sat in my Houston office a few weeks later and did a harshly critical inventory of my meager accomplishments: I'd spent a small fortune in time and money trying to unravel a mystery and still didn't know the answer. I could prove Anzor's innocence but couldn't get him out of prison. I could disprove the official version of Freddie's murder but couldn't offer a persuasive alternative. I had received informal support from a few retired intelligence professionals but hadn't succeeded in getting any formal support from the US government. I was completely out of good ideas.

And then the postman delivered that day's mail. The package wouldn't fit in my box and so was waiting for me at security: a thick manila envelope with no return address and a smudged postmark. I tore it open without much thought of its contents. Inside were three inches of Xeroxed documents bound by a rubber band.

It was an English-language translation of the Georgian investigation file. I flipped through the first several pages without realizing what I was looking at. The reality of what it was and what it meant dawned on me very slowly. The political officer's report of our meeting at the American embassy in Tbilisi had reached someone who cared about Freddie's murder, and that someone had decided to help me.

And I never knew whom to thank. Some of the file was irrelevant—documents related to a drug dealer who had committed a series of violent carjackings on the Old Military Road; interviews with people who'd been victims of other crimes on the same day; Marina Kapanadze's personnel file from the Sheraton Metechi Palace.

But most of it was pure gold. There were copies of witness statements from Anzor and his two companions; from the policemen at the roadside post; from nurses and doctors at various hospitals; and from the family in the village of Arsha with whom the foursome had Sunday lunch. These materials were rich in details that contradicted much of the testimony given at Anzor's trial.

However, the documents that were of most immediate relevance to my investigation were recorded statements by people who'd actually seen and heard the murder of Freddie Woodruff—three passengers in the Niva and seven people at the Natakhtari Drain.

And Georgian investigators had interviewed them all.

CHAPTER 16

OFFICIAL INTERROGATIONS

Otar Djaparidze was a cruel man. Large, brutal, efficient, and clever. A competent and ruthless investigator for the Georgian prosecutor general. It was a fearful thing to fall into the hands of Deputy Chief Djaparidze. And it was into those meaty hands that Eldar Gogoladze had been delivered.

It was 4 a.m. on August 9—a mere seven hours after the murder—and Djaparidze sat across the table from the chief of Shevardnadze's personal protection force. Gogoladze was generally disliked by his peers and hated by his subordinates. They considered him a closed and arrogant man who seemed always to be engaged in some hidden game. Nevertheless, he had risen from obscurity to a position of responsibility with meteoric swiftness. Obviously Gogoladze had a powerful patron. And that alone made him dangerous.

In the cat-and-mouse game of interrogation, every interview starts with the undeniable: the core set of facts that both the interrogator and the witness accept as true. This interview was no different. It was undeniable that Gogoladze had taken a US diplomat on a day trip outside the city. It was undeniable that in so doing Gogoladze had violated ministry regulations requiring both prior authorization of such a trip and a chase car with bodyguards. It was undeniable that the US diplomat had been killed while on Gogoladze's unauthorized and inadequately staffed day trip. And it was undeniable that Gogoladze had a problem.

But Djaparidze also had a problem.

The intentional murder of a CIA station chief was a bold act. And to kill the American spy while he was with the chief of Shevardnadze's personal protection force was audacious. The act emphatically proclaimed the perpetrator's belief that the objectives were worth the risk of retaliation. At 4 a.m. on the morning after the killing those objectives appeared both obvious and unavoidable—disruption of Shevardnadze's "special relationship" with the US and isolation of the nascent Republic of Georgia.

The prosecutor general believed that a thorough and professional investigation of the murder would lead to a perpetrator who was both audaciously bold and in a position to benefit from these foreseeable consequences. And in the minds of nearly every Georgian there was only one entity that fit that description: Russia.

And therein lay the crux of Djaparidze's problem. The Shevardnadze regime might not survive if it accused powerful Russian forces of murdering the American spy. Any perpetrator who was strong enough to confront the CIA was certainly strong enough to destabilize the fragile Georgian government. On the other hand, Georgia might not survive if it rebuffed a US demand for justice. Western financial and military aid were all that kept the country afloat.

The strategy for how to investigate and avenge Woodruff's murder was an intensely political decision affecting Georgia's survival. And the State Council had not yet made that decision. As a result, in the hours immediately after the murder Djaparidze was not able to investigate in a manner that would definitively lead either toward or away from the real killer. He could not afford to create a record that was inconsistent with the government's ultimate political choice. In practical terms that meant he could not afford to pin down the specifics of Gogoladze's testimony.

It was undeniable. And both the interrogator and the witness knew it.

After being warned about the penalties for giving false evidence, Gogoladze testified that he had left the Sheraton Metechi Palace for Kazbegi at approximately 11 a.m. on August 8. He was driving his private white Niva—an inadvertent contradiction of a claim by the Ministry of Internal Affairs that Woodruff was killed while riding in an official government vehicle. There were three people in the car with him: Woodruff, Marina Kapanadze, identified as Woodruff's "girlfriend," and Elena Darchiashvili, whom Gogoladze quaintly identified as his "acquaintance."

According to Gogoladze the trip to Kazbegi had been made at Woodruff's request: He wanted to see the Darjal Valley. Gogoladze had called ahead to a distant relative who lived in the area and instructed him to prepare for a visit. However, Gogoladze was silent as to whether he had complied with ministry regulations requiring that he inform the local police commanders about his travel plans. Djaparidze did not press the point.

The two couples saw the sights of Darjal and then stopped at the village of Arsha for dinner with Gogoladze's relatives. "We didn't drink alcohol," said Gogoladze, an unnecessary detail that the autopsy would expose as a deception.

"We started on our way to Tbilisi from Arsha village at about six or seven p.m.," said Gogoladze. "I was driving the car. Elena sat next to me and Marina sat behind me. Fred sat in the back seat on the right. We made some stops on our way to see the sights. Fred had a camera with him and he took pictures."

"Did anyone have a gun?" asked Djaparidze.

"My passengers had no firearms," said Gogoladze. "I had an Austrian Glock nine millimeter pistol."

Djaparidze made a note, but he did not ask to see the gun. Neither the Glock 9 mm nor any of Gogoladze's other guns were ever inspected or tested.

"After we passed Natakhtari village but before we reached the old Nerekvavi police post, I saw several people dressed in military uniform," said Gogoladze. "One of them was armed with an automatic weapon. When I approached them—or even had already passed them—I heard a shot. After that, Marina Kapanadze started screaming."

Armed men in uniform near a police post. What Gogoladze had described could have easily been an official roadblock and his failure to stop a legitimate basis for deadly force. It was a possibility the interrogator needed to exclude.

"Did they signal you to stop for inspection?" Djaparidze asked.

"No, they didn't signal me to stop," said Gogoladze. "I drove on to the police post and told the people in militia uniforms what had happened—that I had a wounded man in the car and that the accident took place one hundred to two hundred meters from their post."

"Did they say whether they had heard the shot?" Djaparidze inquired.

"The militiamen said that they didn't hear any kind of shot," said Gogoladze. "Fred had a head injury, so I left the road police post and took him to the hospital in the town of Mtskheta—but they didn't have any electricity. So I took him to Hospital Number Two in Tbilisi. He was already dead when we got there."

"When was he killed?" asked Djaparidze.

"Between nine and nine-thirty," said Gogoladze.

"And who killed him?" asked Djaparidze.

Gogoladze paused before answering. "I don't know who fired the shot at us," he said.

It was a stunning admission. Only four hours before, Gogoladze had arrested three young men saying that "they killed the American." Now he claimed to know nothing of the shooter's identity. As I reread the interview I realized that this was not a factual inconsistency. It was more in the nature of an offer. Gogoladze would give vague testimony free of inconvenient facts if the government would overlook his derelictions of duty. He would help them place the blame wherever they wanted, provided they didn't place any blame on him.

Apparently, Gogoladze would rather be seen as a bungler and a coward than be punished for violating ministry protocol. Such moral flexibility could be useful to the investigation—and was completely consistent with Gogoladze's character—but Djaparidze needed to test the limits of how much shame the security chief was willing to heap on himself. To do so the deputy chief inquired about one of Gogoladze's more contemptible acts of incompetence.

"You mentioned that you had a gun," he said. "Did you shoot back at the killer?"

"No," said Gogoladze, "I didn't shoot in return—but after I left Fred's body at the Tbilisi hospital I called my colleagues and we went to the scene of the accident."

A quick change of subject, a suggestion of vigorous police action, a hint of professional embarrassment.

"We didn't find anybody there," he said. "But when we went to the old Nerekvavi police post, the militiamen had already detained four people—Genadi Berbitchashvili, Gela Bedoidze, Iosif Bedoidze, and Anzor Sharmaidze. One of them had a Romanian-made Kalashnikov automatic rifle. It had a bullet in the chamber."

Perhaps it was a mistake: a result of stress or hours without sleep. Or perhaps it was intentional: a response to the shaming. Either way, Gogoladze had for the first time identified a fourth person who was allegedly arrested at the old Nerekvavi police post—Iosif Bedoidze, father of Gela Bedoidze. It was a troubling detail, an inconvenient fact, and a subtle reminder of Gogoladze's ability to invent problems for the investigation. Djaparidze recorded the information but did not ask any follow-up questions.

The witness statement was ambiguous and cunning. It sketched an outline of facts but did not dictate the identity of the perpetrator. It allowed the government to choose exactly how much truth it could tolerate and exactly how much justice it could afford. It left every option open.

Gogoladze signed the statement a few minutes after 5 a.m. and left the deputy chief's office. Djaparidze's night was over. But he would be back at the station in a few hours to interview the two women from the Niva.

Elena Darchiashvili was already known to the police as a victim. Her husband had a violent temper and was jealous of his wife's beauty. He had responded to her many infidelities by scalding her with boiling water—twice. The couple had divorced in 1988. After the divorce Elena moved to her mother's house on Kekelidze Street. The life she led there attracted the attention of her more conservative neighbors. "She likes men very much," one neighbor told police detectives. "They often give her a ride at night."

Djaparidze interrogated Elena three times regarding the Sunday excursion to Kazbegi. The first interview began at 6 p.m. on August 9 with a standard series of questions: name, address, marital status, Communist Party membership. Elena was an ethnic Russian born and raised in Tbilisi. A non-Party woman, she had an advanced education and worked as an engineer at the Railroad Construction Institute. She claimed to be married and to live with her husband on Tchitaya Street, a transparent lie since her divorce from Guram was a matter of public record. The fabrication may have been an attempt to hide a misdemeanor violation of police regulations: She had failed to register her 1988 change of address to Kekelidze Street.

Elena had first met Gogoladze in 1986 when he worked as chief of the October District Police Station. The station occupied two floors of the house where Elena was living with her husband and daughter.

"After the October District Police Station moved from our house, I rarely saw Eldar," Elena told Djaparidze. "Sometimes we talked by phone—but very seldom."

It was another lie. According to the Georgian investigation file, it was well-known within the security services that Gogoladze had maintained a sexual relationship with Elena for seven years. In my experience, people lie in order to gain advantage or to avoid loss. And I wondered which of these was motivating Elena.

"When did you first know about the trip?" asked Djaparidze.

"Eldar called me at my mother's house the night before," she said. "He invited me to Kazbegi, where he was going with his foreign friend and the foreigner's girlfriend."

Gogoladze arrived in the Niva a few minutes after 9 a.m. on Sunday morning. He and Elena exchanged stories about their children as they drove to the Sheraton. "When we arrived at the hotel, I saw a tall man coming toward us," she said. "I asked Eldar whether I should sit in the back seat. He asked the foreigner in English then told me to remain in my place. The foreigner got in the car, gave me his hand and said, 'Freddie.'"

Woodruff gave directions as Gogoladze drove through the labyrinthian streets of Tbilisi to the home of Marina Kapanadze. They followed Nutsubidze Street up the hill and past the ropeway station. Like many things in Georgia, the aerial tram was dangerous and no longer worked. Three years before fifteen people had fallen to their deaths when the cable broke. It had not yet been repaired.

When they arrived at Marina's glum gray apartment block, Gogoladze asked whether Woodruff would go upstairs to fetch her. "Fred told us that Marina's mother didn't like him and he stayed in the car," said Elena.

In a few minutes a girl came out of the building. She was dressed in a short jean skirt and a red T-shirt. She was carrying a linen bag in her hands. "There was something in the bag," said Elena. "I thought it was a jacket."

The girl, who introduced herself as Marina Kapanadze, sat in the back seat behind Gogoladze. She and Woodruff spoke together in English. "I studied English at school," said Elena, "but I didn't understand much of the conversation."

The quartet left Tbilisi at about 10 a.m. They traveled north via the Old Military Road. It was the only way to or from Kazbegi.

The trip took about two hours. They stopped along the way to buy vegetables. "Around noon we arrived at a little village—I don't remember the name—and Eldar called on his friend Archel," said Elena. "Archel, who'd brought us some fish, got in the car and directed us to his sister's house—but we didn't stay. Eldar said he wanted to find a place where we could make a fire and have lunch."

They spent almost an hour driving bumpy mountain roads looking for an ideal picnic spot. Gogoladze made a stop near a *shashlik* shop, a homely little restaurant that served skewered meat grilled on a spit over an open fire. Woodruff, Gogoladze, and Marina went inside while Elena waited in the car.

I tried to visualize the picture she was painting: A meandering journey over deserted roads to an isolated location. An American spy traveling to the Russian border without official permission or bodyguards. A lawless frontier rife with smugglers and thieves. It was an excellent place for a private meeting. And an important private meeting was excellent bait for a trap.

"Was there anybody else in the shop?" asked Djaparidze.

"I don't know," said Elena. "There were two empty cars parked near the building. The passengers could have been inside the shop."

After fifteen minutes the trio came out and the drive continued. Finally—after more than an hour and a half—Gogoladze stopped. Instead of a bucolic vista, Gogoladze chose to picnic by a shack that sometimes served as a snack bar. The destination seemed hardly worth the effort.

The cookout was cut short by rain. The little group huddled by the snack bar until Archel invited them back to his house for dinner. "We stayed at Archel's house for about two hours," said Elena. "During dinner Fred told us that he had four children and that he liked Georgia very much. He said this was his third trip to Georgia and his second trip to the Darjal Valley."

"What did Woodruff tell you about the purpose of his visit?" asked Djaparidze.

"I don't know what he was doing in Georgia," said Elena. "I didn't even know he was an American diplomat until I saw it the next day on the television news. And as for the trip, as far as I could see there was no special purpose in our excursion."

Woodruff complained that he wasn't feeling well so Archel's wife, a pharmacist, gave him a dose of the Russian antibiotic Biseptol. After that, the foursome went to the car for the return trip to Tbilisi. "Woodruff slid into Marina's place behind Eldar," said Elena. "She told him to move—and he did—back to his place behind me."

They made two stops because of Woodruff's stomachache. "The first time Fred went for a walk with Eldar," she said. "The second time we stopped to drink some spring water at Narzan."

"And other than this?" asked Djaparidze. "Was anything unusual before the shooting?"

"No, nothing," she said. "Nobody stopped us, there were no cars on the road, and I didn't see anybody following us. Woodruff didn't talk much. He didn't feel well. And he seemed sad."

"Tell me about the shooting," said Djaparidze. "What did you see?"

"I'm a little nearsighted, so I can't be completely sure," said Elena. "And it was already dark as we approached the old roadside police post. But I saw an athletic figure who stood apart from a group of men. He raised his hand as if he wanted to stop the car, but Eldar didn't slow down. In two seconds we heard the sound of a shot. Eldar asked if anybody was hurt, there was a pause, and then Marina screamed. She said, 'Fred is killed!' "

Elena described the wound, the blood—and headlights shining through the hatchback window. "It was maybe thirty seconds after the shot," she said. "I saw two round lights very close to us—but I didn't see the car. And it never went by us.

"By then we had passed the police post. Eldar stopped the car near a light-colored Jiguli that was broken down on the side of the road. There were some guys in dark civilian clothes standing there," she said. "Eldar asked them if they'd heard a shot. They said they hadn't heard anything."

"Did anyone have a gun?" asked Djaparidze.

"None of the guys by the Jiguli had a gun," she said. "I think Eldar had a gun, but nobody else did."

Marina abandoned the back seat and crowded in next to Elena. Her clothes were bloodstained, her fingers sticky, her hair matted. Gogoladze was so unnerved he flooded the car. The young men from the Jiguli push started the Niva and watched it race off toward the nearby city of Mtskheta. Woodruff fell over sideways on the back seat.

"The first hospital we went to was closed. There was a guard at the front gate," Elena said. "He got in the back seat next to Fred and guided us to another hospital."

However, there was no electricity at the second hospital—or anywhere else in Mtskheta. "The medical staff came out carrying candles," she said. "They checked Fred's pulse and said he was still alive—but he'd have to be taken to Tbilisi because they didn't have a specialist who could treat him."

"What time was that—when they said Woodruff was still alive?" asked Djaparidze.

"It was nine-thirty p.m.," said Elena. "I remember the time distinctly because as we left the Mtskheta hospital Eldar asked Marina what time it was and she answered 'Half past nine.' "

On the way Gogoladze contacted the ministry offices by radio. It was his first attempt at such communication. He was trying to find out which hospital had electricity and if it could treat Woodruff's wounds. With their help he made his way to Tbilisi Hospital No. 2 on Kamo Street.

"The doctors from the Kamo Street Hospital came out and checked Fred's pulse," said Elena. "They couldn't feel it."

Woodruff was dead. The doctors loaded his body onto a stretcher and hurried it inside the hospital.

"While we were waiting, we all went out to examine the car," Elena volunteered. "There was no bullet hole anywhere on the car."

Elena was clearly an amateur—a woman with no experience in the intelligence business. And amateurs tended to be both talkative and unpredictable. But as an independent witness, her revelation about having inspected the Niva was important: If there was no bullet hole, how did someone outside the car shoot someone inside the car?

"One other thing," said Elena. "At the hospital Eldar asked me whether I'd noticed anything. 'Didn't I hear a shot in the car? Didn't I think Freddie might have shot himself?' The questions were strange to me. There was nothing like that at all."

Elena reported that after Eldar had delivered Woodruff's body to the hospital he ordered one of his employees to take her home. It was a puzzling professional decision. It created the risk that someone might intimidate or coach her before the authorities could memorialize her story.

I couldn't help wondering whether that was the point. Nevertheless, Elena had been informative and revealing. The same could not be said of Marina Kapanadze.

In 1993 the only Georgians who spoke fluent English were intellectuals, diplomats, or spies. Marina was fluent in English. But she was neither an intellectual nor a diplomat. She worked as a waitress in the Piano Bar at the Sheraton Metechi Palace.

The Sheraton was the hub of American presence in Georgia. The US embassy had set up its temporary offices on the fifth floor. The hotel restaurant was the only place in the country you could get a hamburger. And each evening the expatriate community—diplomats, journalists, soldiers, spies—would congregate on the tenth floor to drink away their loneliness and boredom. The Piano Bar was an excellent place to meet Americans.

In an authoritarian country, jobs in a Western hotel are typically awarded by the security services. Maids, bellmen, waitresses, drivers—they are rich sources of information about the activities and interests of foreign guests. Georgia was no exception. "The Ministry of State Security was responsible for selecting the employees at the Sheraton," Avtandil Ioseliani told me. "We did not select Marina Kapanadze. Nevertheless, she became a barmaid at the foreign currency hotel."

"We knew she was a spy," he said, "but she wasn't our spy."

Djaparidze's interrogation of Marina Kapanadze began on August 9 immediately after Elena's. I imagined the impression she must have made on the investigator: almond-shaped face, large intelligent eyes, plump lips, buxom breasts, and feminine hips. She was a voluptuous woman with obvious sexual charms. And she was perfectly comfortable in the silence. This was not a witness that the deputy chief was going to be able to bully or manipulate.

"How well did you know Woodruff?" he asked.

"I've known Fred a long time," said Marina. "This was his third visit to Georgia. And when he was here I saw him almost every day. He lived in the hotel and used to spend his evenings in the bar."

"Where did you meet?" asked Djaparidze.

"In the Piano Bar," she said. "I started working there in January, and I met him in February on his second visit to Georgia."

The rhythm of the interrogation was already apparent. It would be a cross-examination, not a conversation. Marina would answer each question concisely and then stop talking.

When dealing with such a witness, an interrogator must pay special attention to anything the witness volunteers. Unsolicited revelations are intentional and purposeful. They are an attempt to guide, mislead, manipulate, or confuse. Such informational nuggets are weapons in the hands of a professional.

Djaparidze continued. "What was the nature of your relationship with Woodruff?" he asked.

"He was very friendly with all the employees in the Piano Bar," she said. "We liked him very much. He was restrained, courteous, charming—and he had a good sense of humor."

"And you personally?" asked Djaparidze. "What did you and Woodruff talk about?"

"Sometimes he told me interesting stories about his travels. Sometimes he taught me new American expressions or told me about American customs. And sometimes I told him about Georgian culture. He liked our people and was interested in our everyday life. I remember him saying that he had never been so sad to leave a place and never so eager to return."

"And what about his work?" he asked. "What did you know about Woodruff's work?"

"I knew that he worked at the American embassy, that he was a diplomat," she answered.

Djaparidze waited in silence for Marina to elaborate—but she said nothing.

"When did Woodruff first invite you to Kazbegi?" asked Djaparidze.

"July fourth," she replied.

"A month ago?" said Djaparidze. "How is it that you remember the exact date?"

"It was at a party," she answered. "All the hotel employees were invited to the American embassy to celebrate their Independence Day. Fred was there and he asked me to accompany him to Gudauri and Kazbegi. He used to say that he liked those places very much and that when he retired he would buy a house there."

My mind spun with the implications. Woodruff had been planning his trip to Kazbegi for more than a month. It was a significantly different picture from the spontaneous unapproved and inadequately staffed outing described by Gogoladze. A month meant that Gogoladze had had more than enough time to obtain ministry permission and bodyguards. A month meant that Woodruff had had more than enough time to arrange a surreptitious meeting in the mountains. A month meant that someone else had had more than enough time to plan an assassination.

"Are you saying that on July fourth Woodruff invited you for an August eighth outing to Kazbegi?" asked Djaparidze.

"No, no—not for that specific date," said Marina. "I didn't know the date we were going until August sixth. He came in the Piano Bar on Friday night just as we opened. He said he wanted to go 'somewhere in the direction of Gudauri'—that he'd been there before, liked it, and wanted to go again."

"Did you go with Woodruff on his first trip to Kazbegi?" said Djaparidze.

"No," she answered. "I'd never been there before—and I was very curious to see how he was going to organize it."

"What do you mean?" asked Djaparidze.

"You know—the gas shortage, the bandits, the wars. Fred told me that Eldar Gogoladze was helping him. I'd known Eldar for about a year—knew that he was chief of Shevardnadze's security team—and figured that if we were with Eldar we'd be safe. I told Fred that I'd go if he promised to get me home on time."

I balked at her claim of only having known Eldar for a year. Obviously, she was trying to suggest theirs was a casual relationship, a passing acquaintance, a vague familiarity. But the security service documents had confirmed the existence of a long-term sexual liaison between the two.

Her characterization was clearly a misstatement—but was it diffidence or deceit?

"Who knew that you were going to Kazbegi?" asked Djaparidze.

"My manager in the Piano Bar—Marina Ivanova—she knew Fred had invited me out of town. I told her about the trip when I asked for the day off. Other than that, I didn't tell anybody."

"When did you leave for Kazbegi?" asked Djaparidze.

"Around nine-forty a.m.," said Marina. "They all came to my house—Fred, Eldar, and a woman I didn't know. I later learned that her name was Elena. They were in Eldar's white Niva."

"How did Woodruff know where you lived?" asked Djaparidze.

"Last Sunday—the first of August—Fred had invited me to a birthday party for one of his colleagues," said Marina. "After the party he took me home in one of the embassy's cars. I remember one time he told me 'I was in your neighborhood and wanted to visit you.' We laughed about it. I guess he just remembered my address."

The trip to the mountains was uneventful. Gogoladze drove; Elena sat in the front passenger's seat next to him; Marina sat behind Gogoladze on the left; and Woodruff sat beside Marina on the right.

"We stopped several times on the way," Marina said. "Once at a farmers' market to buy some vegetables, several times to look at the scenery, and once at the Narzan Spring to drink fresh water. Fred had a Canon camera and took lots of photographs. We wanted to picnic in the open air—but it started raining so we went to the home of Eldar's friend, Archel. We got there about four p.m. and Archel's wife made dinner for us. We didn't stay a long time because we wanted to get home on time."

"Did anyone drink alcohol at dinner?" asked Djaparidze.

"Oh, yes," she answered. "Archel acted as toastmaster and made sure that everyone drank wine. I had maybe a glass and a half. Fred drank three or four glasses. Everybody else drank about the same."

"Did Archel's wife give anything to Woodruff?" Djaparidze asked.

"Yes," said Marina. "Two things. Fred had a stomachache so she gave him some Biseptol tablets. And as we were leaving she gave him some country-style knitted socks."

"When did you leave?" asked Djaparidze.

"About six-thirty p.m.," answered Marina. "I remember looking at the clock because I wanted to know when we'd be getting into Tbilisi."

The return trip was punctuated by a few stops. "Fred was sightseeing, taking pictures," she said. "By the time we got out of the mountains it was dark. After we'd passed Natakhtari—but before we'd reached the old police post—I saw a group of four or five men in the headlights. Some of those men—maybe two or three—were standing together on the side of the road. I could see the silhouette of a car behind them, but I couldn't see well enough to make out the model. Another man—standing a little bit apart from the group—raised his hand as if he was signaling us to stop. Just then I saw that one of the other men had an automatic rifle and was aiming it at us. We drove past them so I couldn't see in the darkness—but I heard the sound of a shot."

"Can you describe the man with the rifle?" asked Djaparidze.

"I can't identify his face, but he was a little more than medium height and was wearing a striped *telnyashka*," she answered.

"Which kind?" asked Djaparidze. "Long-sleeve or tank top?"

Marina seemed to hesitate a moment before answering. "A sailor's tank top," she said. "You know, the kind that leaves your shoulders mostly bare."

Marina had described in detail a peculiar kind of muscle shirt that was typically worn only by enlisted men in the Soviet navy.

The alleged location of the murder was nowhere near the sea. Presumably there would not be very many sailors in and around Natakhtari wearing sleeveless *telnyashka*. It was a critical clue that could influence the direction and outcome of the entire investigation. And it seemed too good to be true.

In his file Djaparidze had a photograph of the three young men Gogoladze had arrested for allegedly killing the American. Genadi Berbitchashvili was wearing a long-sleeved T-shirt with thin horizontal stripes; Anzor Sharmaidze was wearing a short-sleeved black T-shirt; and the third young man—Gela Bedoidze—was wearing a sleeveless *telnyashka*. During his interrogation, Gogoladze had admitted that he did not know who killed Woodruff. Thus, when he arrested the three young men he had no reason to believe that any one of them was actually responsible for the murder. The young men had been randomly selected for arbitrary arrest. Nevertheless, Marina's testimony now implied that this accidental arrest had netted someone who was dressed in the same eccentric fashion as the murderer.

It was an extraordinary coincidence. And I have learned to be very suspicious of any extraordinary coincidence.

"What about the rifle?" Djaparidze asked. "Can you describe it?"

"No," she said. "I don't know what type of gun it was—but when I saw it I was afraid."

"Can you describe the other men?" asked Djaparidze. "What they looked like? What they were wearing?"

"No, I can't identify any of those other men," she answered. "I couldn't see their faces and I can't say what they were wearing."

It was just as I had expected. A single detail: easy to remember, easy to communicate, impossible to disprove. It was almost as though Marina had spoken to someone who was present when the three young men were arrested.

"When did you realize that Woodruff was wounded?" Djaparidze asked.

"When we first heard the shot, three of us screamed," she said, "but Fred was silent. Then he moved . . . clumsily. I thought he was teasing us to make us think he'd been shot. I turned and looked at him and saw that something was wrong. His head was bleeding. That's when I screamed and told Eldar to stop."

"Did you see a car following you at the moment you heard the shot?" asked Djaparidze.

"I'm not sure," answered Marina. "To tell you the truth, at that moment I couldn't have told you who was standing in front of me. But I remember looking back when I heard the shot. And I don't remember seeing any headlights."

"And did Gogoladze stop?" asked Djaparidze.

"Not immediately," said Marina. "It didn't seem possible that Fred could have been hit. We didn't hear the sound of broken glass or metal. But there was so much blood. Eldar finally stopped the car and Fred slumped over in the back seat. I was covered with blood. I just couldn't stay there. I got in the front seat with Elena."

"And what was Gogoladze doing?" Djaparidze asked. "Did he have a gun? Did he shoot back?"

"Eldar?" she said. "Eldar had a gun—but he didn't shoot. He was crying and saying things like 'Oh, my God! Fred! Oh, my God! What a tragedy!'"

"Did Woodruff have a gun?" Djaparidze asked.

"No, only Eldar," said Marina. "Nobody else had a gun."

"Was Woodruff dead?" asked Djaparidze.

"No, not dead," said Marina. "I could hear his breath whistling. Eldar was shouting, 'I heard him wheeze! Quickly! He is alive!' Suddenly I saw a group of people. Eldar stopped the car again and I jumped out. 'Help!' I shouted. 'Somebody shot our friend!' I was hysterical. I have no idea if they even replied."

"What time was it?" asked Djaparidze. "When Woodruff got shot, I mean—what time was it?"

"When we stopped by that group of people I looked at my watch," she answered. "I remember that the crystal was coated with Fred's blood. And that I rubbed it off so I could see. It was nine-fifteen p.m."

They raced on to the Mtskheta Hospital, but it had moved.

"Some fellow showed us the way to the new place," said Marina. "But there was no electricity. I ran inside to get help and saw the staff walking around with candles. They told us that they couldn't do anything for Fred, that we'd have to take him to Tbilisi."

The Niva sprinted off toward the city. "When we got to Tbilisi we could see lights on the embankment—which meant they had electricity. So we went to Hospital Number Two on Kamo Street. A doctor came out to examine Fred and told us he was dead."

Having already recorded Elena's testimony about inspecting the Niva for damage, Djaparidze raised the subject with Marina.

"Yes, we checked out the car after we arrived at the hospital," she said. "There wasn't any damage—no bullet hole, no broken glass, no damage. After a while men from the security services took me to the Railroad Ministry Building to make a statement. Then they took me home."

I finished reading the three interviews and sat at my desk mulling over what I'd learned. I made a list of the key facts and rearranged them like puzzle pieces.

Marina had identified as a potential suspect one of the young men arbitrarily arrested by Gogoladze. This testimony tended to redeem Gogoladze's sullied reputation and at the same time steer the investigation away from other lines of inquiry. In my mind, the alternative theories that Marina did not want explored all involved the purpose of the meandering trip to the Russian border. Both Gogoladze and Marina had omitted any reference to this part of the day's activities. Only Elena—the amateur—had spoken about it. And only Elena had been left in the car when the three professionals visited the *shashlik* shop. It was not a normal way for a group of holiday makers to behave—leaving their road-weary companion alone in the car while they went into a restaurant.

Maybe this encounter in the mountains had something to do with the murder, I thought. Maybe the other witnesses could tell me the truth of what really happened at Natakhtari.

CHAPTER 17

A REPORTER'S QUESTIONS

Georgian investigators took statements from seven people who were on the Old Military Road at or near the time Freddie Woodruff was murdered. But none of those people testified at the trial.

It was a calculated omission. If any of these seven had publicly recounted what they'd seen and heard, then the neatly constructed case against Anzor Sharmaidze would have collapsed.

Eteri Vardiashvili—the woman who was misidentified in the regional judge's order as "El. Vardiashvili"—had walked from her house in Natakhtari to the Drain sometime after 8 p.m. on August 8. Her husband (who worked as a security guard at the adjacent greenhouse) had driven the family cows up to the property that morning and she'd come to take them home.

"I always drive my cattle home before sunset," she told the investigator.

She collected the animals near the greenhouse and herded them past the guards' barracks and out through the gate. She (and the cows) turned left and made their way along the wall that screened the barracks from the highway. About thirty meters north of the gate—on the edge of the gravel apron that marked the turnoff to the Drain—she saw a white foreign car.

"It was parked under the big tree," she said in her witness statement, "with its front facing the highway."

There were four men standing by the car. They were wearing uniforms and appeared to be guardians. Eteri didn't stop to talk to the men. She'd overheard them threaten to slaughter her cows and was afraid to linger. She drove the cattle north along the roadside all the way back to Natakhtari. And, she told the investigators, at no time did she hear a gunshot.

These last statements were problematic for the prosecutor general. The witness was walking the same stretch of road where Gela Bedoidze (allegedly) ran out of gas and she didn't see him or his car. And she was walking there at the same time that Anzor Sharmaidze (allegedly) shot Freddie Woodruff and she didn't see or hear the murder.

It was little wonder that the government chose not to disclose this testimony to Anzor's defense team.

A second witness saw the same thing from a different perspective.

Merab Gelashvili was driving north on the Old Military Road at approximately 9 p.m. Just in front of the turnoff to the Natakhtari Drain, he saw a man sitting on a round object in the middle of the highway. The man was facing west—toward the gate leading to the Drain—and (as far as Merab could tell) the object on which he sat was an automobile tire. As he was passing the man, Merab saw a light-colored car parked on the west side of the road and the silhouettes of two or three men nearby it. He didn't see any weapons and he didn't hear the sound of a shot, but he did see one or two southbound cars stop suddenly at that location as he was driving away.

One of those southbound cars was driven by Ramin Khubulia, an assistant chief at the Ministry of Internal Affairs. He told investigators that he drove past the Natakhtari Drain at about 9 p.m. "It was starting to get dark but I was not yet using my headlights," he said.

Ramin saw four men in guardian uniforms and assumed they were colleagues from his ministry—so he stopped to bum a cigarette. "I asked one of the young men whether they were militiamen from the Ministry of Internal Affairs, but he denied it," Ramin said.

As he continued trying unsuccessfully to get a cigarette, another one of the guardians demanded that Ramin give them a spare inner tube or tire. The man's tone was disrespectful and his attitude was aggressive—not at all the way the assistant chief was used to being treated.

Ramin looked over at the guardians' car but couldn't see whether it did *in fact* have a flat tire. "It was white, it was foreign, and it didn't have any license plates," he said. "And it was parked in a very strange way: It was on the roadside but it was facing the road."

He didn't like the situation—the men's belligerence, the car parked for a quick getaway—so he got back in his automobile and drove home. It wasn't until the next day that he learned there'd been a shooting in the area.

I paused to think.

The whole scene seemed oddly familiar: a car broken down on the side of the Old Military Road; a single guardian trying to flag down drivers; a few other young men in uniform clustered around a disabled vehicle. And then it struck me—it was exactly the setting that Gela, Genadi, and Anzor had described when they testified in court.

The lie they'd been forced to tell had apparently contained elements of truth.

I looked back at the time line. The interviews of witnesses from the Old Military Road were conducted in the days and hours immediately before Gela, Genadi, and Anzor gave their official statements. Those official statements seemed to borrow heavily from the reality described by the witnesses from the Old Military Road. However, nowhere in their official statements did Gela, Genadi, or Anzor mention the four guardians who were, according to the witnesses from the Old Military Road, less than one hundred meters away from the spot where Anzor allegedly shot Freddie Woodruff.

It was a conspicuous omission. Why, I wondered, did the Georgian authorities want to erase the presence of those four guardians from the official story of the murder? And—assuming they did want to erase their presence—why did the Georgians give the Americans un-redacted witness statements that so explicitly cast suspicion on the guardians?

Another one of the locals who saw the guardians was Badri Chkutiasvili. He had a farm across the highway from the Natakhtari Drain and was staying there overnight to guard his vegetables. Around 9 p.m. he and one of his laborers (a man named Vasiko from the village of Pasanauri) went up to the guard shack at the Drain to watch TV. As he crossed the Old Military Road, Badri saw a light-colored foreign car parked near the wall separating the road from the guard barracks.

"Both doors on the right side of the car were damaged," he said. "And the car wasn't parked parallel to the road—its front was facing the road and its rear part was on the grass."

He also saw four young men near the car. They appeared to be changing a flat tire. One of the young men was wearing a long-sleeved blue-and-white-striped *telnyashka*—the kind of T-shirt worn by Soviet seamen and (on the night of his arrest) Genadi Berbitchashvili. However, Badri specifically recalled that (unlike Genadi) this young man had no beard. There was a second man—slightly taller than the first—dressed in a guardian jacket and civilian pants. There were two other men but Badri couldn't make out any details.

"I couldn't see them because it was already dark," he said.

As soon as they got behind the wall, Badri and Vasiko saw that there were no lights on in the guard shack. They assumed that the electricity had gone off and so stopped to smoke a cigarette.

"We were hidden behind the wall," Badri told the investigator. "We couldn't see the four guardians and they couldn't see us. But we could hear how they stopped cars and asked for gas and an inner tube. After a little while we heard a loud noise—a kind of crackle—that sounded like a gunshot. But we didn't pay much attention to it: These days we hear gunfire on the highway all the time. But less than a minute later we heard a woman scream. 'My

God, they killed a man!' she said. The scream was coming from the same spot where the four guardians were standing—just beside the foreign car—and we thought the guardians had killed a man."

Badri and Vasiko were frozen in terror—but they could hear everything clearly. One voice said that the wounded man should be taken to the hospital; another voice answered that he could not start his car; a chorus replied that they would help push. The two frightened farmers took this as a sign that it was safe to come out of hiding.

"There were two guardians pushing the car," said Badri. "But I didn't see the other two guardians. The car was a light-colored Niva. One man and two women were sitting in the front seats and another man was laying down in the back seat by himself. One of the guardians reached in and lifted up the man's head. 'Take him to the hospital,' he said. 'He may yet live.' Vasiko and I helped push the Niva and—after five or six meters—the car started and the driver went off in the direction of Tbilisi."

In the conversation that followed, the guardians denied that they'd stopped the car, denied that they'd heard a shot, and denied that they'd seen a bullet hole in the glass or metal. One of them—the man wearing the blue-and-white-striped *telnyashka*—washed blood off his hands in a puddle and self-consciously declared that none of the guardians had a gun. "We should thank God that we're unarmed," he said. "Otherwise, we'd be accused of a crime we didn't commit."

A couple of guards from the Drain showed up and asked who was responsible for the gunshot.

"The guardians answered that it wasn't a gunshot at all," Badri said. "That when they were pumping air into the tire, the valve had come out and made a big noise."

About five minutes later—their car somehow suddenly fixed—the guardians drove off in the direction of Tbilisi. Badri recalled that they had explained the timing of the repair by claiming that one of the cars they'd just stopped had given them gas and an inner tube.

I tried to imagine the scene.

Badri swore that while he was standing behind the wall he heard the guardians stop cars on the highway and ask drivers for an inner tube. Even if one of those drivers had given the guardians an inner tube in the minutes before the shooting, they would still have had to install it and inflate it by hand—exactly what they said they were doing when the valve allegedly exploded "like a gunshot." Assuming that the valve did in fact explode, then the guardians would have had to repair the valve, reinstall the inner tube, and reinflate the tire. All of this activity would have taken time and attention. But the light-colored Niva (and the mortally wounded American diplomat) arrived less than a minute after the alleged valve explosion.

The minutes between the arrival of the Niva and the departure of the guardians were simply not enough time to make the necessary repair—particularly in light of the fact that two of the guardians were busy push-starting the Niva and the other two guardians were nowhere to be seen.

The more I thought about it, the more I suspected that the guardians had been waiting for the Niva and were only pretending to have a flat. Badri hinted that he suspected the same thing too.

"The next day my father told me that the foreign car had been parked in that place since noon," he said.

The guardians were parked two thousand meters from Natakhtari and five hundred meters from the Nerekvavi police post. But they hadn't gone to either place for help. Instead, they sat in the August sun for nine hours and left immediately after the murder.

It seemed too coincidental to be a coincidence.

Two days later Badri was reinterviewed by an assistant prosecutor general and added a few curious details to his story. He now claimed that—prior to the Niva stopping and the woman shouting about murder—he had been in a position to see the guardians clearly. He had watched as they stopped several different cars, and he recounted for the investigators the models of automobiles involved.

"They stopped a 2109 car," he said. "Afterwards, they told us that they asked the 2109 driver for a tube and he gave it to them."

The VAZ-2109 is a four-door hatchback commonly referred to as the Lady Samara. It was the kind of car that Ramin Khubulia was driving that night. According to Ramin, he stopped to ask for cigarettes about the same time that Badri was lurking by the wall. According to Badri, he only saw one 2109 car stop for the guardians. So presumably the 2109 car that Badri saw was Ramin's.

But Ramin said that he didn't give anything to the guardians. And that meant the guardians were lying about the inner tube.

Finally, Badri identified the guards who had walked down from the water tower to ask about the gunshot. The first was Giorgi Tserekashvili. The second was his brother, Tamaz Tserekashvili.

It made me smile to realize how I'd stumbled onto the truth: There were two male witnesses named Tserekashvili and (contrary to the indignant claims of the regional judge) I had not attempted to pass off *Tamaz* Tserekashvili as *Giorgi* Tserekashvili. Rather, I had (without really realizing the implications) found new evidence—or at least evidence that was new to the defense.

And it must have set off alarm bells at the Prosecutor General's Office. Because Tamaz Tserekashvili had told the investigators that one of the women in the Niva had accused the guardians of murdering Freddie Woodruff.

"The screaming lady was telling the two guardians who pushed the Niva that their friends had killed the man," Tamaz Tserekashvili said. "She meant that those who shot at them were also dressed in guardian uniforms."

Men wearing guardian uniforms had killed Freddie Woodruff. And the hysterical woman in the Niva had seen them do it. Perhaps it was the other two guardians that were nowhere to be seen. Or perhaps there were even more uniformed men standing on the side of the Old Military Road between Natakhtari and the Drain.

Based on the description, I assumed that the screaming woman was Elena Darchiashvili. She was the amateur among the intelligence professionals in the car. She was the one most likely to panic. And there had not yet been time or opportunity for Eldar and Marina to frighten her into absolute silence.

What she said was, I believe, exactly what she saw—and exactly why she was so terribly afraid to ever talk to me.

Just about that moment, another witness, Lali Tserekashvili, passed by the Drain on her way to Tbilisi. She'd hitched a ride with a stranger and was sitting alone in the back seat of his Moskvitch sedan.

"There were three or four men dressed in guardian pants and striped shirts," she said. "They had automatic guns in their hands and were arguing with a man standing near a Niva. There was another man standing two or three meters away from the guardians. He was below average height and dressed in a white shirt and a tie. He had sunglasses on. And he wasn't talking to anybody."

Most of what she reported was consistent with the other witness statements. But the information about a short man in a white shirt and tie was entirely new. No one else had mentioned a man in civilian clothes wearing sunglasses at night.

Who was he? I wondered. And why was he there? Was this the man from Mongoose who later claimed credit for the murder of the CIA officer in Georgia? Was this Vladimir Rachman, the man arrested at the train station and freed as a result of pressure from the Russian Ministry of Defense?

I'd gotten to the end of the witness statements and was still only at the beginning of the mystery. The Georgian investigators had done an outstanding job of identifying, locating, and interviewing a disparate group of people who'd been at the Drain at or near the time of Freddie's murder. But there was a glaring omission. There was no record of any attempt to interview the guardians or the short man in the white shirt and tie.

Having studied their work, I couldn't believe that the Georgian investigators had simply failed to do their duty. They had demonstrated themselves to be first-class professionals. And if they didn't interview the guardians, it wasn't because they hadn't thought of it. It was because someone kept them from doing it.

And then I remembered my conversation with Dell Spry. If the man in the white shirt and tie was Rachman, then it was the Russian Ministry of Defense that had prevented the Georgian investigators from interviewing him. And if the Russians had prevented the interview of Rachman, then perhaps they had done the same thing for the guardians.

Perhaps. But only perhaps.

I was becoming overwhelmed by the data. I had a huge box of jigsaw puzzle pieces and no idea how to differentiate the real from the fake, the relevant from the irrelevant, the true from the false. What I needed was a guide—someone with expertise in solving unsolvable puzzles, someone who could give me a paradigm for judging the reliability and placement of each individual piece.

What I needed was Bob Baer.

Fortunately, the peripatetic ex-spy was in America at the time. We met for dinner in Oakland, California: me, Bob, his wife Dayna, and Adam Ciralsky. During his earlier life as a CIA lawyer, Adam had represented Bob and the two had become friends.

When I arrived at the restaurant they were already deep in conversation about NATO's allegedly erroneous bombing of the Chinese embassy in Belgrade. In 1999, eight years before our dinner, B-2 bombers from Whitman Air Force Base in Missouri had dropped five JDAM GPS-guided precision bombs on geographic coordinates provided to NATO by the CIA. Secretary of Defense William Cohen claimed that the targeting was an error—that "our planes attacked the wrong target because the bombing instructions were based on an outdated map."

But my dinner companions disagreed. "That was no mistake," said Bob. "The Serbs had recovered the wreckage of a downed F-117 and sold it to the Chinese. Our plane was in the basement of their embassy and we destroyed it."

Such is table talk among spies. I was seated across from Dayna, a willowy beauty who seemed far too delicate for her rough-

and-tumble husband. I was surprised to learn that she had also worked at the CIA—but as a social worker. It was for me an unthinkable thought.

"The Agency hires social workers?" I asked.

"Sure," she said. "They would point at someone and say, 'Tell us what's wrong with them. We don't want you to fix them, we just want to know what's wrong.' And after doing that for a while, I went into covert ops—technical surveillance and security. I was the girl with the machine gun on the back of a motorcycle. That's how I met Bob."

She smiled broadly. Her expression was warm, disarming, and ever so slightly mischievous. This was an exceedingly smart woman and she was clearly enjoying the fact that she'd shocked me.

Her husband rescued me from the embarrassment of speechlessness by asking about my investigation.

"So how much will you tell me?" he asked.

It was an incisive question. When I first began this project, I struggled with the issue of how much to reveal to people who asked me about it. There was a strong temptation to be secretive—to hide my agenda and obscure my strategy. After all, discretion regarding such things is obligatory for trial lawyers and de rigueur for spies. But this was not litigation and the SVR was not bound by the rules of court. So I'd chosen a completely different tack.

"Whenever somebody asks me something about my investigation," I said, "I tell them everything I know about the topic. I never know the true identity of the person to whom I'm talking, so I never try to hide anything from anybody. I don't talk in code and I don't use encrypted e-mail. It may be silly, but I don't try to keep anything secret."

A chuckle rumbled out of Bob's barrel chest. "That's not silly," he said. "That's why you're still alive."

I felt a surge of panic but pushed it aside. For now, I had the attention of an expert and I didn't intend to waste it. So I started at the beginning and told him everything. He listened without interrupting until I got to Vladimir Rachman.

"The police stopped him at the train depot and did a random search," I said. "They arrested him for possession of military paraphernalia—a silencer and two cans of tear gas."

"That's bullshit," he said.

"No, no—" I stuttered. "That's what Dell Spry told me."

"I don't care," he said. "It's bullshit. That's not how things happen. No Georgian policeman is ever going to stop a Russian unless somebody tells him to."

I was suddenly very confused. Bob seemed to be saying that Rachman hadn't been arrested at the train depot. But if that was true, then FBI special agent Dell Spry was an unreliable source of information, and that seemed impossible.

I was working as fast as I could to unpack the riddle. And then it hit me: It wasn't the objective facts Bob was rejecting, it was the subjective explanation of the facts. Bob didn't deny that Rachman had been arrested; he denied that Rachman had been arrested *as the result of a random search*.

He could see that I'd figured it out and he smiled—an odd kind of smile a man might make if he'd never seen one in person but read about them in a book. Nevertheless, I felt the warm sensation of approval. I was just beginning to enjoy it when I remembered: I was dealing with a master manipulator and I needed to be very careful.

My eyes must have betrayed the thought because the smile disappeared and the big man grunted. "Find the guy who ordered Rachman's arrest," he said. "He's the link between what you know and what you don't know."

It was a daunting task and I had no idea how to accomplish it. But Bob had exploded the logjam of my thoughts by asking a common sense question: How do things really work in that environment? And at least with respect to Rachman that was a question I could answer.

Both Rachman and I were strangers in the strange republic of Georgia. We didn't speak the language, we couldn't read the signs, and we didn't know our way around. We both depended completely on local Georgians to feed us, house us, drive us, and generally help us do the jobs we were hired to do. Without that local assistance, we were both helpless.

This somewhat pedestrian insight allowed me to formulate an achievable goal: to identify the people who had provided Rachman's logistical support. And if I could find those people, then presumably they could tell me who had him arrested.

One of the ancillary effects of this insight was that it gave meaning to a previously enigmatic section of the FBI letterhead memorandum. That section—entitled "Spetsnaz Group Alpha"— discussed the deep bonds of loyalty that exist among current and former members of this elite special operations force. "They have been trained to lean on each other for support and trust each other for discretion," the memo said. "It is not unthinkable that a former Group Alpha member would have the assistance and support of a current Group Alpha member."

Most of the remaining text had been blacked out by the censors. But the section concluded with what now appeared to be an obvious reference to Rachman's arrest. "███████ was ██████ days after the shooting death of Fred Woodruff."

The message was clear: The FBI believed that then-current members of Georgian Group Alpha had provided logistical support to Rachman in connection with his assassination of Freddie Woodruff.

So, in hopes of finding the man who'd ordered Rachman's arrest, I went looking for some of the most lethal special operators in the world. But I wasn't entirely sure I wanted to find them. My first step was to turn to Mousia Semenova, a woman with an uncanny knack for finding people inside the former Soviet Union. She listened patiently as I described what I needed and then changed the subject.

"I know a Russian journalist living in Paris," she said. "She's smart, experienced, and well connected. I think that if you tell her your story, it will lead to something interesting."

I had learned not to resist such detours. And so I made contact and booked a flight.

Natasha Gevorkian was a sultry and voluptuous bohemian. The daughter of a KGB officer, she'd been born in Armenia and raised in Georgia. She was a celebrity among Russian journalists and had been chosen to coauthor the first and only authorized biography of Vladimir Putin. We met over coffee and traded stories. Hers were better.

"In 1997, Saint Petersburg mayor Anatoly Sobchak was accused of corruption," she said. "Putin—who was deputy mayor of the city—publicly refused to denounce him. It was a very unusual display of loyalty and it caught Yeltsin's attention. You see, Yeltsin had a problem: When you're riding the tiger, it's impossible to get off. So Yeltsin summoned Putin to Moscow for an interview. 'If I make you president of the Russian Federation, will you be loyal to me in the same way?' he asked. 'I don't want to be president,' whined Putin. 'I want to be an oligarch.' Yeltsin laughed at him. 'You won't be *an* oligarch,' he said. 'You will be *the* oligarch.' "

Natasha's dark eyes twinkled. She took a deep drag on her cigarette as an excuse to make me wait for the punch line. "They struck a bargain," she said. "Yeltsin promised to make Putin president and Putin promised to never investigate Yeltsin or his family for corruption. And—as the whole world knows—Putin is president and Yeltsin died rich."

It was a marvelous tale and she told it well. But the conversation was about more than captivating anecdotes. I was being vetted. She was trying to decide if she could trust me. And for Natasha, trust was a matter of life and death.

"I am close to the oligarchs who oppose Putin," she said. "And that has made me an enemy of the state. I was there when Alexander Litvinenko was dying of polonium poisoning—and I don't want to die that way."

We talked for several hours before apparently I passed the test. Coffee had become dinner had become coffee again. She pushed the cup away and lit another cigarette. "I have a meeting tomorrow with Irakli Okruashvili," she said. "I think you should come."

Okruashvili was the first prosecutor general with whom I'd met, the one who had turned down the Woodruff family's initial request to reopen Anzor's case. Since that day in 2004 he'd fallen out of favor with Saakashvili and been prosecuted for extortion, money laundering, and abuse of power. He'd come to France seeking political asylum. Natasha was right. Okruashvili was someone to whom I was eager to speak.

We met at Café de Flore on the boulevard Saint-Germain. It was one of those in-between days that come at the end of winter. We crowded around a small outdoor table until a cold drizzle drove us inside. Okruashvili was a study in understated elegance: black cashmere blazer, black collared sweater, gray herringbone slacks, black Italian loafers. He didn't look like any political refugee I'd ever seen. He and Natasha greeted one another in Georgian and then switched to English for my benefit. He knew who I was but didn't remember meeting me twice before. Nevertheless, he seemed content to speak freely.

"Next month the Georgian court is going to sentence me in absentia to fifteen years in prison," he said, seeming curiously unfazed by the prospect. "My application for asylum is scheduled for hearing in Paris the month following—but I don't expect to get it. It would be a bad precedent: a determination by France that Georgia engages in political repression."

I turned the conversation toward the murder of Freddie Woodruff and the continued incarceration of Anzor Sharmaidze.

"I don't have any direct knowledge about the Woodruff murder," he said. "But logic dictates that it was the Russians. After all, no one else had an interest in doing it. As for Sharmaidze, I attended a cabinet meeting in which we decided to release him. It was just before Bush's visit and *60 Minutes* was going to do a story—we didn't want bad publicity in the West. Did they not let him go?"

It had been four-and-a-half years since my first visit to Georgia and I was still surprised at how casually the local elite treated the total destruction of innocent lives.

"No," I said. "They did not let him go."

"Must have been Misha," he said. "He's disconnected and unrealistic, not at all aware of the real situation in Georgia. All he cares about is retaining his power, increasing his wealth, and fighting with Putin."

Okruashvili put down his café crème and looked at me as though for the first time. I had the feeling that something important had occurred to him and he was wondering whether to waste it on me. After a few seconds of silence he spoke. "Misha is going to go to war in Abkhazia and South Ossetia," he said. "It's already been decided: He will try to retake the provinces before George Bush leaves office."

It was March 2008 and the election was eight months away. Okruashvili was predicting war before November. He must have sensed my ambivalence because he immediately began trying to prove himself as a knowledgeable and trustworthy insider.

"I was in Misha's inner circle," he said. "I was with him at least four hours every day since the beginning. I know his secrets." He began naming the sources of Misha's wealth and the identities of his contract assassins. He identified Misha's principal allies in Washington and his primary CIA advisors in Tbilisi. He described defects in the official story of Zhvania's death and offered to help find a witness who could unravel the mystery of Woodruff's murder.

"Shota Kviraya will have all the details," he said. "He lives in Moscow now and spends all his time drinking—but I can put you in touch with someone who knows his location."

For some reason Okruashvili really wanted me to believe his forecast of imminent war. It didn't take me long to figure out why. It was the old bugaboo: He thought I was a CIA officer and he was hoping that his early warning would ingratiate him with the US government. I couldn't promise a reward from the Americans, but I could tell anyone who'd listen that war was coming to the Caucasus. And I did so later. But I'm not sure anyone heard me.

Just before he left the café, Okruashvili returned to the topic of Misha's upcoming military adventure. "He's going to need US support," he said. "And he's going to be very sensitive about how he and Georgia are portrayed in the Western press."

I appreciated his saying this, but the topic was already in my mind. This was the crisis that would allow me to leverage American opinion and force the Georgian government to release Anzor.

But I would need to be ready. I flew home to Houston and hired a technologically adept student to scan my entire file to a flash drive and run it through an optical character recognition program. From that day forward, everywhere I went I carried a dozen years of evidence on a lanyard around my neck.

I had it with me six months later when the Georgian army began an artillery barrage on the South Ossetian city of Tskhinvali. It felt odd and a little terrifying to watch an armed conflict unfold and know the backstory behind the bloodshed. But the thing that really confounded me was the timing. The Russo-Georgian War started on August 8, 2008—exactly fifteen years to the day since the murder of Freddie Woodruff.

Russia accused Saakashvili of "aggression against South Ossetia" and launched a large-scale land, air, and sea invasion. Tanks poured through the Roki Tunnel, and ground troops opened a second front in Abkhazia. It was the first time since the fall of the Soviet Union that the Russian military was used against an independent state.

And the mismatch soon became a rout. On August 12—four days after the war began—Russian president Dmitry Medvedev proclaimed a unilateral cessation of his "peace enforcement" operation. At the time of this announcement there was no credible military force standing between the Russian army and Tbilisi. Misha had made a massive miscalculation and Georgian independence now hung by a single thread. Without vigorous American support the little country would be reabsorbed into the Russian empire.

I watched these events unfold with a growing sense of regret. This was the crisis I had hoped to leverage—the moment when Georgia's need for positive Western publicity could be exploited to secure Anzor's release. But I was missing the moment because I didn't have an ongoing partnership with a Western journalist.

But that was all about to change. On August 19 I received an e-mail from a man named Andrew Higgins. He identified himself as a correspondent for the *Wall Street Journal* and said that he wanted to talk with me about the murder of Freddie Woodruff.

"I've kept an eye on this case—from a distance—ever since '93, when I happened to be in Tbilisi at the time of the killing," he said. "I've always thought the official version of what happened was, to put it mildly, somewhat fishy."

I called him immediately. The idea for Higgins to contact me had originated with Thomas Goltz. The two veteran reporters were lamenting the frustrating reality of their chosen profession: A journalist has a front-row view of history but is very seldom allowed to intervene in a way that makes someone's life better. But then Goltz remembered me. "There is a story you can tell," he said to Higgins, "a good story. And telling it will save someone's life."

Higgins was leaving for Tbilisi in a week and wanted a quick rundown of my fifteen-year obsession. I tried to condense it but was defeated by the task. And so I leapt into the darkness.

"Let me go to Georgia with you," I said.

Three days later I was standing in the Paris bureau of the *Wall Street Journal* handing a virtual stranger an electronic copy of my entire file. This was my last best chance. And I held nothing back.

I'm not sure what Higgins had expected, but he seemed surprised by what he read. "You've got a lot more here than just theories," he said.

I gave him contact information for Georgia Woodruff Alexander, Dell Spry, and Irakli Okruashvili. He spoke with each of them in turn and quickly concluded that the official story of Freddie's murder had "more holes than Swiss cheese."

By the time we boarded the red-eye to Tbilisi, I had an ally. We flew together with Cindy McCain and her Secret Service detail. I later realized that the wife of Senator John McCain was only one in a series of American dignitaries who cycled through

Tbilisi during the crisis. Together these government VIPs provided a kind of human shield protecting the city from the insult of Russian invasion.

We got to the Marriott Hotel on Rustaveli Avenue at about 4 a.m. It was the new standard of luxury built after the Rose Revolution. And even in the wee hours of the morning it was a beehive of activity. The Georgian government had installed a big map in the hotel lobby. It showed troop deployments and was staffed twenty-four hours a day by representatives from the Ministry of Foreign Affairs. They were there to persuade the international press corps that Georgia was an innocent victim of Russian aggression.

But Higgins never stopped to talk to them. "They aren't news," he said. His investigation of the story was methodical, disciplined, and smart. He read everything, talked to everyone, and believed only what he could prove. He had an eye for irony and a nose for bullshit. And he really wanted to know why I'd done all this.

"I don't know," I said. "Seemed like the right thing to do at the time."

We went over and over the same material—each time from a slightly different perspective. He would press me on key points, asking for documentary proof, third-party witnesses, and independent verification. Soon the tone of his questions began to shift: less confrontational, more collegial. He'd begun to expect that I would have evidence for my assertions—and to believe that I would tell him the truth.

But he still wouldn't let me go with him on the interviews. He'd go off to Shevardnadze's compound or Bedoidze's hillside shack and I would sit in the hotel and brood. I was an advocate and I wanted to advocate.

"Trust the process," I told myself. But it wasn't easy. I had invested an enormous amount of time and treasure in an untested theory: that well-timed use of the Western news media could induce the Georgian government to give Anzor justice. I had, in effect, appealed my case to the American public. And I was hoping that the power of the press to generate negative public opinion in America would be sufficient to cause Misha Saakashvili to do the right thing in Georgia.

As far as I could tell, the timing was perfect. The Georgian government was frantically trying to cultivate and manipulate Western public opinion. Misha had lost the military war. He was scrambling not to lose the propaganda war.

I spent an inordinate amount of time trying to get Irakli Batiashvili to talk with Higgins. The former minister had been pardoned after serving only six months in prison—but he had apparently been permanently scarred by the experience of incarceration. The layers of security that now surrounded him prevented my direct contact.

And then I got a telephone call from his fifteen-year-old daughter, Irina. Could I meet her mother, Maya Batiashvili, for coffee in thirty minutes? The circumstances of the invitation seemed designed to make me hurry. I rushed out of the hotel and jogged down the sidewalk. Before long I was sweating. It was hot and noisy in the city. I was out of breath when I arrived at the coffee shop. Irina and Maya were waiting for me inside. They sat facing the door with their backs against the wall. And they looked nervous.

The girl started talking as soon as I sat down. "Mother doesn't speak English," she said. "She's here to tell you what Father says. And I'm here to translate."

Maya rattled off the message in Georgian and Irina nodded.

"Father says he can tell you what you want to know about the murder of Freddie Woodruff," she said. "But if you want him to tell you who killed the CIA man and why they killed him, then you must give him certain assurances first."

"Certain assurances," echoed Maya in English. It was obvious that she didn't understand the words and equally obvious that she recognized this was the exact sound that her husband had told them to make. "Father said you would know what that means," she said. "Certain assurances."

I felt a sudden surge of adrenaline. My vision became sharper, my hearing more keen. Time slowed down and my reflexes sped up. I was terrified. Notwithstanding all of my denials, Irakli Batiashvili still believed that I was an agent of the US government. And—based on this belief—he was offering to give me everything I wanted in exchange for a promise of US support and protection.

I could buy it all with a lie.

I took a deep breath before I answered. I was certain that if Irakli misunderstood me in even the smallest detail, then some-one—perhaps even me—might die. "I am just a lawyer," I said. "I do not have authority to give you any assurances on behalf of the US government. If you need those assurances before you can tell me what happened to Freddie, then you absolutely must not tell me what happened to him."

Maya listened as her daughter translated and hope slowly melted off of her face. She left the café without ever having a cup of coffee. Irakli never told me his secret. Nevertheless, I learned a lot from his offer.

The former minister was one of those people who'd asked me about my investigation and with whom I'd openly shared my evidence. Thus, implicit in his offer to tell me the truth about Freddie's murder was an informed judgment that I did not yet know the whole truth. And since he thought that I worked for the US government, he was also implying that the Americans didn't know the whole truth either. But there was also an implied representation in his offer: that Georgian investigators had dis-covered the identity and motive of the killer. The information his offer provided was tantalizing and encouraging. And it gave me confidence that it was really possible to solve this puzzle.

American diplomats continued to rotate through Tbilisi, and Higgins continued to interview witnesses. He landed an audience with Saakashvili two days before Vice President Dick Cheney came to town. "Misha was eager to talk about anything except Anzor," Higgins said. "Whenever I started asking questions about the Woodruff murder, he would lose interest and say it was time for him to do something else."

Soon Higgins finished talking and started writing. He asked me for a little more help with the documents but was otherwise guarded about his conclusions. "Don't worry," he said. "I think you'll be satisfied."

At night I sat in the hotel café and watched the young wives of Georgia's political elite compete for pride of place. The table at which a woman sat and the status that it implied depended directly on whether her husband's fortunes were rising or falling. It was a junior high lunchroom with life-and-death implications.

I left the country unsure whether I had actually accomplished anything. Higgins thought that his article would be published within a few days, but that didn't work out. The 2008 financial crisis exploded in September and sucked up all the newsprint in the *Wall Street Journal*. For sixty days they wrote about one topic only: the worst economic disaster since the Great Depression of 1929. Then—on October 18, 2008—they wrote about Anzor Sharmaidze. And the next day the Georgian government released him from prison.

CHAPTER 18

CONFESSIONS OF AN OLD SOLDIER

There wasn't anything new or surprising in Higgins's article. The witnesses each reiterated the statements they'd previously made to me: Shevardnadze said it was a common crime; Gogoladze said that he was the intended target; Bedoidze said he was tortured and gave false testimony; and Anzor said he was framed—everything I'd been saying to anyone who would listen. The difference was that Higgins said them on the front page of the *Wall Street Journal*.

The day after publication, someone from the Ministry of Justice called Anzor's attorney, Tamaz Inashvili. "We've granted your application for parole," the man said. "Go out to Ksani Prison and pick up your client."

It was welcome news but somewhat unexpected: No one had submitted an application for parole on Anzor's behalf. Nevertheless, Tamaz picked him up and drove him home via the Old Military Road.

But Anzor was not yet free. Parole released him from prison but left his conviction intact. His status as a felon deprived him of all social benefits and made him effectively unemployable. He was an outlaw and an outcast.

A week later he called me in Houston. I had anticipated the call and imagined how the conversation would go: He would gush with gratitude and I would modestly deflect his praise. But that's not exactly what happened.

"You have to give me money," he growled.

"What do you mean give you money?" I sputtered. "I thought you were calling to thank me!"

"Yeah, yeah—thanks, you saved my life," he said. "But now you have to help me live it."

I confess that I felt some relief that I had avoided the embarrassment of effusive appreciation. And I did admire the cool logic and pragmatism of Anzor's response to my generosity. But what surprised me most was that in the face of his apparent ingratitude I felt absolutely no disappointment or resentment.

"Okay," I said, "let's figure out how we can get you some money."

The simple truth was that whatever I'd done I hadn't done it for Anzor Sharmaidze as an individual. I didn't actually know the man. And as a consequence, the fact of his gratitude or ingratitude didn't really matter to me. What did matter was that my success had changed the way that certain intelligence officers related to me.

When I initially started working on this case, the default assumption within the intelligence community was that I was an annoying and potentially dangerous dilettante. But by successfully engineering Anzor's release over US and Georgian objections, I had demonstrated myself to be both credible and moderately resourceful. As a result, the presumption regarding me changed: Professional operators with knowledge of both Freddie's murder and my work no longer assumed me to be an incompetent amateur.

And some of them reached out to help. A year before Anzor's release a US government spokesman had suggested that my efforts on behalf of the convict were merely a publicity stunt. A month after the release, an intelligence officer from the same agency contacted me.

"Freddie and I were friends," he told me. "And I was the first American to view his body. It was fairly obvious that he was dead, and that he'd been dead for some time. But I took a pulse anyway."

According to the officer, he was present when seventy-two hours after the murder the FBI shooting team discovered the bullet hole in the rear hatch of Eldar's Niva. "It was a very hard-to-find bullet hole," he said. "The projectile had gone through the rear window gasket and changed trajectory slightly as it passed through the metal skin of the car."

He didn't think anyone could have planned such a shot. And it was on this basis, the improbability that a shooter could intentionally hit the gasket, that he and other government officials concluded that Freddie's death was a tragic accident. But this conclusion didn't logically follow from the evidence. As far as I could see, the improbability of hitting the gasket only meant that the shot wasn't fired with *the intent to hit the gasket*. It didn't mean that the shot wasn't fired with *the intent to hit Woodruff*. If Anzor could allegedly fire his weapon and accidentally hit the gasket, then surely an assassin could fire his weapon and accidentally hit the gasket. Thus, the location of a bullet hole was not evidence that Freddie's death was an accident. And by the same token it was not evidence that his death was the result of intentional murder.

It was at best evidence of *a bullet that might have killed Freddie*. But that didn't prove it was *the bullet that killed Freddie*. Nevertheless, the intelligence officer insisted that it did prove that. "Everything—blood spatters, trajectories, caliber, wound examinations—definitively proved that Freddie was killed by a round that passed through the Niva from the back/outside of the vehicle and struck him in the back/top of the head," he said.

This was a half-truth. The FBI shooting team had *in fact* determined that Freddie was sitting in the back seat of Eldar's Niva at the time he was murdered. But without the shooter's bullet and Freddie's brain there was no way for them or anyone else to prove that the round had "passed through" the back hatch.

The more I thought about the intelligence officer's judgments, the less persuasive they seemed. He had without much evidence or analysis chosen to disregard the many witnesses who examined the Niva during the first twenty-four hours after the murder. In his opinion, Deputy Minister Avtandil Ioseliani, Eldar Gogoladze,

Marina Kapanadze, and the senior investigators in the Georgian forensics lab were either lying or mistaken when they said there was no bullet hole in the hatchback. And the intelligence officer had no easy answer to the FBI investigation report from the Bonn-based legal attaché. Special Agent George Shukin had examined the Niva the day after the murder and confirmed that the metal skin and glass of the car were undamaged. He was a credible witness and difficult to dismiss. All the intelligence officer could say was "It was a very hard-to-find bullet hole."

There was another graphic piece of evidence that needed to be accounted for—the horrific damage to Freddie's skull. The gaping entry wound implied a much bigger projectile than the 5.45 × 39 mm bullets that Anzor's AK-74 used. CIA officer Bob Baer had told me that based on the nature of Freddie's injury he believed the shooter used a Dragunov sniper rifle, the long gun of choice for Russian assassins. In its 1993 configuration, that weapon fired a 7.62 × 54 mm steel-jacketed projectile, a bullet with a diameter of 7.92 mm. Thus, a Dragunov round was too wide to fit through the 8.5 × 6 mm bullet hole found in the Niva and reported in the Georgian investigation file. And according to Dell Spry, the irregular shape of this hole was caused by key-holing—when a bullet tumbles in flight and as a result strikes the surface at an oblique angle. But if a 7.62 × 54 mm Dragunov round struck the hatch at an oblique angle, it would have made a massive hole in the Niva. The only conclusion that accounted for all the evidence was that the Niva was stopped and the hatch was open at the time of the shooting.

I had originally believed that Freddie was shot at the Natakhtari Drain. But the witnesses who were present on the side of the Old Military Road said they heard a gunshot and "less than a minute later" the Niva and the mortally wounded Freddie arrived from the north. These same witnesses reported that, upon arrival, Elena told the guardians that their friends had killed Freddie. This suggested the presence of guardians farther up the road.

The witnesses said the guardians had been parked at the Drain since midday. That meant that if the shooter was at the *shashlik* shop in the mountains so that Marina could "showcase" Freddie, he'd had a second vehicle. And if he had a second vehicle, then he could have used it as a prop to give Eldar an excuse to stop the car. The shooter lay in wait as his team flagged down the Niva and asked for gas; Eldar opened the hatch and stepped back; the shooter killed Freddie. Since Eldar was not in the driver's seat he was not at risk of being hit by a bullet that passed through Freddie's head. But at the same time, because he was outside the car when Freddie was shot, Eldar wasn't splattered with blood and brain. The chief bodyguard solved the problem of this damning cleanliness by delivering Freddie to the hospital and immediately going home to shower and change clothes.

But Eldar was an egoistic and self-important little man. And kindness to strangers was simply not in his nature. If he stopped to offer aid to a stranded motorist, then Freddie would have become immediately suspicious. And this would have made it hard to hold him in the back seat of the Niva. As I talked this through with Special Agent Dell Spry, he reminded me of Occam's razor. "The simplest answer is probably the right one," he said. "We believe that Marina may have pointed a gun at Freddie, relieved him of his weapon, and told him not to move. The theory was attractive to us because it neatly explained three independent consequences of the encounter: the size of Marina's reward, the magnitude of Elena's terror, and the mystery of Freddie's missing gun."

I had for the first time harmonized the forensic facts with the testimony provided by the witnesses who were present on the Old Military Road. The major pieces of the puzzle had come together and I now knew *how* Woodruff had been murdered.

I called Mousia to share my progress and to ask for advice: Where could I get a Niva hatchback door to shoot with a Dragunov round? But she quickly brushed my question aside. "I've found someone who can tell us about the guardians on the side of the road," she said. "He was in Georgian Group Alpha in 1993. And I found him through the Alpha veterans' Facebook page!"

Kote Shavishvili was retired from government service and working in the private sector. He occasionally traveled for business, and we arranged to meet in Cyprus. It was an easier connection than Tbilisi and provided me the illusion of Western security.

Mousia flew in from Moscow. Obliging banks, a temperate climate, and a euro-based economy had combined to make Cyprus a favorite destination for Russians. There were several nonstop flights a day and they were all full.

I was waiting for her at the bottom of the airstairs as she came off the plane. "Come," she said. "I have a present for you."

We stood near the baggage cart at the side of the plane as handlers unloaded passenger luggage. Mousia clapped as a man with a wide Slavic forehead wrestled an automobile hatchback door out of the hold and onto the cart. He looked back inside the plane and then yelled to her in Russian.

"Where's the rest of the Niva car?" he asked.

Mousia and I carried my prize to the hotel. The receptionist was from Rostov-on-Don and conducted the whole transaction in Russian. I was beginning to get the sense that Cyprus had been colonized.

We were scheduled to meet Kote that evening at a restaurant near the beach. Mousia and I arrived early but he was already there waiting.

A bald man in his early sixties, he had the hardened body of an athlete. His hands were calloused and his gray mustache was bushy. He was three inches shorter than me, but the straightness of his posture made him look taller. He was the kind of man who is easy to respect—a man of action for whom guile is an embarrassment. I liked him immediately.

The restaurant he'd chosen served real Georgian food made by real Georgian cooks. The air was thick with the coriander smell of traditional red and green bean soup. And Kote was comfortable in his role as gracious host.

"What can I do for you?" he asked.

I told him who I represented and why they had engaged me. "They are simple religious people," I said. "And they want to honor their dead."

He pulled out the Cross of St. Nino hanging around his neck and smiled warmly. "I am a believer too," he said.

I summarized the statements from the roadside witnesses and told him my suspicions about the guardians. He listened closely, but I was pretty sure he already knew everything I was telling him. I got to the end of the narrative and stopped without asking him a question. The three of us sat in silence while he looked at me. It was obvious that he was thinking, but I couldn't tell what. Finally, he spoke.

"If you were going to carry out an operation like this, the assassination of an American CIA officer by a foreign shooter, then I was the man in Georgia you would call for logistical support."

His words had been carefully chosen. It was not a confession. It was a conditional admission about routine practice. He paused to check my reaction and then continued.

"If you're going to shoot someone, you need to put the shooter, the weapon, and the target in the same place at the same time. And if your shooter is foreign, then he needs someone local to organize the intersection of these three elements and to provide him support before, during, and after the operation. In 1993, I was second in command of Georgian Group Alpha under Igor Giorgadze—and it was my job to organize such things and to provide trained operators for support."

My heart was racing. This was exactly what KGB officer Stanislav Lekarev had told me in Moscow: The murder of Freddie Woodruff was organized through Giorgadze and facilitated by Georgian Group Alpha. But one important element of Lekarev's surmise was missing from Kote's description—the involvement of Russian military intelligence.

The old Georgian soldier must have heard my thoughts because he replied to them directly. "Eldar Gogoladze was GRU," he said.

It was the same thing that Irakli Batiashvili had said about Gogoladze. But I didn't let on that I'd heard it before. "I thought he was KGB," I said.

"He was KGB," he said. "And GRU. And CIA. He was a triple agent. GRU took him out of a police substation and put him into Georgian KGB. And when the Americans came they recruited him to the CIA. In fact, that's what the men in Group Alpha called him—'the CIA agent.' But his ultimate loyalty was always to Russian military intelligence."

It was a head-spinning revelation. But I finally understood why mafia chief Jaba Ioseliani had chosen Eldar as the head of Shevardnadze's personal protection force and why Shevardnadze could not fire him. Eldar was in business with GRU and GRU was in business with Mkhedrioni.

"What was Eldar's role in the murder?" I asked.

"Eldar was the messenger," he said. "There was someone from Mkhedrioni that Freddie wanted to meet and Eldar was the conduit for arranging that meeting. Marina—who was also in Mkhedrioni—was there to make the introduction for Freddie."

He stopped talking, but I had the feeling he wanted to say more. He pursed his lips and furrowed his brow just enough to make the lines around his eyes stand out. He looked bitter. "They were both very well rewarded for their service," he sighed.

"What do you mean?" I asked.

"In GRU and KGB, the job you get after you retire depends on the perceived value of the contributions you made during your career—the more valuable your contributions, the better your job. I was Soviet Group Alpha; I fought in Afghanistan; I retired as a general—but my contributions weren't valuable enough to get me any job at all. That's why I'm stuck providing security for an Internet poker site."

Kote was a proud man. And clearly he felt insulted and demeaned. He wanted to complain to someone. "Eldar never lost his contacts in GRU," he said. "They protected him and—after he got out of prison—they gave him an executive position at Cartu Group. They even rehired him at Cartu after you got him fired."

"They?" I asked. "I thought Cartu belonged to Bidzina Ivanashvili."

"Not really," he said. "Cartu is funded—indirectly, of course—from a GRU slush fund. Ivanashvili is the face, but it's not all his money."

It was a fantastic accusation, and I had absolutely no idea whether it was true. Nevertheless, it did provide a plausible excuse for Eldar's employment in a position for which he was so obviously unqualified. And it did explain why he would be fired from Cartu after admitting on television that Woodruff's murder was the work of "a great regional power."

But I had neither time nor inclination to pursue this line of inquiry. I did not want to distract Kote from his grievance. I was aiming at something and I needed him to be angry.

"What about Marina Kapanadze?" I asked.

"Oh, yes," he said. "She was rewarded too. She got a job in the West—working for the Russians. The Ministry of Defense, I think."

"And what about the shooter?" I said. "I know he was a professional—"

"He was no professional!" Kote shouted. "One professional does not steal another professional's tools!"

His outburst quieted the restaurant, but it didn't matter. I had what I needed: an implicit admission that he had provided logistical support to the shooter and that the shooter had betrayed him by stealing a silencer and two canisters of tear gas.

Kote was the missing link between what I knew and what I didn't know. And his outrage explained the shooter's inexplicable arrest. As a deputy in the Ministry of Internal Affairs, he could easily have had the thief detained. And as a member of the Alpha brotherhood, he would have had every reason to do so.

I had trouble going to sleep that night. I kept thinking about how close the shooter came to disappearing without a trace. But the FBI had identified him because he stole from a comrade and the comrade had him arrested. Thus, a complex operation to assassinate an American operative was put at risk because of petty dishonesty and righteous retaliation. The whole episode was utterly banal. And exactly how things happen in real life.

I wanted to test the credibility of Kote's indictment of Gogoladze by finding Marina. If she was *in fact* employed by the Russian Ministry of Defense, it would make his claim about GRU involvement more believable. Up until now, I had always been too afraid to meet her. After all, she was a very dangerous woman and I was a threat to her comfortable life. But I had accumulated sufficient contacts in the intelligence world that I believed I could learn what I needed to know without actually having to talk to her. And so, using the good offices of a cooperative US government employee, I hired two agents from a European intelligence service to find Marina Kapanadze.

They failed. But in the process of failing they located her son in a suburb of Athens. A few years earlier, the young man had been arrested by Georgian authorities for stealing almost $1 million from an airport reconstruction project. According to the European agents, immediately after the arrest the Georgian prosecutor general received immense pressure from the Russian Ministry of Defense. Whether for that reason or another, the prosecutor general released the young man and terminated the investigation.

It wasn't a smoking gun, but it did imply that someone in the Kapanadze family had enormous influence in Moscow.

It occurred to me that the FBI had conducted an extensive investigation to determine whether Eldar and Marina were complicit in Freddie's death. Almost all the documentary evidence regarding this inquiry had been redacted from my FBI FOIA files. However, Dell Spry believed that in light of my success in liberating Anzor, the FBI special agent who took over the post-Ames investigation might be willing to talk to me.

And so I reached out to Dave Beisner. A legendary veteran of FBI black ops, Beisner was a crusty curmudgeon. And he didn't mince words about the Georgians with whom he'd dealt. "They all lie," he said. "All of 'em. You can't believe a word that comes out of their mouths."

On the basis of his experience, Beisner believed that the only way to ascertain the truth from a Georgian was using a polygraph. And so he'd taken one to Tbilisi. This information filled in a gap in my time line. I had travel authorizations for two special agents and a polygrapher, but I didn't know the identities of the human subjects.

They were Eldar Gogoladze and Marina Kapanadze.

"I wired 'em up and asked 'em a single question," he said. "'Were you reporting to anyone about Freddie Woodruff's movements?' They both denied it and I got no indication of a deception. So I closed the case."

It was hard for me to follow the logic of his process. He seemed to assume that *if* Gogoladze and Marina were not reporting on Freddie, *then* Freddie's death was not a murder. But that was, as lawyers like to say, a non sequitur: The conclusion did not logically follow from the premise. Just because they weren't reporting didn't mean it wasn't a murder.

More troubling still was his assumption that a polygraph would work effectively on Georgians. As a US government report noted in 1990, among some Eurasian cultures, lying on behalf of the state is fulfillment of a person's highest duty and gives the deceiver a calm consciousness and immense joy. There is no guilt, and therefore, there is no observable pattern of physiological reactions to guilt.

The more I thought about it, the more I suspected that the Bureau wanted to stop working on the Woodruff murder and used the polygraph as a scientific justification for that decision. Nevertheless, they'd been suspicious of Gogoladze and Marina up to the very last minute.

I'd all but given up on ever finding Marina when I got a call from journalist Eliso Chapidze. "Do you believe in coincidence?" she asked.

Eliso had been in Western Europe for a seminar and was flying back to Tbilisi. Her plane stopped in Istanbul, and a matronly looking Georgian woman sat down in the seat next to her.

"I am Marina Kapanadze," she said.

For the next two hours they talked about Freddie Woodruff. Marina was charming and sentimental and sad. She claimed to have cared deeply about Freddie. And at one point she cried. "His death ruined my life," she said. "It followed me everywhere. And in the end, I was forced to leave home and move away."

She now lived in Athens and worked for a company that sold Russian military equipment. And she just happened to have a recent photograph with her colleagues. "It was Marina standing in the middle of a bunch of Russian army generals," Eliso said. "The generals were all in uniform, but Marina said they were retired."

The barmaid had become an arms dealer. And I had learned about it because of a chance encounter on an airplane. My first reaction to this impossibly improbable coincidence was panic: My idle curiosities had become the subject of a Russian intelligence operation. A hostile foreign power was apparently monitoring my communications, analyzing my strategies, and steering my investigation.

I felt naked and exposed. However, after a few sleepless nights I began to ponder *why* the Russians would organize this meeting with Marina. It seemed obvious that they wanted to confirm that Marina had been rewarded for valuable service to Russia. And— since Marina didn't talk about anything other than Freddie and her current job with the Russians—they clearly weren't trying to persuade me that her "valuable service" was somehow *unrelated* to the Woodruff murder.

So why almost twenty years after his death would the Russian special services go to so much effort in order to confirm that killing Freddie had been a valuable service to Russia? I suspected that the answer to this riddle was somehow related to the reason they had killed him in the first place. According to experts, there were two competing theories as to why the Russians might have done that: One theory said the murder was related to the Russian drug trade and the other theory said the murder was related to the Russian spy Aldrich Ames.

And since Marina was Mkhedrioni and Eldar was GRU, there was a good chance they would have been involved either way.

I spent a long time thinking about Russian involvement in drug smuggling. It was a well-documented historical fact and one that even the Russians had tacitly acknowledged. Admittedly, my perspective was severely limited; nevertheless, I was unable to imagine any benefit to the Russians if I or anyone else ultimately attributed Freddie's death to trespass on an old smuggling operation. As far as I could see, if drugs were the true motive for the murder, then the Russians would have been better served to leave Marina in Athens and me in ignorance.

But they had intentionally chosen to inform me—to confirm the fact of their relationship with Marina and confirm the fact of her valuable service to Russia. And so I turned to the second theory: that the murder of Freddie Woodruff was related to the Russian spy Aldrich Ames.

I immersed myself in the details of his betrayal. I read the declassified congressional reports and consumed a half-dozen biographies of his deceit. I talked to a broad cross section of witnesses, from the FBI special agent in charge of the Ames investigation to the Washington, DC, lawyer in charge of the Ames defense.

And I continued my correspondence with Aldrich Ames himself.

Pursuant to a plea agreement, Ames had been sentenced to life in federal prison. He was housed in the Allenwood medium security facility in central Pennsylvania. Under the terms of his plea, the CIA reviewed and censored all of his incoming and outgoing mail. This effectively prevented any substantive dialogue about the Woodruff murder. In addition, the Agency exercised absolute authority to approve or disapprove his visitors. And they exercised that authority to refuse my and his requests for a face-to-face visit.

The CIA knew who I was and it didn't want me to talk to him.

Around that same time I received a handwritten postcard from G. L. Lamborn in San Antonio, Texas. "I understand that you and Dell Spry (an old acquaintance) have been looking into the Freddie Woodruff case," he wrote. "The case has bothered me for almost two decades. I believe I may be able to help you as I was uniquely involved in the mid-90's. I'd like to see it closed and the results made known."

I wrote back immediately and scheduled a visit for Sunday afternoon.

Lamborn had just gotten home from church when I knocked at the door. We sat in the dining room because the living room had been surrendered to rows of double-facing library shelves. Books in several languages seemed to have spilled out of the back bedrooms and down the hall before conquering the parlor.

"Let's deal with the issue of my bona fides," he said. He handed me his passport and a badge identifying him as retired CIA. This was obviously something Lamborn had done before and he had a protocol.

I fumbled for my own passport but he stopped me. "It's all right," he said. "I know who you are."

Lamborn was an angular man: lean, dry, athletic. He dressed like a Baptist deacon, but his military bearing made the costume look like a uniform. I could see immediately that he was disciplined, intense, and dangerously patient. But what struck me most profoundly about Lamborn was his unusual combination of astonishing intelligence and genuine humility. This was a forceful man who'd spent his life cultivating a fundamental respect for people.

"I took over Freddie's branch chief job in 1995," he said. "I was there when the FBI was investigating whether the murder was related to Aldrich Hazen Ames."

It was a surprising disclosure.

Lamborn had written a book and I had read it before driving over to San Antonio. In it, he revealed himself to be a specialist in both influence operations and counterinsurgency. That kind of expertise would normally place him in the Agency's Special Activities Division and outside a normal rank-and-file posting. But after a moment's quick reflection I realized that his skill set was probably the perfect résumé for a Transcaucasia branch chief.

"I spent twenty-six years at the Agency," he said. "I was in the Directorate of Operations, the Directorate of Intelligence, and in the Office of the Director."

It occurred to me that this might be the man who sent me the translated Georgian investigation file. Or the man who prevented me from visiting Ames in prison.

"I never heard of you until I retired," he said. "And I never sent you anything. I contacted you because Freddie's murder has bothered me for twenty years and I think it's time somebody solved it."

He talked a little about the mechanics of the murder. He assumed without discussion that Anzor was innocent and the criminal trial had been a charade.

"Dave Beisner let slip that a professional sniper had been hired to kill Freddie," he said. "I have no idea where that bit of information originated."

And so I told him. He listened without moving as I described Dell Spry's invitation to a noisy Georgian wedding; the unlikely arrest of a Russian at the train depot; the witness testimony about guardians on the Old Military Road; and Kote's eruption when I referred to the shooter as a professional.

"Why do you trust Kote?" he asked.

It was a crucial question and one that I'd struggled to answer since the beginning of my investigation: How do you trust someone that you know lies to you?

"I believe that—if you can identify what a person cares about more than anything else in the world—then you can trust that they will always be doggedly devoted to that thing. You then interpret their words and actions through the lens of their heart's desire. As for Kote, I believe he is a patriot who values personal honor and professional integrity above all else. His volcanic response to the shooter's dishonorable conduct emanated from his center and was, therefore, trustworthy."

I felt vaguely embarrassed by my sophomoric psychobabble. But it was an intimate question and I had given an intimate answer. And Lamborn seemed satisfied. At least, I assumed he was because he handed me a five-page single-spaced memorandum laying out his conclusions regarding the murder of Freddie Woodruff. We went through it together.

"Narcotics had nothing to do with Freddie's murder," he said. "Ames was giving the Russians everything we knew about drug smuggling in the region. And with that information they could easily evade our net—all they had to do was change the shipping arrangements. There was simply no need to kill a CIA ops officer like Freddie in order to protect their drug trade."

In a few sentences he had demonstrated the central flaw in a theory it had taken me weeks to discount. This was going to be fun.

"It is much more likely that Ames got drunk and revealed details that identified him as a Russian spy," he said. "Perhaps he even tried to recruit Freddie. But whatever he did, he said enough that Freddie's entire demeanor changed radically overnight."

This compelling narrative melded together the time line, the character of the players, and the evidence regarding their demeanor. Lamborn was accounting for every fact.

"As far as we know, Freddie didn't put anything regarding Ames 'in traffic' to headquarters. However, this failure to document is completely reasonable. It is a very serious thing to accuse a fellow officer of being a spy for another intelligence service. And should the accusation later be proved false and unfounded, the would-be accuser could himself be in serious trouble. Freddie knew he was due to rotate back to headquarters shortly, and he may have thought it best to discuss these matters behind closed doors at Central Eurasian Division."

Lamborn had introduced a powerful and previously unknown factor into the analysis, the bureaucratic culture of the institution.

These customary practices informed each employee's operative reality and to an extent that is hard to underestimate influenced every interaction with the institution.

"No matter how drunk he was that night, when he woke up Ames was sober enough to realize that he had committed a serious indiscretion. He may have contacted his Russian handler upon return to Washington or he may have triggered an emergency clandestine meeting while still in Tbilisi. Either way, he definitely would have told the Russians about his drinking binge with Freddie and the security problems it had created. The Russians understand CIA culture and would assume that Freddie was waiting until he returned to headquarters to report about Ames. This gave them a window of opportunity to silence Freddie and protect their highly valuable penetration of the CIA."

"I suggested this to Ames's handler, Victor Cherkashin," I said. "He said it was a nice theory but that Freddie was rotating back to headquarters in two weeks and the KGB simply couldn't move that fast."

For the first time, Lamborn laughed. "You wouldn't believe how fast they can act when they want to," he said. "And remember, this is Russia's backyard. In 1993 they had all the assets they needed right there in Georgia."

Lamborn's analysis was predicated on the assumption that Ames was sufficiently valuable to the Russians that they would kill Freddie to protect him. But I wondered whether that was still true at the time of the murder.

"Ames was transferred out of counterintelligence and into counternarcotics in December 1991," I said. "And the FBI formally opened an espionage case against him in May 1993. One KGB officer to whom I spoke suggested that by August 1993 Ames had lost his importance to the Russians and that they killed Freddie not to protect Ames, but to draw attention to him and thereby protect another more valuable agent."

Lamborn became completely still. His eyes were open but unfocused. After a minute of silence he finally spoke. "It is a serious theory," he said. "We don't know whether the Russians knew about our investigation of Ames prior to his arrest. Nevertheless, whether the Russians killed Freddie in order to save Ames or to sacrifice him—his responsibility for the murder remains the same. Aldrich Hazen Ames is the reason why Freddie Woodruff was murdered."

We talked for almost four hours. When it was over, he walked me to the door and shook my hand. "The bottom line is that killing Freddie Woodruff was not accidental and was not carried out by a random shooter," he said. "His murder was professionally planned and carefully executed."

It was exactly what I had suspected when I started this adventure so many years before.

I made two more trips to Tbilisi. The reclusive Bidzina Ivanashvili became the leader of a coalition of opposition parties in 2012 and forced Misha Saakashvili out of power and out of the country. The oligarch's new justice minister promised to reexamine the Sharmaidze conviction but after Anzor was arrested for a petty theft nothing came of the reexamination. As of this writing, Anzor is back in prison—a victim of the continuing sanctions imposed on him as the man who murdered Freddie Woodruff.

The caravan had moved on and it was time for the dogs to stop barking.

I had spent a small fortune in time and money to collect a box full of facts. And I could arrange those facts into a coherent story that accounted for all the relevant details. But was it the truth? Or was it simply as close to the truth as you can get in the murky world of intelligence?

I could not know. But what I did know was that the official version of the murder had deprived Freddie of a warrior's death. It had painted him as the hapless victim of a drunken potshot. It had impugned his tradecraft and besmirched his memory. And it had denied him the immortality of myth.

The director of central intelligence had retrieved Freddie's broken body but had left his honor behind. And now that honor had been recovered. The Georgian and American governments had acknowledged that he had, in fact, been targeted for murder. The Agency had unofficially confirmed that Freddie was assassinated because he was a singular threat to an implacable enemy. The world now knew that Freddie Woodruff was a hero.

It was all the justice a spy could ever hope for.

THE SPY WHO WAS LEFT BEHIND

I believe that Vladimir Rachman assassinated Freddie Woodruff. He and one or two members of Georgian Group Alpha parked their vehicle on the west side of the Old Military Road about a mile north of the turnoff to the Natakhtari Drain. One of the team members flagged down Eldar Gogoladze's southbound Niva and asked for gas or a tire for their stalled car. When Eldar opened the rear hatch, Rachman fired a single shot from his Dragunov at the passenger sitting on the right side of the back seat.

That's what Elena Darchiashvili was talking about when she told the guardians at the Natakhtari Drain that their friends had shot the American.

And it explains why Eldar went home to take a shower. He'd chosen to drive the Niva that day because the two-door car restricted Freddie's movements in the back seat and with the rear hatch open allowed the shooter a clear view of the target. But since Eldar was standing outside when Freddie was shot, he didn't have any of the splatter on his clothes and person that investigators would expect to find if he'd been sitting in the driver's seat. He went home to wash and change clothes in order to eliminate his damning spotlessness.

Rachman had been at the *shashlik* shop in the mountains when Freddie, Eldar, and Marina Kapanadze stopped there for a meeting. He watched Marina identify Freddie as the target and observed Freddie slide into the Niva and sit on the right side of the back seat.

That's why Marina made Freddie scoot over to the right side when later he tried to sit on the left, behind Eldar.

The bullet that Rachman fired lodged in Freddie's brain. But the caliber of that projectile did not match the caliber of the weapon seized from Anzor Sharmaidze; therefore, both Rachman's bullet and Freddie's brain were made to disappear.

Marina was concerned that Freddie might have photographed Rachman or his vehicle at the *shashlik* shop. So immediately after the shooting she exposed all five canisters of Freddie's 35 mm film.

Rachman received logistical support from Georgian Group Alpha. They provided him with housing, transportation, weapons, and personnel, including the four guardians at the Natakhtari Drain. The guardians at the Drain acted as a blocking force and a control for oncoming traffic.

In addition, Georgian Group Alpha equipped Rachman with a silencer and two canisters of tear gas. He didn't use this matériel to assassinate Freddie but tried to steal it anyway. In response, the Georgian Group Alpha commander had him arrested. These tit-for-tat insults were key to the FBI unraveling the truth about how Freddie was murdered.

The plotters delivered a message through Eldar offering Freddie a Sunday afternoon meeting with a Mkhedrioni operative at a *shashlik* shop in the mountains near the Russian border. Because of the Mkhedrioni connection, Marina was invited along to make introductions. Elena was brought along to make the cover story of a Sunday picnic more believable; however, she was excluded from the meeting at the *shashlik* shop.

The location of the meeting was carefully chosen. The Old Military Road was the only way in or out of the valley. Thus, the plotters had a kill zone through which Freddie was required to pass. Rachman chose the area just south of Natakhtari for the actual attempt because it was close enough to the mouth of the valley to allow him and his team to make an easy escape.

Eldar and Marina were GRU operatives, and they both would have had to know from the beginning that the true purpose of the excursion was to murder Freddie. They did their jobs and they were handsomely rewarded for their participation in the conspiracy.

Elena was not an intelligence professional and therefore not a reliable coconspirator. But the events of that day and the threats of what would happen to her if she talked had so frightened Elena that twenty years later she was still hysterical.

I believe that the SVR, working through colleagues in the GRU, hired Vladimir Rachman to assassinate Freddie Woodruff.

While he was in Tbilisi on Agency business, Aldrich Ames got drunk and compromised himself to Freddie. He revealed enough information that Freddie began to suspect that Ames was a traitor. This suspicion explains both the radical change in Freddie's demeanor and his angry exchange with Ames at the Piano Bar.

Ames knew that his drunken declarations to Freddie could terminate his usefulness to the SVR and put him at risk of arrest in the United States. He requested an emergency secret meeting with his SVR handlers in order to inform them about his breach of operational security. That meeting probably occurred in Tbilisi. In the absence of a plan to neutralize the effect of his disclosures, Ames would not have left Georgia—a place that allowed for easy and immediate escape to asylum in Russia.

The SVR was informed about CIA culture and knew that Freddie would wait to communicate his suspicions about Ames until he could do so in person at CIA headquarters. This gave the SVR a window of opportunity to kill the messenger before he had delivered the message.

The SVR probably didn't know that Ames was already under investigation for espionage. But they did know that Ames's most recent position at the CIA did not afford him access to valuable intelligence and that his prospects for advancement at the Agency were not good. His days as a high-value Russian agent were limited; nevertheless, the SVR instructed Ames to return to the US and contracted with Rachman to assassinate Freddie.

But the SVR did not kill Freddie because it was good for Ames; they killed Freddie because it was good for the SVR. If their goal had been simply to protect Ames, they could have invited him to fly across the border and retire in Moscow. Instead, they chose the extreme sanction of violent murder, a dramatic and largely unprecedented act that could easily draw attention to the very agent they were ostensibly trying to preserve.

The only rational explanation for the SVR's decision to send Ames back to America and kill Freddie is that they chose to sacrifice Ames in order to protect a more valuable and more highly placed intelligence asset. It is possible that the object of this support was the traitorous FBI special agent Robert Hanssen; however, this seems unlikely since even the SVR did not know Hanssen's true identity.

I believe that errors and omissions by US government officials contributed to the murder of Freddie Woodruff.

Ames got drunk and told Freddie a secret. That disclosure led inexorably to Freddie's murder. But the FBI and CIA already knew Ames's secret. FBI special agents had already searched his home and office; were already eavesdropping on his conversations; and were already following him twenty-four hours a day. They could have arrested him at any time. Instead, they permitted him to travel to the former Soviet Union.

If the FBI had prevented Ames from going to Tbilisi, Freddie would not have been murdered. If the CIA had informed Freddie about Ames's treason, Freddie would have been prepared and would not have responded to Ames's drunken confession in a way that incited panic in Ames.

The FBI and CIA chose to expose Freddie to Ames's treachery without warning him about the risks. This decision put Freddie in harm's way and ultimately led to his death. It also led to the sabotage of the FBI investigation of his murder. A thorough investigation of Woodruff's murder was not in the interest of the officials who had authorized Ames to go to Tbilisi. Nor was it in the interest of those who wanted to avoid any suggestion that Ames was responsible for the murder of an American intelligence officer and therefore should not escape the death penalty.

And that's how Freddie became the spy who was left behind.

ACKNOWLEDGMENTS

W hen I first began my investigation into the murder of Freddie Woodruff, I hoped to discover what a moderately-empowered curious man could accomplish by himself. I very quickly learned the truth of this naively arrogant ambition: By myself, I could do almost nothing.

Whatever success I achieved in liberating Anzor Sharmaidze, redeeming Freddie Woodruff, or writing a book is due almost entirely to the generosity of other people who helped me. They are giants upon whose shoulders I was privileged to stand. I have named many of them in the text but I would like to highlight a few here.

Pride of place belongs to Lali Kereselidze. She gave me a voice, credibility, and a spot on her fold out couch. She was my confidant, advisor, factotum, and friend. Without her, my quixotic quest would have been stillborn and Anzor might well have died in prison.

Of equal importance was Tamaz Inashvili, a man of extraordinary integrity and professionalism. He persisted in supporting Anzor for more than a decade and was there to drive his client home when the government finally released him. Without his assistance, I could not have navigated the labyrinth of Georgian justice.

The journalists with whom I worked were both my sword and my shield. Their reporting kept me safe and their influence gave me leverage. It was because of Thomas Goltz, Eliso Chapidze, Jamie Doran, and Andrew Higgins that I was ultimately able to move the Georgian government.

ACKNOWLEDGMENTS

One of the highlights of this adventure was the privilege of meeting and working with CIA operations officers and FBI special agents. These shadow warriors are men and women of the highest quality—selfless patriots who make enormous sacrifices to preserve our way of life. Without the guidance and direction provided by Bob Baer, Dell Spry, and G. L. Lamborn, I would most certainly have failed and most probably have been killed.

Chief among those who sacrificed is the family of Freddie Woodruff. His widow and children are entitled to the utmost respect and deference. I have tried hard to tell this story in a way that honors them as Freddie's living legacy. If I have failed at any point to achieve this goal, I offer my most sincere apology.

Throughout this project I have had the passionate support of friends, family, and the coffee klatch at the Croissant Brioche Café. Beverly Davis was my Sancho Panza and Dulcinea. Without her my adventures wouldn't be nearly as much fun. Tony Gorry and Michael Crawford were my sounding boards, readers, and critics. They made the lonely work of writing easier and the product clearer. Elena Tognini was my faithful friend and fellow traveler. She gave me confidence, courage, and the irrational belief that I could actually do this. Mousia Semenova adopted my idealistic campaign as her own and routinely demonstrated a startling ability to do the impossible. My cousin John Spence inquired, encouraged, and suggested that I include a map of the Byzantine Empire. And Mirka Jalovcova helped and supported me. She made me bold, gave me perspective, and (more than once) held me while I cried.

I have never had an editor before and have profited from the experience. Colin Harrison and his team at Simon & Schuster made this book better. Any flaws or mistakes that remain in the text are entirely my own.

And finally, it was the humanity of Georgia Woodruff Alexander that challenged and inspired me to seek justice for Anzor. Without her compassion, courage, and commitment there would be no investigation, no litigation, and no book.

APPENDIX

Time line of Aldrich Ames's CIA career from 1983 to his arrest for espionage:

September 1983 Ames is made counterintelligence branch chief for Soviet operations, responsible for analyzing selected CIA operations involving Soviet "assets."

September 19, 1984 Ames's wife files for divorce on grounds of mental cruelty. Ames later testified that financial pressures arising from this divorce led him to first contemplate engaging in espionage.

April 16, 1985 Ames walks into the Soviet embassy and hands the receptionist an envelope addressed to the KGB resident. The envelope contained proof of his identity, documents about two or three cases that CIA Moscow Station was running, a phone directory for Soviet Eurasian Division management personnel, and a demand for $50,000. He is asked to return in a month.

May 15, 1985 Ames returns to the Soviet embassy. He is taken to a private room and handed a note saying the Soviets have agreed to pay him $50,000 and will (as Ames suggested) continue using arms control specialist Sergey Chuvakhin as the intermediary. The note is given to him by Victor Cherkashin, who is (at the time) the KGB counterintelligence chief in Washington, DC.

June 13, 1985 Ames provides Chuvakhin with copies of documents that identify more than ten top-level CIA and FBI sources who are then reporting on Soviet activities. Ames later admits that part of his rationale for exposing these operations to the KGB was that he sought to protect his own role as a KGB informant by eliminating those KGB assets who could be in the best position to tell the CIA of his (Ames's) espionage. Over the subsequent years, Ames provides the Soviets with information on more than a hundred Soviet and East European operational endeavors. This results in the virtual collapse of the CIA's Soviet operations.

October 1986 The CIA names a four-person analytical group known as the "Special Task Force" to look at cases known to be compromised and to identify any commonalities among them.

The FBI creates a six-person analytical team known as the "ANLACE Task Force" to investigate the origin of its loss of two human intelligence assets.

November 1989 A CIA employee, who knew Ames well, reports to the CIA Counterintelligence Center that the formerly impecunious Ames seems to be living beyond his means.

April 1991 The FBI and CIA investigation teams join forces to search for and identify the source of their intelligence losses.

December 1991 Ames is assigned to the CIA's Counternarcotics Center in charge of an antinarcotics task force for the Caucasus region. This appears to have been the first assignment that took into account the security concerns that had been raised about Ames.

October 1992 The joint CIA-FBI investigative unit is relatively certain that Ames is the spy for whom they are looking, although others remain under suspicion.

January 1993 The joint CIA-FBI investigative unit begins briefing the FBI and other appropriate officials on its work, and begins contemplating turning the Ames investigation over to the FBI.

March 1993 The joint CIA-FBI investigative unit delivers its final report and, on the basis of this report, the FBI begins an intensive investigation of Ames. The Foreign Intelligence Surveillance Court issues orders authorizing electronic surveillance techniques against Ames's home and office. The Bureau employs other surveillance techniques including mail cover (i.e., deriving information from envelopes addressed to and from Ames) and the installation of a clandestine monitor in his car.

May 12, 1993 The FBI formally opens an investigation case against Ames. They initiate round-the-clock surveillance of Ames using the Bureau's Special Surveillance Group.

CIA director James Woolsey advises White House chief of staff Tony Lake regarding the fact and status of the Ames investigation. Lake subsequently informs President Bill Clinton.

June 11, 1993 The FBI begins wiretapping Ames's home and office telephones pursuant to a FISA warrant.

June 25, 1993 The FBI conducts a search of Ames's office at the CIA. Approximately 144 classified documents are located in his work area, most of which do not relate to his official duties.

July 1993 Ames travels to the Republic of Georgia for the opening of the headquarters for the Black Sea Basin Intelligence Sharing Initiative.

August 8, 1993 Freddie Woodruff is murdered near Natakhtari in the Republic of Georgia.

September 1993 Ames travels to Turkey on official business related to the Black Sea Basin Intelligence Sharing Initiative.

October 19, 1993 The FBI searches Ames's home and installs listening devices.

February 21, 1994 FBI special agent Dell Spry arrests Ames.

February 22, 1994 Aldrich and Rosario Ames are formally charged with espionage.

April 28, 1994 Ames pleads guilty to espionage and is sentenced to life in prison without possibility of parole.

INDEX

ABOUT THE AUTHOR

Michael Pullara is a Texas trial lawyer. He represents plaintiffs in complicated commercial disputes and, on a pro bono basis, individuals suing for violations of their human rights. During his thirty-eight-year career he has represented death row inmates seeking free exercise of religion, American oil companies suing Italian mobsters, Arabs suing for damage caused by US military action in Iraq, and small business owners suing international telecoms for fraud and breach of contract. *The Spy Who Was Left Behind* is his first book.